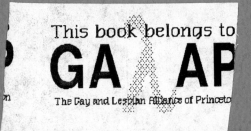

BIG BILL TILDEN

The Triumphs and the Tragedy

by FRANK DEFORD

 Simon and Schuster · New York

This work is an outgrowth of a two-part magazine series
written by Mr. Deford for *Sports Illustrated*
(January 13, January 20, 1975).

All the pictures in the photograph section, except the first three,
are used with the permission of the New York *Daily News*. The
photographs of Tilden's parents are courtesy of the Tilden
family, and the third photograph is courtesy of Manuel Alonso.

Designed by Irving Perkins
Manufactured in the United States of America

1   2   3   4   5   6   7   8   9   10

Library of Congress Cataloging in Publication Data

Deford, Frank.
    Big Bill Tilden.

    "This work is an outgrowth of a two-part magazine
series written by Mr. Deford for Sports Illustrated."
    Includes index.
    1. Tilden, William Tatem, 1893–1953.   2. Tennis.
I. Title.
GV994.T5D43   796.34'2'0924 [B]   75–45011
ISBN 0–671–22254–6

Contents

6 · CONTENTS

For André Laguerre

Acknowledgments

This work was originally intended only as an article for *Sports Illustrated* magazine, but early on in the research I was convinced that there was much more of a story to be told. Roy Terrell, the managing editor, and Art Brawley, the tennis editor, accepted that judgment and encouraged me to take the extra time for a thorough study of the man. *Sports Illustrated* eventually published two long articles in the January 13 and 20, 1975, issues, but more than that: the editors' early support and confidence in the project were crucial to its turning into this book.

Naturally, I am also in the debt of the many people who granted me interviews. Since I spoke with a hundred or more persons, it would be foolish and inconsiderate of me to single out some for thanks while neglecting others. I must, however, offer a special appreciation to the family—to William T. Tilden III and Mrs. Miriam Ambrose, who were always gracious and helpful, even when they were not convinced that it was desirable to exhume some of the more painful memories of their uncle. I must also cite Dr. Carl Fischer, who was not only a valuable and devoted source but responsible for my meeting so many other valuable sources.

Many old acquaintances of Tilden's spoke to me, and spoke candidly, because they believed they bore him that obligation. Tilden, after all, liked having people talk about him. I know from the reaction to the magazine pieces that some of these people felt I had been unfair—that it was enough just to write of his greatness, to remind us of his glory, and that we should remain silent about his sadness. Well, I'm sorry; Big Bill's motto was "Truth, though the heavens fall."

I never met Tilden, never even saw him play, but in Philadelphia, one rainy spring night in 1974, in a high-ceilinged room at the Bellevue-Stratford Hotel, I dreamed quite vividly that he came to see me. Either that, or his ghost did—one or the other. For me, it was after a sad day of reading about family tragedies in nineteenth-century newspapers and talking to very old people about long-ago childhoods. As I remembered the dream the next morning, Tilden had wasted little time with me on pleasantries or reminiscences but had gotten right to the point of his visit, which was to instruct me in how to write this book.

I have thought about this, and I feel certain that if he did know that some guy was going around, twenty years after his death, asking about him, inquiring after him, writing a book about him—if he knew this, he would be tickled pink. I'm also pretty sure he would throw a fit about much that is in this book. But then, he never did like what anybody wrote about him.

F. D.

Westport, Connecticut
December 16, 1975

Part One

CHAPTER ONE

"I'll play my own sweet game"

WITH any artist who attains the ultimate in his craft, there must be one moment, an instant, when genius is first realized, when a confluence of God's natural gifts at last swirl together with the full powers of endeavor and devotion in the man to bear him to greatness. Virtually always, of course, that moment cannot be perceived, and it passes unnoticed, but with Big Bill Tilden it was isolated, forever frozen in time. He knew precisely when he had arrived, and, thoughtfully, he revealed it.

This happened on Centre Court at Wimbledon in 1920. Tilden was already twenty-seven, and although he had never won a major championship, he had reached the finals. It was his first trip abroad, and to his delight the British, unlike his own countrymen, had taken to him right away. Americans always only grudgingly granted Tilden recognition, never mind respect, largely because they were emotionally hung up on Big Bill's main rival, Bill Johnston, who was affectionately known as Little Bill, or even, in the soupiest moments, Wee Willie Winkie. Johnston was five feet eight, a wonderful cute doll-person from the California middle class, and all Americans (Tilden prominently included) were absolutely nuts about him: the little underdog with the big heart who cut larger fellows down to size.

By contrast, at six feet one and a half inches tall, 155 pounds, angular and overbearing, a Philadelphia patrician of intellectual pretension, Big Bill was the perfect foil for Little Bill, and the great American villain. Until 1920 he had also cooperated by remaining a loser with a healthy reputation for choking in important matches. The year before, in the finals at Forest Hills, Johnston had defeated Tilden in straight sets, and so it was assumed that Wimbledon would serve as the stage where Johnston, the American champion, would duel Gerald Patterson, the Wimbledon defender, for the undisputed championship of the world.

Unfortunately for hopes for this classic confrontation, Johnston was waylaid in an early round by a steady English player named J. C. Parke. Not until the next day, when Tilden routed Parke, avenging Little Bill's defeat, did Big Bill move front and center as Patterson's most conspicuous challenger. Of course, from the moment Tilden strode upon their grass that summer, the British had been enchanted with him—his game, his manner, his idiosyncrasies: "this smiling youth, so different from other Americans." A woolly blue sweater Tilden wore seems to have positively enthralled the entire nation, and the London *Times* exclaimed that "his jumpers are the topic of the teatable."

While little Johnston struck the British as just that, a pleasant little sort, the lean giant caused them admiration and wonder: "Of great stature, he is loosely built with slender hips and very broad shoulders . . . in figure, an ideal lawn tennis player." His game they found so arresting—"There is no stroke Mr. Tilden cannot do at full speed, and his is undoubtedly the fastest serve seen"—that one of the more poetic observers even rhapsodized, "His silhouette as he prepares to serve suggests an Egyptian pyramid king about to administer punishment."

Seeing Tilden for the first time, unprepared for that sight, was obviously a striking experience. Not so much in what exactly they said but in their evident astonishment and determined hyperbolic reach do the British of 1920 best intimate what an extraordinary presence Big Bill Tilden must have been. Yet perhaps even more important, the British understood immediately that here was a different sort of athletic temperament. The Americans were not to fathom this in Tilden for years, if indeed many of them ever did. But Tilden had played only a handful of matches in England that summer before he was assessed perfectly in the sporting press: "He gives the impression that he regards lawn tennis as a game—a game which enables him to do fascinating things, but still a game. . . . When he has something in hand he indulges his taste for the varied at the expense of the commercial."

Pleased at the attention given him, even more gratified that his playing philosophy was appreciated, Tilden grew assured, and, boldly and not without some conceit, he began to enunciate his theories of the game. When not at the courts or attending the theater, he spent all his time writing in his hotel room, and within three weeks he had completed his first book, *The Art of Tennis.* "The primary object in match tennis is to break up the other man's game" was, significantly, the point he most emphasized.

Patterson, meanwhile, remained quite confident. An Australian, the nephew of the great opera star Nellie Melba, he was not only the defending Wimbledon champion but star of the team which held the Davis Cup. He was at his peak and generally recognized above Johnston as the ranking player in the world. At Wimbledon Patterson had only to bide his time scouting the opposition and practice at his leisure, for in those days the defender did not play in the regular tournament but was obliged only to meet the "all-comers" winner in a special challenge round.

Patterson's supremacy seemed all the more obvious after Tilden appeared to struggle in the all-comers final against the Japanese, Zenzo Shimizu. In each set Tilden fell far behind: 1–4 in the first, 2–4 in the second, 2–5 in the third. He won 6–4, 6–4, 13–11. Nobody realized it at the time, but it was one of Tilden's amusements, a favor to the crowd, to give lesser opponents a head start. Tilden had whipped Shimizu 6–1, 6–1 in a preliminary tournament the week before Wimbledon, and he certainly had no intention of cheating his Centre Court fans with that same sort of lopsided display. In the final set Big Bill tested himself and kept things going, largely just by hitting backhands and nothing much else.

"The player owes the gallery as much as an actor owes the audience," he wrote once; and Paul Gallico summed it up: "To his opponents it was a contest; with Tilden it was an expression of his own tremendous and overwhelming ego, coupled with feminine vanity." Big Bill never really creamed anybody unless he hated them or was in a particular hurry to get somewhere else.

Certainly he was not ever anxious to hastily depart Centre Court at Wimbledon, and he returned for the championship against Patterson on Saturday, July 3. Big Bill found this date especially felicitous; an obsessive patriot, he noted that, for an American, July 3 was the next best thing to July 4. He further buttressed this omen by somehow obtaining a four-leaf clover that he was assured had once grown under the chair that Abraham Lincoln used to sit in on the White House lawn. And so, with that talisman safely ensconced in his pocket, he set out to become the first American ever to win the Wimbledon men's championship.

Patterson had a strong serve and forehand, but his weakness was an odd corkscrew backhand that he hit sort of inside out. And so, curiously it seemed, Tilden began by playing to Patterson's powerful forehand. The champion ran off the first four games with dispatch and won the set 6–2. But then, as Tilden changed sides for the first time in the second set, he spotted a good friend, the actress Peggy Wood, sitting in the first row with a ticket he had provided her, and he looked straight at Miss Wood, and with a reassuring nod, that kind delivered with lips screwed up in smug confidence, he signaled to her that all was quite well, that it was in the bag, that finally, at the age of twenty-seven, he was about to become the champion of the world.

Miss Wood, of course, had no notion that she would be used as a conduit for history; nor, for that matter, could she understand Tilden's cockiness. He had lost the first set 6–2; he was getting clobbered by the best player in the world. But down the five full decades, and more, that have passed, she cannot forget that expression of his, nor what followed. "Immediately," she says, as if magic were involved, "Bill proceeded to play."

In that instant he had solved Patterson's forehand, and the champion, his strength ravaged, had nothing but his weakness to fall back upon. *The primary object in match tennis is to break up the other man's game.* "A subtle change came over Patterson's game," the *Guardian* correspondent wrote in some evident confusion. "Things that looked easy went out, volleys that ought to have been crisply negotiated ended up in the net." Tilden swept the next three sets at his convenience, losing only nine games, and toward the end it was noted for the record that "the Philadelphian made rather an exhibition of his opponent."

Big Bill did not lose another match of any significance anywhere in the world until a knee injury cost him a victory more than six years later. Playing for himself, for his country, for posterity, he was invincible. No man ever bestrode his sport as Tilden did for those years. It was not just that he could not be beaten, it was nearly as if he had invented the sport he conquered. Babe Ruth, Jack Dempsey, Red Grange and the other fabled American sweat lords of the times stood at the head of more popular games, but Tilden simply was tennis in the public mind: *Tilden and tennis*, it was said, in that order. He ruled the game as much by force of his curious, contradictory, often abrasive personality as by his proficiency. But he was not merely eccentric. He was the greatest irony in sport: to a game that then suffered a "fairy" reputation, Tilden gave a lithe, swashbuckling, athletic image—although he was in fact a homosexual, the only great male athlete we know to have been one.

Alone in the world of athletics, nearly friendless and, it seems, even ashamed of himself, there was seldom any joy for the man, even amidst his greatest tennis triumphs. It's quite likely that in his whole life Tilden never spent a night alone with an adult, man or woman. And his every day was shadowed by the bizarre and melancholy circumstances surrounding a childhood he tried to forget; certainly it is no coincidence that he did not blossom as a champion until just after he discarded the name of his youth.

He had been born on February 10, 1893, and christened William Tatem Tilden Jr., which he came to hate because everyone called him Junior or June. Finally, arbitrarily, around the time of his twenty-fifth birthday, he changed the Junior to the Second, II. That onus officially disposed of, June became Bill and then, even better, Big Bill.

He had been introduced to tennis early. It was an upper-class game, and the family he was born into was rich, of ascending social prominence, and even greater civic presence. The family mansion, Overleigh, was located in the wealthy Germantown section of Philadelphia, only a block or so from the Germantown Cricket Club. The Tildens belonged, of course, and the club was indeed to be the site of many Big Bill triumphs, but the family summered at a fashionable Catskill resort, Onteora, and it was there that young June learned the game of tennis, in the last year of the nineteenth century.

The first clear vision of him as a player does not arise, however, until about a decade later, when Tilden was playing, with little distinction, for the team at his small private school, Germantown Academy. This day he was struggling on the court, slugging everything, all cannonballs, when Frank Deacon, one of his younger friends, came by. Even then, as a schoolboy, Tilden was always closest to children years younger than he. At the end of a point, which, typically, Tilden had violently overplayed, hitting way out, Deacon hollered to him in encouragement, "Hey, June, take it easy."

Tilden stopped dead, and with what became a characteristic gesture, he swirled to face the boy, placing his hands on his hips and glaring at him. "Deacon," he snapped, "I'll play my own sweet game."

And so he did, every day of his life. He was the proudest of men and the saddest, pitifully alone and shy, but never so happy as when he brought his armful of rackets into the limelight or walked into a crowded room and contentiously took it over. George Lott, a Davis Cup colleague and a man who actively disliked Tilden, was nonetheless this mesmerized by him: "When he came into the room it was like a bolt of electricity hit the place. Immediately, there was a feeling of awe, as though you were in the presence of royalty. You knew you were in contact with greatness, even if only remotely. The atmosphere became charged, and there was almost a sensation of lightness when he left. You felt completely dominated and breathed a sigh of relief for not having ventured an opinion of any sort."

Tilden himself said, "I can stand crowds only when I am working in front of them, but then I love them." Obviously the crowds and the game were his sex. For a large part of his life, the glory years, all the evidence suggests that he was primarily asexual; it was not until he began to fade as a player and there were not enough crowds to play to that his homosexual proclivities really took over. But ahh, when he was king, he would often appear to trap himself in defeat, as he had against Shimizu, so that he could play the better role, prolonging his afternoon as the cynosure in the sun, prancing and stalking upon his chalked stage, staring at officials, fuming at the crowd, now toying with his opponent, then saluting him grandly, spinning, floating, jumping, playing his own sweet game, reveling in the game.

And yet, for all these excesses of drama and melodrama, his passion for competition was itself even superseded by another higher sense: sportsmanship. Tilden was utterly scrupulous, obsessed with honor, and he would throw points (albeit with grandeur, Pharisee more than Samaritan) if he felt that a linesman had cheated his opponent. Big Bill was the magistrate of every match he played, and the critic as well. "Peach!" he would cry in delight, lauding any opponent who beat him with a good shot. And, if inspired or mad enough at the crowd or at his rival, he would serve out the match by somehow holding five balls in one huge hand and then tossing four of them up, one ofter another, and pounding out four cannonball aces—bam, bam, bam, bam; 15–30–40–game—then throwing the fifth ball away with disdain. That was the style to it. Only the consummate showman would think of the extra ball as the closing fillip to the act.

"He is an artist," Franklin P. Adams wrote at Big Bill's

peak. "He is more of an artist than nine-tenths of the artists I know. It is the beauty of the game that Tilden loves; it is the chase always, rather than the quarry."

Further, even more unlike almost all great champions in every sport, whose brilliance is early recognized, early achieved, Tilden was required to make himself great. Very nearly he created himself. Only a few years before he became champion of the world, he could not make the college varsity at the University of Pennsylvania. He taught himself, inspired himself, fashioning a whole new level for the game in the bargain.

Withal, it is probable that the very fact that he was homosexual was largely responsible for the real success he achieved in tennis; he had none elsewhere. Urbane, well-read, a master bridge player, a connoisseur of fine music, he held pretensions to writing and acting as well as tennis, but these gossamer vanities only cost him great amounts of stature and money, and even held him up to mockery. For all his intelligence, tennis was the only venture that June Tilden could ever succeed at, until the day he died in his cramped walk-up room near Hollywood and Vine, where he lived out his tragedy, a penniless ex-con, scorned or forgotten, alone as always, and desperately in need of love from a world that had tolerated him only for its amusement. "He felt things so very deeply," Peggy Wood says. "He was not a frivolous person, And yet, I never saw him with anybody who could have been his confidant. How must it be like that? There must have been so many things deep within him that he could never talk about. I suppose he died of a broken heart." It seems he did.

To the end, in the good times and the bad, he searched for one thing above all: a son. He could not have one, and so he would find one for himself, make one, as he made himself a great player to honor the dead mother he worshipped. But the boys he found, whom he loved and taught, would grow up and put away childish things, which is what any game is, what tennis is, and ultimately, what Big Bill Tilden was. He was the child of his own dreams, always, until the day he died, age sixty, his bags packed, ready once again to leave for a tennis tournament.

CHAPTER TWO

"Bill would adapt and lick them all"

IN 1920, when Tilden became champion of the world, tennis was a game with a very limited constituency. Only five nations entered the Davis Cup, and although a few public parks players, such as Bill Johnston or Vinnie Richards, had surfaced in the United States, it was still an upper-crust sport the world over. As physically testing an activity as it is, tennis had for so long been associated with effete ladies and gentlemen that it had taken on the image of a sissy game, one that it really was not to shake completely for yet another half-century, till the 1970s. In the best traditions of sophomoric wit, lawn tennis was referred to as "long penis" on the campuses; and in the sports departments it was the cynical summation that any player could earn a top ranking so long as he had "ten years of practice and a millionaire father." Young Allison Danzig was distraught when he joined the New York *Times* sports staff and was assigned the tennis beat, one that no red-blooded sportshawk would take.

If there was a prototype player of this period, it was one named Richard Norris Williams, who was always listed as R. Norris and always known as Dick. A wealthy Philadelphia socialite, born abroad, raised in Switzerland, he came back to the United States, most of the way, on the

Titanic, went to Harvard, and was the national champion in 1914 and 1916. Although Williams was only a couple of years older than Tilden, he was as much a prodigy as Tilden was a late bloomer, and so he always seemed much older, and was even something of an idol to Tilden—especially after Williams whipped Big Bill's older brother, Herbert, in a club match in Philadelphia. From all accounts, Dick Williams also must have been about the nicest guy around, and Tilden really liked the man, if he was also somewhat jealous of his easy popularity.

Tilden wrote a good deal of tennis fiction, none of it inspired, much of it trite. He peopled his stories with characters based on his acquaintances, making no effort to disguise them. There was a Gerald Palmerson, for example, who was obviously Gerald Patterson, Billy Jolson (Johnston), and even a lanky player named Tilton who pops up in the supporting cast occasionally. The one character who appears most often, and in a featured role in every instance, is a paragon of a man named Dick Thomas. That, of course, is Dick Williams. Dick Thomas, the character, was Tilden's stylized version of Dick Williams; nobody could be so good and noble as Dick Thomas. He spent most of his time in the stories saving younger players (usually Buddie or Brickie) from moral degradation and instructing them in points of honor. "I would rather have you licked like a sportsman than win like a rotter," he informs his young chum in the climax of "Brickie's Game Point."

And in "Food for Thought," in which young Frank Russell of Yale plays the juvenile lead, there is this exchange:

> "Dick," Frank said slowly, "you're a darned good sport."
> "No I'm not, kid. It's just part of tennis to play the game fair."

And so on.

If somewhat overstated by Tilden, who was always given to extremes, that was the prevailing spirit in tennis at the time. It was a gentlemen's diversion. Dick Williams, the real-life person, embodied all this. He played world championship matches with about the same attitude as most people have for mixed doubles down at the playground at four-thirty on Tuesdays. Oh sure, Williams would have certainly rather won than lost, but in either case he didn't want the result to get in the way of the playing. As a consequence, he hit every ball as hard as he could, and ideally so that it would kick up the chalk on the baseline. He did that because playing that way was what gratified him.

Obviously, with such a small margin for error, Dick Williams could blow hot and cold. When he was on, when his bombs were clicking into the corners, he was invincible. Of course, after a time he would go off; but it was all a lot of fun for Dick. In 1923, at the very height of Tilden's powers, when no one in the world could even stay with him on the court, Williams came up against him in the finals—best three-out-of-five sets—of the Pennsylvania State championships at the Merion Cricket Club. It was one of Williams' days. According to the best memories, which have probably been only slightly exaggerated, Williams won the first set in six and a half minutes, allowing Tilden a total of three points. Not three game—*no* games; three points. In the second set Williams was still operating at about 98 per cent of peak efficiency, and he won that 6–1. So: 6–0, 6–1 against the greatest player of all time at his peak. But then the magic began to drain out of Williams' racket, the balls started going out by an inch or two, and Tilden won the last three sets and the match. Nonetheless, Big Bill always said that no man in history ever played tennis like Dick Williams played tennis in those two sets.

Many years later a reporter went to Philadelphia specifically to talk to Williams about that match. Williams died shortly thereafter, but he was still in full command of his faculties; he just didn't remember the match at all. Nothing. Which match? What did it matter, all those old matches? It had all been only a game, one set like any other. When Williams served as Davis Cup captain in 1926, he got up and left the stadium before Tilden and René Lacoste faced off in the concluding match, because someone asked him if he'd like to fill in as a fourth for doubles. Tilden seriously injured himself during the Lacoste match, and because the U.S. had already clinched the Cup, he wanted to default; but since the captain was off somewhere playing doubles, Tilden figured he better stick it out, and in the process he further damaged the knee. But why would Dick Williams want to sit around and watch some meaningless Challenge Round match if he could get into a nice game of doubles? That was the world of tennis that Big Bill came to.

For the sake of propriety the ladies and gentlemen who played at their clubs were obliged to cover themselves. Pristine white was obligatory, for it least revealed patches of sweat. Even on the hottest days it was the custom for the men to wear long flannel pants and regular long-steeved Oxford shirts; sometimes the shirts were also of flannel. On a humid day it was nothing for a player's clothes to pick up ten pounds of moisture and for the players to lose even more of their own weight. Little Bill Johnston was supposed to have weighed at least 125 pounds, but Dr. Carl Fischer, a top amateur player who was also an osteopath, swears that he once weighed Johnston in at 103 after a particularly grueling match on a humid day.

The other equipment was relatively primitive. In the middle of matches Tilden would often switch and go barefoot or play in his stocking feet because he could get more traction that way than in the rudimentary sneakers of the time. Such a simple item as a warm-up jacket didn't even exist, and although part of the reason for this was sheer affectation, Tilden often wore his regular camel's hair coat to the court. He, more than most players, broke strings all the time, and once manufacturers found that there was more money in using lamb gut to make surgical sutures, it was difficult to obtain quality strings. As much as tennis balls vary in their properties today, there was even greater disparity then. The British ball was made with a plug in it until 1924, and in no case were new balls put into play every few games as they are now. As a result the balls would pick up grass stains or clay stains, be hard to see and harder to hit. Usually the balls tended to sail. "People conveniently forget that the balls were much faster in those days," René Lacoste says. Tilden played with a Bancroft racket with a handle that measured 5⅜ inches in circumference; it weighed 14¼ ounces, heavy by today's standards (by 1937 Tilden himself was down to toting a 13½-ounce racket with a 4¾-inch handle). In his prime, when he used the 14¼-ounce racket, he strung it tightly, with at least sixty-five and sometimes seventy pounds of pressure. Of the modern players, Arthur Ashe most closely resembles Tilden physically, being slightly shorter and the same weight; also, Ashe has the big serve. He strings his rackets with sixty pounds of pressure, which is considered extremely taut nowadays.

There were few indoor courts and the lighting was uniformly bad in all of them. There was no professional instruction to speak of in the United States. Tilden's brother, Herbert, six years his senior and an intercollegiate doubles champion while at Penn, taught him to play. As late as 1910 there was only one lawn tennis pro in the country (although there were a handful of others who taught all the racket sports—squash, court tennis, etc.), and when the

West Side Tennis Club moved from Manhattan to Forest Hills in 1914, it had to send to England for a pro. By 1920 there were still perhaps no more than a score of teaching professionals in the United States, and they were thought of as servants more than teachers. "George, the professional," Tilden refers to a character in one of his short stories, exactly as he might say "Bridget, the maid." There is no evidence that Big Bill ever deigned to consult a pro in his whole life.

And the very thought that he, or any of his fellows, would actually make a living of lawn tennis! In a story entitled "The Amateur," which was published in 1924 and is as snotty a piece as Tilden ever wrote, he looked with utter disdain upon an indigent young player who was forced to take a club teaching job in order to pay the doctor's bills for his desperately ill mother. Tilden makes it clear that turning tennis pro is perfectly analogous to a young lady turning whore: "God! How he hated the money that was dirtying up the game he loved." The one saving grace to the whole disagreeable tale was that the young pro's "good breeding kept him in his place far more than a man who was not aware of social niceties." And yet, if professional teaching of tennis was déclassé, professional playing was simply nonexistent. The first pro tour was not organized until 1926, when a promoter named C. C. (Cash and Carry) Pyle signed up Suzanne Lenglen, the Maid Marvel, and Vinnie Richards, plus a couple of spear carriers.

Indeed, in 1920 it was still considered rather tacky in some quarters that lawn tennis should fetch a player any notoriety whatsoever. Thus when Tilden played in the tournament at the Queens Club prior to Wimbledon, his first opponent was listed only demurely as a Mr. Hogan. Others in the field were shyer still and followed the custom of taking what was known as a *nom de racquette.* Cuniculus,

A. Lone and L. Tennis were all mysterious adversaries in this tournament. The present Wimbledon stadium was not constructed until 1922, so in 1920, when Tilden upset Patterson, and again the following year, when he beat Babe Norton of South Africa in the Challenge Round, the world's premier tournament was still held in a pastoral setting where there were seats for hardly five hundred people, and, as one observer wrote, the whole scene resembled "a delightful vicarage garden party." The players themselves often called the lines. As late as 1926 at Forest Hills, Tilden sat in as a linesman when he was not playing.

And yet, as quaint as all this sounds, who is to say that the competition then wasn't every bit as good as it is today? To be sure, the pool of talent was not nearly so large. Once seeding was introduced in the early 1920s, the best players almost always had a breeze to the quarterfinals. But as there were fewer stars, so too were there fewer tournaments of consequence. When Tilden played at Forest Hills or in the Davis Cup, he was primed, at his best. The results were truer then precisely because there were not so many of them—and Tilden won every match with everyone at their best. Obviously, if Tilden were playing today he could not go for seven years without a defeat in a major tournament, because he would be playing ten or eleven months a year (or twelve, knowing him), flying all over the world, running a string of tennis camps on the side, filming commercials and making appearances on *The Merv Griffin Show*. But this takes nothing away from what he accomplished under the conditions he was faced with in his era. Every time it counted, he beat the person he was playing.

An athlete, no less than a general or a statesman, must be judged by what he accomplished in his time. That is the only appropriate standard. Since some athletic proficiency can, however, be precisely measured, since we know that people run faster and jump higher all the time, as they also live longer and grow bigger, it is as easy as it is fashionable to conclude that no athlete of the 1920s could beat any reasonable representative of the 1970s. But to what purpose?

Johnny Weissmuller, the Olympic swimming champion of Tilden's era, has had his best times lowered by adolescent girls. Are we to say then with a straight face that Johnny Weissmuller at his peak was a lesser athletic presence than some fourteen-year-old girl? If we are—and that is what the bald figures tell us—then it is also to say that kids in the Little League would strike out Babe Ruth, that Jack Dempsey would be knocked out in the Golden Gloves, and that Tracy Austin, the U.S. fourteen-and-under girls champion from Rolling Hills, California, would have beaten Big Bill Tilden in straight sets in the first round at Forest Hills in 1923. It is also to say that Napoleon was a failure as a general because he didn't know how to deploy air power and that Jefferson was an inconsiderable mind because he couldn't change a tire.

Anyway, if players are progressively better, a prime reason is that they had Tilden to build on. It was he who first made a science of tennis, mastered every stroke, conceived every stratagem. The greatest talent and genius resided in one. He could hold forth for an hour or more on nothing but how a ball spun. For every stroke he had at least three different varieties, for every attack a defense. And that is important, because although there may have been fewer top players then, there was more variety.

Without manuals, jet planes, videotape or teaching conventions, each player grew up with his own style. Manuel Alonso, a high-ranking world-class Spanish player who lived for many years in the U.S., Tilden's contemporary, says now, "The beauty of that time was that each individual *was* a certain game. And no matter how good Bill may have been, his greatest capacity was at adapting.

These players today all do the same thing against each other. Bill would adapt and lick them all, one by one, before they knew what he had done to them."

Significantly, the one player who gave Tilden the most trouble—and the one whom he egregiously overrated—was Henri Cochet, whose style it was to hit everything on the rise, that is, to meet the ball before it reached the apex of its bounce. Tilden had never seen anyone do that with proficiency and consistency before he encountered Cochet, and so he had worked out no reliable defense. Cochet really quite intimidated him in his last amateur years, when Tilden was over the hill and the Frenchman was at his peak. Of course, a few years later, as pros, when they were both over the hill together and when Tilden had fathomed the Cochet game, he beat him regularly.

Johnston was the only other player ever to hold an Indian sign on Tilden and was, in fact, perversely responsible for the totality of Tilden's great game. He had to improve in order to beat Little Bill. Then, once Tilden did reach his peak, Johnston was the only remotely serious competition, and he but occasionally. There is one school of thought that Tilden never exhibited his ultimate ability except for the odd game here and there because when he was capable of his best there was no one capable of drawing that from him. After he won a couple of Wimbledons, Tilden saw no need whatsoever to waste a lot of time every summer going over to England and back just to prove the academic point that he was champion of the world. In just about so many words he said that the Mountain could come to Mohammed, that the world championship would be settled wherever he chose to play. Naturally, this kind of hurt the British, not to mention the gate, so in 1923 the United States Lawn Tennis Association prevailed upon Little Bill to go over to Wimbledon as a consolation prize. Johnston won the championship with an economy of effort, losing exactly four games in the finals, and then he came back to the United States and lost to Tilden in the Nationals, winning only nine games. The gap was that great.

How Tilden zoomed to this estate, coming from nowhere to catch up to and then pass Johnston, and everyone else, is as fascinating as any part of his saga. Indeed, given the fact that throughout tennis history champions have been invariably divined (if not already crowned) by age twenty, then what Tilden pulled off, frog-to-prince, is simply impossible. Big Bill was never the best anywhere in his life until suddenly he was best in the world. In his own family his brother, Herbert, was better; in his small private school somebody named Buddy Mann could beat him; and at Penn he couldn't even make a very ordinary college varsity. A teammate named William D. Stroud, who was to become an eminent cardiologist, used to regularly beat out Tilden for the sixth and last singles position, and when he entered the National Collegiate Athletic Association Tournament as a sophomore, Tilden was routed 6–1, 6–3 in the *qualifying* round by one Eli Whitney of Harvard; that is, he wasn't even good enough to get into the tournament.

By comparison, Johnston made the top ten for the first time as a teenager and was ranked number one in 1915 at age twenty. Tilden, twenty-two that year, reached number seventy. The next year he was admitted to the U.S. Nationals, whereupon he promptly went out in the first round, overcome by the talents of Harold Throckmorton. Carl Fischer was one of Tilden's protégés during this period and especially close to him. He says, "If you had asked me around 1915–16 if I thought Bill Tilden would ever be national champion, I would have been stunned. I just would have replied, 'Whatever would make you ask me a foolish question like that?' "

But, obsessed, Tilden went about building his game piece by piece, almost as a child tries to collect every bubble gum card in the collection. "I began tennis wrong," he said later. "My strokes were wrong and my viewpoint clouded." He would create the first complete game. To this end he entered every rinky-dink tournament that would have him: Beach Haven, Ocean City, Buck Hill Farms, the Delaware State. In winter, on milder days when there was no snow on the ground, he would hit endless balls against a backboard, or in harsher weather he would go inside and work out on squash courts (although he had too full a backswing ever to be a champion squash player). He began coaching at Germantown Academy, where he learned foremost to learn from his students. If a boy said, Why does a ball do such-and-such? Tilden would hit a hundred or a thousand or two thousand himself until he could provide an answer. He went to other schools as well, giving free lessons, talking tennis to whoever cared. Winters he gave fundamental clinics (without balls) in a country club ballroom. He took a job writing for the Philadelphia *Evening Ledger*, much of which involved covering tennis. Except for one odd interlude during the winter of 1915–16 when he went up to the Catskills and posed as a model for a photographer who was illustrating a book of Robert Service poems, Tilden does not seem to have ever been far from tennis during this transitional period.

At last in 1917, coincidentally as many players went to war, Tilden made a quantum jump as a player, capping the year by reaching the quarterfinals in the so-called Patriotic Tournament, which was substituted for the Nationals. Big Bill was himself inducted into the Signal Corps shortly thereafter, diagnosed for flat feet, and dispatched to Pittsburgh, where he served out the hostilities under a commanding officer who enjoyed tennis and gave Private Tilden plenty of time to practice. On July 6, 1918, in Chicago, Big Bill won his first U.S. singles title, the Clay Courts, beating Chuck Garland despite a wrenched ankle;

and by the time he reached Forest Hills he was still undefeated for the year and co-favorite along with Lindley
Murray, the defending champion. Of course, it was a grossly
devalued field, with many of the better players, notably
Johnston and Williams, still away at war.

Even against these slim pickings Tilden failed to dis-
tinguish himself, however; although when Murray did
rout him in the finals, Big Bill had a manifold excuse. He
played that match with a huge boil on the Achilles tendon
of his right ankle, but since it was always his determination
not to mention injuries, lest they detract from an opponent's
accomplishment, few realized that he had lost under such a
painful handicap. As a consequence, when Johnston came
out of the service and Tilden beat him two or three times
in the summer of 1919, there was a general tendency to dis-
regard these results. The conventional wisdom remained
that the Philadelphian was a frail competitor whose prominence during the war was accounted for only because much
better players had been in places less convenient to Forest
Hills than Pittsburgh.

Wishful thinking may also have been factored into this
popular equation, for Tilden was beginning to leave an
impression as a person as well as a player. "He wasn't con-
ceited yet," his friend Carl Fischer remembers, "but the
better he became, the more opinionated, the more belliger-
ent. All of his personal liabilities were accentuated by his
success." Tilden was perhaps even more insufferable than
usual at Forest Hills this time because he had whipped
Johnston in straight sets on the grass at Newport a couple
of weeks before, and he really believed now that he had the
goods. Al Laney, the perceptive tennis writer for the New
York *Herald Tribune,* remembers that when Tilden upset
Dick Williams in the semifinals to stand but one match
away from the national title, "people appeared to be horrified at the result, and there was a certain resentment

against Williams that he had permitted himself to be beaten by such a fellow."

Little Bill, always the people's choice, saved the day by stopping Tilden in the finals. The turf was soggy from two days of rain, and all the experts opined that this had muted Tilden's big guns. But Big Bill himself thought otherwise; he was sure that Johnston had done him in by exploiting his backhand. This was the one loophole in the complete game. Tilden didn't have a hard backhand drive. He did have a lovely backhand slice, but he could not attack off it, and Johnston had pounded it to death, moving in to pick off the soft returns and crunch Tilden with them. It wasn't even close: 6–4, 6–4, 6–3.

As far as he had come, so incredibly fast, Tilden seemed to have reached his limit just short of the top. Two years running he had gotten to the national finals but had failed to win so much as a set. Any sensible, normal twenty-six-year-old man with a family and a mortgage would have gone back to tending the store at this point. Bill Tilden went to Providence, Rhode Island, instead and taught himself how to hit a backhand drive.

In Providence he took the ostensible job of selling insurance for the Equitable. In fact, he earned his real keep by playing tennis with a young protégé named Arnold Jones, whose father was an insurance executive who owned one of the few indoor courts in the country (it still stands too, if in a somewhat dilapidated condition, the Valley Forge of American tennis). Tilden lived with the Joneses, and apart from brief ritual forays into the occult insurance realm, he spent the whole winter hitting backhands alone or with young Jones, or chopping wood to build up new muscles in his arms. The backhand drive required a new grip, a new swing and new thinking. It would be the equivalent, say, of Nolan Ryan spending his entire winter learning how to throw a knuckleball. Jones was a fine young player, the national sixteen-and-under champion, but he was certainly no match for Tilden. Nonetheless, the new backhand was so foreign to Big Bill that for much of the winter Jones beat him consistently. But he persevered in what had become by now a compulsion to develop the last frame in the complete game, and by the summer, at Wimbledon, he beat Gerald Patterson and stood at last at the summit.

The only dispute to that claim remained Johnston (and his innumerable fans). Because Tilden had not personally defeáted Little Bill at Wimbledon, there were many who considered his victory there a fluke and who suggested that Big Bill was just minding the championship for the rightful owner. So, on an overcast Monday in September of 1920, ten thousand people packed into the wooden stands at Forest Hills, most of them content that they were about to witness Johnston taking back what was properly his. Both men, the American holder and the Wimbledon holder, had lost only two sets apiece in their march to the finals, both were fit, and they had no excuses.

Tilden spent the night before at a friend's house nearby, listening to what he called "foreign music" till eleven, when he took a peaceful night's sleep. After a typically large breakfast, he drifted over to the West Side Tennis Club early and bided the morning playing auction bridge. John McCormack, the Irish tenor, had bet ten dollars on him and came by once to urge Big Bill to win. "What will you do for me if I win?" Tilden asked.

"Anything. What can I do?" McCormack replied, somewhat taken aback.

"Sing me Rachmaninoff's 'When Night Descends,'" Tilden snapped. McCormack mumbled that he would and left. Off and on during the bridge game Little Bill would drop by and peer in.

Then, when the rain held off, the two took the court, the Philadelphian and the Californian. It was not until after this match that they became, universally, Big Bill and Little Bill. Tilden in his camel's hair coat, the big sash tied, carried an armful of rackets to the arena, Little Bill but two, and soon they began under gray, forbidding skies. It was called then the greatest U.S. final in history, one that was interspersed with the most incredible tennis and goings-on.

It began, however, rather prosaically, and not at all like Tilden either: 6–1 for him in the first set. Significantly, it was his new backhand drive that swept him along. Johnston would never win off that wing again. Tilden might have coasted to an easy victory too, but volleys landed short, and Johnston then would get back into the point, time and again, with perfect lobs. Tilden's greatest weakness, relatively, was always his overhead. Despite the fact that that shot much resembles a serve, at which none was better than Big Bill, he could never duplicate his service intensity on the overhead. He seldom slammed but trusted to placement, and this day he was not so precise. Johnston scurried back. When he got well ahead in the second set, Big Bill gave up the ghost and let Little Bill run it out at 6–1. Then, having traded lopsided sets, the two Americans got down to playing what was characterized in the press the next day as "mechanically perfect tennis amid incredible drama."

At high pitch of performance, Tilden won the third set 7–5, and after an intermission he took command in the fourth as well. Rain began to spatter, however, and just as a point began, Tilden understood the umpire in the chair to call off the action. For some reason, never clear, the tournament referee emerged onto the court at this point, overruled the umpire and awarded the point to Johnston. Tilden, shaken and fuming, brought new electricity to the court. Soon he stood but two points away from the match, but Johnston somehow retrieved a short volley and won his way back. It was never that one man faltered, only that the other raised his game. Now, inspired, Johnston raised his. He broke Big Bill and held for the set: 7–5. Four sets, a dead tie: 6–1, 1–6, 7–5, 5–7.

Nearby on Long Island, at Mitchel Field in Garden City, an army photographer, Sergeant Joseph Saxe, climbed into the back of a JN-Curtiss one-engine airplane that was piloted by Navy Lieutenant James Murray Grier, a distinguished member of the famous Lafayette Escadrille and, like Tilden, a Philadelphian. It was his assignment to fly the plane over the Forest Hills stadium so that Sergeant Saxe could take photographs that could be displayed for recruiting purposes. Taking photographs of exciting events from airplanes was considered a pretty romantic calling at that time.

Lieutenant Grier flew over the stadium at a height of five hundred feet the first time, and the novelty rather amused the crowd, relieving it for a moment of the incredible tension building on the court. Both Tilden and Johnston paused for a second and watched the plane. Lieutenant Grier took the JN-Curtiss up to nine hundred feet for the next pass, high enough to be only barely distracting, but then, as Sergeant Saxe wanted some closer shots, the pilot brought the plane down to three hundred feet the third time by and barely four hundred on his fourth pass. Now the crowd responded with some evident irritation and watched rather peevishly as a point ended and Lieutenant Grier took the plane around for one more fly-through. He climbed a bit higher and had just reached an altitude of about five hundred feet, turning back over Queens Boulevard, when the crowd noticed that the engine noise was somewhat different. Both players, near the net, also turned their heads toward the JN-Curtiss.

Of momentum, it moved along just a bit more as Lieutenant Grier worked the controls in desperation. But he found no response; the plane choked out and quit, and at first it seemed to appear to glide serenely toward the earth. Such a peaceful arc, it all seemed part of the maneuver. Only at the last, tail straight up, did it horribly plummet; and for an instant, to the players and those in the far stand, it seemed that the plane might dive into the crowd itself.

At the last it disappeared behind the stand and hit the ground barely two hundred feet away. The impact was such that Tilden felt the ground shake under his feet. The motor slammed three feet down into the sod, and the two men were dashed to pieces. Immediately about a third of the people in the stadium left their seats and hurried to the crash, where many of them began to comb the hot wreckage for souvenirs.

The umpire even feared a panic. Better to keep the show rolling. "Can you go on?" he asked Johnston, and the tiny man just said, "Yes," and calmly turned and walked back to the baseline to receive serve.

"How 'bout you, Bill?"

"Right," Tilden replied, and without any more ado he turned to an ashen-faced ball boy and held out his hand for two. Then he moved to the line, put his first one in, and from there the two men went back about their business, no less brilliant than before. With Tilden's serve pounding away, twenty pure aces on the day, Johnston could never get control of the match. Tilden took the break he needed and closed out the set at 6–3.

It was while they were extricating the bodies from the ground that Tilden came to the net and shook Little Bill's hand and stood there, undisputed, best in all the world.

Chapter Three

"Whatever he wanted to do, he did it, and he did it in style"

TWO months later, on November 15, 1920, Tilden and Johnston, with Sam Hardy as captain, and a couple of spares sailed from San Francisco to Auckland, New Zealand, on the S.S. *Niagara*. There, at the Domain Cricket Club, they won back the Davis Cup over the international combine of Australia and New Zealand, which was known as Australasia. It was the first time the United States had won the Cup since 1913, and the first of seven straight Cups that Tilden and America were to take, which is still the record. Tilden had won Wimbledon, Forest Hills, and led his country to the Davis Cup in six months' time—all of which he would repeat in a shorter span the next summer.

So, conveniently as the Roaring Twenties burst upon America, tennis had its mythic colossus to go with the Sultan of Swat and the Manassa Mauler and the Wheaton Iceman and all the rest. Tilden remained a cloudier figure than the other heroes, because homosexuality was a taboo subject then; and while many people knew the secret (the USLTA shuddered that it would become common knowledge), the general public did not. Glaring at a linesman, as he had at young Frank Deacon, Tilden could appear swish and bitchy—"Who *is* this fruit?" Ty Cobb is supposed to have said the first time he saw Tilden—but any effeminacy vanished in the action. Tilden always appeared much more mincing in the theater than on the court, although, of course, questioning line calls was indisputably theater to him. "He had too much power to be effeminate playing, no matter how effeminate he was on the stage," says Gloria Butler, a long-time pupil and younger friend of Tilden. "It was a funny mixture, but then, Bill was a funny mixture in every way."

Playing, he moved with a grace that compared itself naturally to the dance, which he also had a talent for. He was a superb ice skater as well. Slim, double-jointed, with long arms and legs, Tilden had the perfect athletic build. The boxing coach at Yale watched him play and then tried to get him to take up the ring, marveling that he possessed "the most amazing footwork I've ever seen." Although it is doubtful that Tilden ever hit more than a dozen golf balls in his life, he won a bet for a friend once by stepping up and hitting a drive about two hundred yards, straight down the fairway.

Big Bill had wide clothes-hanger shoulders that tapered down to thin hips, so that while he reached more than six feet one in height, he never weighed more than 175, and that only when he was in his fifties. Like a child who insists that he is five and a half years old as soon as he reaches his fifth birthday, Tilden was always very particular about listing his height as six feet one *and a half.* He worked at the illusion of size—Big Bill!—and almost all his contemporaries still living refer to him offhand as having been six three or six four. They are amazed to learn the truth and are often reluctant to accept the lower figure. It just doesn't seem possible that Big Bill Tilden was only six feet one and a half.

Growing up unassured and undistinguished, Tilden always seemed to have a hat on his head, which was the fashion of that period. However, as soon as he achieved some prominence, he began going hatless and rarely thereafter was covered. He wanted to be recognized, and he was, almost universally—abroad as well as in the United States. Who the hell was Babe Ruth in France? Le Grand Bill was the one they all knew, everywhere in the world. Just in case anybody should miss him, towering hatless over smaller people in hats, Tilden made it a point to bring along some rackets wherever he went. When he sailed to Germany in 1926, he lugged a complement of thirty-six rackets.

While Big Bill was not a handsome man, women found him of distinctive appearance, striking. Mrs. Charles Garland, the widow of a good contemporary player, regarded him with these curious extremes: "apish, but attractive." His eyes were small and became slits when he laughed; he had a wide straight mouth of little expression, a high forehead with thinning hair slicked back, small ears and the lantern jaw that passes down the generations of Tilden men. But then, very little attention was paid to his face; it was his presence and character that defined him.

He was a jumble of contradictions. Far from being the homosexual dandy, Tilden was a sloppy dresser. He bought the cheapest suits at a Philadelphia store named Jacob Reed; they hung on him formlessly, and often could be dirty as well. Although he was never less than immaculate on the court and would rail at some poor protégé who dared wear pants with a grass stain, he was often forgetful when it came to getting things cleaned, himself included. Since Tilden had a compulsion about not appearing nude in the locker room, and was literally never seen undraped by men who knew him for much of his life, what he would deem a lack of privacy sometimes made it difficult for him to take a shower even when he remembered to.

He trained, as he lived, strictly by his own peremptory dogma. For instance, he couldn't abide soft drinks, so he declared that they caused gas and cut a player's wind. Yet he drank potfuls of coffee—burning or he would send it back—each cup larded with at least three or four heaping spoonfuls of sugar. Moreover, for six months a year, most years, he chain smoked, taking it up after Forest Hills, puffing away till the spring. In this case, since he thoroughly enjoyed cigarettes, he announced that they had no effect on wind whatsoever, although he also somehow arrived at the conclusion that smoking did affect eyesight. As his own eyesight diminished naturally with age, he became more dubious about cigarettes and forbade his students to smoke. He didn't really smoke anyway, but, very much like an old lady, he would hold the cigarette between thumb and forefinger, take short little drags and blow the smoke out without inhaling much, if at all.

In any event, he had amazing stamina; Vinnie Richards called him "inhuman" in this respect. He could just run other players into the ground. Dr. Carl Fischer remembers once when Tilden drove nonstop from California to Pennsylvania in three days, just pulling over for a couple of catnaps (and this was long before any Interstates). Then he went out as soon as he arrived and played a couple of matches. Five sets a day was not uncommon with Tilden at any time in his life, literally till the day he died.

Basically, what he ate was cholesterol. Although he took room service or dined out most days of his adult life, he ate, as he dressed, quite prosaically, and if served something downright exotic—chicken, say, or fish—he would push it around his plate, "picking at it," according to one hostess, or hiding it under other food he left untouched. Lamb chops were on the borderline of acceptance; he would eat the eye, but nothing else. All in the world that he wanted were steaks, which he consumed meal after meal, and often right before a match. Some of his grandest feasts came just an hour or so before he stepped onto the court. "You should have plenty of fuel in you," he replied to anyone who would dispute him in this matter. "Better to be slow for a few games at the start because you are full than it is to be weak-kneed and shaky at the climax because you are hungry." Of course, this soon became a self-fulfilling proposition as Tilden quite convinced himself that he was a slow starter and strong finisher.

A typical Tilden meal, training or otherwise, would start with a huge vat of soup or a fruit cocktail or honeydew melon. That little fruit sampling was about the only healthy thing he ever ate in his life. Then came the steak or two, and some hash-brown potatoes. Some people think they can recall him eating vegetables other than corn, but his nephew and namesake, William T. Tilden III, swears that his uncle would never touch a salad or green vegetable. For dessert he would always have ice cream. He was absolutely nuts about ice cream. And when he polished off cereal in the morning, he would bury it in the thickest possible cream.

Baron Gottfried von Cramm, the German player who was subsequently imprisoned by the Nazis and later married to Barbara Hutton, remembers a typical Tilden evening in Berlin: "Bill was always the center—witty, amusing—interested in everything from the latest gossip to the latest modern art, all the while nourishing himself on giant steaks. He might have three of those in the course of an evening—floating them down with literally gallons of strong coffee, while chain smoking all the time. Quite frequently, those parties would end up in his own suite, so he was always there to the end. But early next morning, looking very much his splendid self, he was at the court. Everyone assumed that Bill just didn't need any sleep and rest at all, and we were much too lightheaded during those years ever to wonder where this all might be leading."

While gluttony, tobacco and nonstop parties were all

quite acceptable to Tilden, he remained absolutely apoplectic on the subject of liquor. Besides burning hot coffee,
the only other thing he ever drank was ice cold water.
Sometimes he'd start the day just by downing a whole
pitcher. The French were so amused with his penchant for
constantly drinking mineral water that, when he played in
Paris in 1928, a glass of water became known as a Tilden
cocktail, and people were actually going around saying,
"I'll have a Tilden."

His antipathy to liquor seems to have derived entirely
from the fact that both his father and his older brother,
Herbert, whom he idolized, had liked to have a few with
the boys. Despite little evidence (virtually none in Herbert's case) that drinking had anything to do with their
deaths, Tilden grew quite convinced that liquor had played
a major part, and he often expressed this judgment as fact.
For himself, he not only became a teetotaler but something
of a scold on the subject as well. And he would never
equivocate. "Alcohol is a poison that affects the eye, the
mind, and the wind," he declared.

In his fiction, where he could trot out his characters to
deliver his most personal messages, the evils of demon rum
are one of a cadre of favorite recurring themes. *Glory's Net,*
his only novel, which was published in 1930, is Tilden's
most personal document, and sure enough, the tennis
champion who is hero of the book, David Cooper, sees his
marriage and career start to crumble because of an occasional weekend highball. Worse, David's younger brother
Billy, who is "a little fresh, but not a bit evil-minded as
kids go today . . . not a consistent necker," himself ac-
cepts a drink at a "queer little cafe in Montmartre." Mary,
David's drippy small-town wife, whom he met at a church
picnic, swoons: "Oh Billy, you mustn't touch liquor. Look
what it does to David."

Happily David at last perceives the folly of his ways, and

a wise David/Tilden advises Billy, "A fellow who drinks is a damned fool, and believe me, I know."

It was Tilden's own accounting that the last drop of alcohol to cross his lips came when he was playing at a tournament on the Riviera in 1930. The tournament, in Monaco, was sponsored by George Pierce Butler, the tobacco tycoon, who knew Tilden personally. It was here too that Tilden met Butler's daughter Gloria, a little girl at the time, who was to be one of the few women ever to gain any sort of personal access to him; Angel Child he called her.

In any event, just before Tilden was to play an early-round match he came down with some frightful stomach cramps from food poisoning and advised Butler that he was going to default. This was disaster for the tournament, and Butler knew it; without Big Bill it was nothing. And so he urged him to play, pointing out that Tilden's opponent was extremely weak, and that if he could just stagger through this match he could get a couple of days off to recuperate before he had to face any substantial competition.

"I can't play, George. I can't even walk," Tilden protested, but at last, as a favor to Butler, he agreed at least to try so that the people could see Big Bill. But he had not exaggerated his infirmity; in pain, he could hardly see the ball, and his unknown opponent was whipping him. Then, at a changeover, Tilden glanced up from his agony and saw Butler walking down the terrace steps to courtside carrying a tray with two glasses. One was a brandy, the other a green crème de menthe.

"Take one of these, Bill," Butler said.

"You know I don't touch the stuff," Tilden replied, and a bit huffily.

"Come on, for God's sake, it will help you," Butler snapped. "Go one, take one."

Tilden, somewhat intimidated by such orders, reached out, grabbed the crème de menthe and tossed it down. Back on the court he steadied and pulled out the match. Of course, Big Bill conveniently dismissed the outcome of the match as any sort of endorsement for liquor and its recuperative properties; instead he only cited the incident as a benchmark for his last drink. "From that day to this, I have never touched another drop," he would intone, ending the story.

His greatest indulgence was bridge, which he played endlessly. If bridge players were not about, he would gladly fall into another game—pinochle, say, hearts or gin rummy—anything but poker, which he had no taste for and never played. Bridge was his delight, though, even if people did not exactly stand in line to play with him. The trouble was that he had to dominate a bridge partner as he did every other person he encountered. "Ohh no, what did you lead that for?" he would whine. "Anything but that." Adela Rogers St. Johns, the writer, who often played with him in Beverly Hills later in his life, found him an intrinsically excellent player, clever and keen, but "erratic and irascible" as a partner. With perfect hindsight he would sneer condescendingly at her: "Of course, partner, if you had just thought to lead a club." Also, because Tilden got so involved with personalities, he was most vulnerable against people he disliked, such as George Lott, whom he could not abide, any more than Lott could stand Tilden. According to Lott, when the Davis Cup team sailed to France one spring, Lott so cleaned out Tilden at the bridge table that Big Bill had to periodically go down to his stateroom and replenish his cash supply from a secret cache he had in his trunk. Purposely infuriating Big Bill at all times, which was second nature to Lott, he always played against Tilden on this trip. Lott's partner was "some Polish countess," while Pola Negri, the movie actress, teamed up with Big Bill. That must have been some group.

But where he could restrain himself and play the cards

instead of the people—and, as Ellsworth Vines says, "not try to squeeze more tricks out of his hand than Jacoby could"—Tilden was a fine player. Some winters he would head South from Philadelphia with an old Germantown pal, Roy Coffin, who was a top all-round athlete. The two would work their way down to Palm Beach, playing a few tennis tournaments here and there. Then, at each town they'd hit, whether to play tennis or just to pass the night, Tilden and Coffin would ask for the town's best bridge players and take them on, like visiting frontier gunslingers. The locals in some little backwater hamlet in Georgia would gather round the hotel to watch Big Bill Tilden play bridge as avidly as they might come to see him play tennis.

During the tennis season Tilden would make home and headquarters of whatever club he was appearing at in a tournament. Without family or close friends or business, the clubs became his whole life—the locker room his bedroom, the bridge table his living room, the court his office. He would show up at ten in the morning on a day when he was not scheduled to play until late in the afternoon, and then spend the day at cards or out on the courts practicing or helping young boys. John Hennessey, a Davis Cup teammate, can remember mornings when Tilden could be found playing tennis with just about any hacker who was around and wanted to hit a few. Or, given the slightest encouragement, he would sit and discourse on the sport, decreeing more or less. "He just hung around all day," says Junior Coen, one of his favorite protégés, who is now a Kansas City broker. "He had to find something to do, and yet, to tell you the truth, I really don't know what he did all day with himself." Each day was unto itself. "He never looked a day ahead or a day back past 1919 either," Coen says. He existed only as Big Bill Tilden, the champion of the world, and perhaps he sensed that when that person was no more, the times ahead would be as sad as they had been in the past.

Basically, of course, Tilden was lonely, and a loner as well. "You've got to realize, he just didn't mix with people," Junior Coen says—curiously but quite intentionally placing an emphasis upon the last word, not the verb. Cocktail parties, where strangers came to inspect Big Bill, both unnerved him and brought out his worst. "He could never be a diplomat," Gloria Butler says. "If he got into a discussion, and he thought he was right, which he always did, he would walk right over anybody."

Al Laney of the *Herald Tribune:* "He could discourse on so many subjects, and you really had to listen because he had a first-rate mind and because he evidenced a certain logic that puzzled you because by then you were convinced that he couldn't possess any logic. And yet, there was never any humor with him. And more than just a lack of humor: there was no joy, no satisfaction, nothing pleasant in his company."

Grantland Rice, the premier sports columnist of the time, who once served on a special tennis committee with Tilden, found him even more distinctly a figure of pity: "He craved affection and respect from mature people, but received it from few. Whenever Bill strayed from the court he was pathetic."

No wonder then, really, that all his life Tilden took refuge in the company of people younger and more immature than he. Junior Coen says, "I don't remember Bill ever having any relationship with an older person. And you know, it's funny, but I never even saw him with an unidentified person, someone he had just happened to meet." A great many people who knew Tilden well doubt that he ever had a real friend of his own age in his whole life.

The fact that red-blooded young American boys of that

time did not even know what a homosexual was probably made it even easier for Tilden to retreat into the children's world. Since people recognize now that Tilden was homosexual, there is a tendency to snicker or grin smugly when talking of his tennis "protégés," but in fact, he never once seems to have made a pass at any of these boys. In the 1920s, when he was in the glory years, his sex drive appears to have been nearly nonexistent anyway, and since Tilden viewed his protégés as potential sons and heirs more than anything else, it would be quite shocking to learn that he ever approached any of them sexually. Of course, it is also true that his protégés tended to be cute little devils, and that Big Bill always seemed to have his arms around them. He was a very handsy guy.

Make no mistake, though, there was within him a genuine affection for his boys: they were his love. With each, he tried to convince himself that the boy would succeed him as champion of the world. That is what he wanted most of all. He was mentor and patron more than instructor to the boys, taking them with him on tour, or showing up at insignificant tournaments where they played. Sarah Palfrey Danzig, later U.S. national champion, and one of the few girls who came under his loving attention, can remember the embarrassment of having Big Bill rout René Lacoste out of bed early one morning and then drag the Frenchman to the courts to watch little Sarah play some other schoolgirl. When Walter Thomas, another of his protégés, twisted an ankle in the national junior tournament, Tilden, the world champion, was out of his seat and first to the boy, to soothe him and massage the ankle as Thomas lay there in the middle of the court. Tilden even played doubles in men's tournaments with some of his boys, and Vinnie Richards was only fifteen years old when he partnered Tilden to the U.S. championship. Sandy Wiener, a special favorite, a local Germantown boy, traveled all over the country with Tilden during school vacations, and at home Tilden would get up early mornings and run him to school in his bright red Marmon.

All of his kids he spoiled shamelessly. He was by nature a very generous, even profligate man, but he would lay it on even thicker for his boys. Literally, he instructed them not to spend a penny. At tournaments, they just signed his name—and not only for meals and an occasional soda pop. Alphonso Smith, another lesser protégé of the '20s, can remember signing for a whole bouquet of flowers he sent a girl he just met and for an expensive airplane jaunt that he took to kill some time.

They just signed Big Bill's name, and the club gladly took care of it. Everything was on the cuff. If Alphonso Smith was going around signing for airplanes and flowers, Tilden was surely chartering whole fleets and leasing a greenhouse or two. Frank Roberts, a venerable tennis promoter in Baltimore, approached Big Bill at his peak about appearing in a tournament there. Tilden replied that he would be delighted to, as long as he received his usual first-class expenses and, as an extra bagatelle, could have Roberts throw a little dinner for some young friends of his. Roberts quickly agreed; after all, he only had to bring him down from Philly.

The young friends, however, turned out to be most of the page staff of the U.S. Senate. Roberts had to pay their train fare over and back from Washington to Baltimore and then set up a typical Tildenic dinner—steak and ice cream—at a fancy downtown hotel. "He and the kids had a wonderful time, all sitting there laughing and stuffing their faces," Roberts says. "Me and Tilden were the only adults there, and he was more like one of the kids. I'm sitting there the whole time trying to figure out how to sell enough extra tickets to pay for this." Other times Tilden simply resorted to friendly persuasion, extortion if you will, by informing a tournament committee on Sunday, say, that he would not be coming in Monday for the week after all unless this particular boy, or these two, or even five or six, were not also suddenly accommodated in the draw.

Whatever the incidental demands, he was always Big Bill. While he was hardly engaged in what could be called a cash-flow occupation, Tilden was paid in stylish currency. "He traveled like a goddamn Indian prince," says Al Laney. Never would he deign to stay, as other players did, in private houses—only the best hotel in town. And a suite—a corner suite if the tournament promoter had his wits about him. On railroads: compartments. If Tilden felt he needed an automobile, he would hire a limousine with driver, twenty-four hours a day, beck and call. "The poor driver had to sleep in the car," Ellsworth Vines says. Miriam Ambrose, Tilden's niece, adds, "I don't think Uncle Bill ever rode in a bus or an underground in his entire life."

In London he always stayed at the Savoy, in Palm Beach at the Poinciana, in Los Angeles at the Ambassador, in New York at the Algonquin. There, he would occasionally take off on long trips, forgetting to check out, running up large, unnecessary bills. It didn't faze him. Peggy Wood, who sometimes sat in on the famous Round Table discussions at the Algonquin, never remembers Tilden joining that exalted barbed company (he would not have been the center of attention), but the hotel delighted in his resident celebrity, and provided him with a sitting room where he could better entertain his acting friends and other VIP's. "He did not want itty-bitty people around him," Miss Wood says. "He had to explain things to them. Bill liked to have big people around."

For the hoi polloi he tendered words like "brainless," "hopeless" and "ingrown stupidity," while, never temperate, he employed "fantastic" for whatever he remotely approved. Citing Greta Garbo, he took to signing autographs with just the last name: Tilden. And if crowds at lesser tournaments acted to his displeasure, he would threaten to leave the court—which, in fact, he did at least twice. He went backstage at the Met to visit with Mary Garden, lavished four hundred dollars' worth of flowers once on Pola Negri, granted President Harding a visit, and then told everybody (after Harding died) that he went abroad to play only as a patriotic favor to his leader. He played bridge with Bernard Baruch and tennis with the Duke of York at Buckingham Palace, after the future king dispatched his royal white Rolls Royce around to the Savoy to fetch him.

Next to royalty, Tilden leaned to actors and actresses the most. "He never talked down to those people," Junior Coen says. "When he was with one of those, you could see that he felt inadequate to them." Two whole chapters in his autobiography are devoted to nothing more, really, than name-dropping. His Hollywood favorites were the brightest of all: Douglas Fairbanks and Mary Pickford, and Charlie Chaplin, who remained an acquaintance, perhaps more, even to the end. Fairbanks, of course, couldn't touch Tilden at tennis, but conveniently he had invented his own game, which was called Dougledyas, or simply, Doug. When he was in California, Tilden used to play Doug all the time at the studio gym with equipment that Fairbanks had made to order. Doug was played with a regular badminton shuttlecock but the racket was a hybrid lightweight tennis racket. One of the rules was that you were permitted to use your body to hit the birdie, and Fairbanks was very good at that.

Tilden was also "linked" in the press to Pola Negri for a time when he was visiting Hollywood, which pleased him no end. He protested too much when people told him that he looked like an actor named Herbert Marshall or, better, bore a stage resemblance to Alfred Lunt. In London he hung around with Tallulah Bankhead and Bea Lillie. "Ahh, we used to go with the cream with Bill," says John Hennessey, a kid then, fresh out of Indiana. Tilden also got involved more personally in the theater by investing much of his inheritance into a variety of plays and movies, most of them starring himself and all of them, just about, flat-out flops. Once Tilden even played Dracula, and everybody at last thought that would work, but the trouble was he could never forbear playing William T. Tilden II.

A special problem he had as an actor was his superb memory. Woe to the poor reporter who wrote something critical of Tilden in February and then didn't see him till June. Big Bill could hurl the offending remarks right back at him, word for word, salting the recitation with smug rebuttal. He would startle people he met briefly (and who had not offended him) when, perhaps months later, he would run into them and casually say, "Hello, Mr. Wilson." On the stage, this manifested itself in memorizing the whole play. He would forget himself and start mouthing the lines being said to him. But then, he also instructed photographers how to take his picture, writers how to write and tournament directors how to run a tournament. He began to speak English with a slight British accent, and what French he could manage with a German accent. Always extraordinarily generous, he lavished expensive gifts on his young friends and anyone else he fancied. If he ventured out from room service, he would surely have a whole table dining with him. And nobody ever beat Big Bill to a check. "Whatever he wanted to do, he did it, and he did it in style," says Junior Coen.

And yet, in bizarre counterpoint to this sumptuous, worldly existence, Tilden all the time also carried on something of a small boy's life back in Philadelphia, where he would go to reside much of every year with two maiden ladies, an aunt and an older cousin. He called them Auntie and Twin, and alone, in all the world, they called him Billy.

They would keep his room, where he had accumulated a couple of thousand phonograph records, exactly as he left it while he gallivanted all around the world. Then he would come back to it to spend hours up there on the third floor listening to his "foreign music" before coming downstairs for the perennial steak dinner. He would leave the house to go hang around with some kids or work in little amateur theater groups. One Christmas at the Germantown Y, Big Bill made a stirring comeback from one set down to beat the local boys' Ping-Pong champ.

He both coached tennis and directed theatricals at Germantown Academy, and was briefly the tennis coach at another boys' school and at Penn as well. For at least two summers he was a counselor at Camp Winnipesaukee in Wolfeboro, New Hampshire. Imagine, if you will, the world's number-one player today taking a month or so off between winning Wimbledon and winning Forest Hills to go off to the Green Mountains and read ghost stories and organize paper chases for twelve-year-olds. That is what Tilden did.

It was the habit of the camp to break for a week in midsummer so the boys could take off on special hiking adventures. Tilden took this time to go to Bretton Woods, New Hampshire, and play in a tournament. While he was there, he learned that one camper and a counselor had been drowned on a canoe trip. He defaulted, drove immediately to Wolfeboro, where he confirmed details, and from there to Boston, where the drowned boy had lived. There he consoled the family and drove the distraught father back to New Hampshire to recover his child's body.

However abrasively Tilden might so regularly strike people, however rude and unfeeling he could appear to be, there was also this incredible measure of kindness within him. For every moment when he offended some adult, there must have been an hour or two of helping some child.

The most loyal of men, he rose to his finest, was his most charitable, at precisely those times when most men would shrink from the scene. Perhaps because there had been so much sadness, so much death come unawares in his own family, he was steeled by tragedy and better able to cope.

Peggy Wood had not seen him for a number of years when, in 1936, her husband died in America while she was in England. Tilden, there on a pro tour, suddenly materialized and took command, ushering her about, buffering her from others. "You see," she says, "he had once long before known me as a friend, and so he acted as if we had always known each other and been together. He was always so kind and generous." Years later, in Los Angeles during the war, when he learned that a young Mexican-American prospect would not be permitted to use the fashionable Los Angeles Tennis Club courts, it was Tilden who put himself on the line, who told the club manager, Perry Jones, a powerful USLTA official, that he would blow the whistle publicly and pull out a lot of other players if the kid's ban continued. Only then did Jones bow and let Pancho Gonzales play on his courts.

Wherever he was, if a junior tournament was held or a dinner honoring young players, Tilden would show up. At the zenith of his career he volunteered to be a scout for the Philadelphia junior team, and he devoted much of his time to checking out the strengths and weaknesses of the New York opposition. In the fall and the spring, in his snappy red Marmon, he would buzz all around to tournaments in the Philadelphia area, carrying some protégé along with him, springing for ice cream after the matches. And just for the fun of it too, no matter how good he became, Tilden loved to keep on playing tennis with his old school pals. Every year, after he won the U.S. championship at the Germantown Cricket Club, he would then go back out on a side court with a bunch of the old neighborhood buddies, and for a five-dollar-a-man bet he would play alone against four men. It was a sucker bet; with four guys to aim at across the net, Tilden could always win points by hitting his opponents. He would wing them in the ankles with volleys, blast them all over with serves, or lob them if they began to cringe and run away. One year he was down 0–5, love–40 before, laughing, he pulled out the set.

Tilden was perhaps even more enthusiastic about his little theater efforts around Germantown, where he was regularly leading man and director as well. When he selected starring vehicles for himself, he leaned toward plays where he could appear in a uniform. *Clarence,* a durable if suspect comedy of the time, was also a special one of his favorites, possibly because the hero was obliged to be a musician and play a saxophone in one scene. To pull this off, a student named Ed Hiestand, who indeed could play the sax, was installed backstage with his instrument, while Tilden with another sax tried to lip-sync the Hiestand effort. Unfortunately, Hiestand recalls, he went on playing long after Clarence/Tilden withdrew the instrument from his lips and began to emote. But undaunted as ever, Big Bill carried on, and eventually he even appeared as Clarence on Broadway in a benefit performance. He once told Frank Deacon's wife, "Dorothy, I'd a thousand times rather be an actor in the spotlight than a tennis player."

Mrs. Deacon he directed as the leading lady in the Belfry Club production of a Lunt-Fontanne opus named *Dulcy.* It was thus on this occasion that Tilden reached the ultimate in his normal everyday omniscience: he halted rehearsals and gave her a long lecture of detailed instructions on the subject of how to kiss. "Bill just always had to dominate," says Gloria Butler. "He had to be absolutely possessive in his relationships. There was no middle way, and he could not adapt himself. He could discuss anything; I can remember sitting up until four in the morning listening to him on every subject. But while he was so interested in so many things, he had a certain contempt for many people. Bill really didn't like people." Like Junior Coen, she placed emphasis on the last word.

Tilden's nephew says it this way: "Uncle Bill was always glad to see you, but at the same time, you knew he would be gladder still when you left."

CHAPTER FOUR

"The American boy . . . loves a fair deal and hates a crook"

THE trouble with Big Bill was that wherever he was—on the courts, in Hollywood, at Auntie's, wherever—he was not in the real world. "Bill wanted everything to be perfect," Sandy Wiener says, adding somewhat wistfully, "and, of course, it isn't." William Tilden III says, "The main problem was that he never grew up. He was champion of the world, but he was always childish, and he saw everything in black and white. *People who were wrong deserved to be punished.* Uncle Bill felt that, down in his heart."

His worst faults were accented off the court by the fact that he was champion on. A certain righteousness crept into his judgments, and he could not tolerate the most innocent of mistakes. Al Laney remembers on one occasion having to sit patiently for half an hour being punished while Tilden hectored him for allegedly confusing "tactics" with "strategy." Big Bill somehow decided that it·was a form of deceit when Babe Norton, the playful little South African, declared before the U.S. Nationals in 1923 that he only had to defeat Dick Williams to win the title. Tilden actually demanded that Norton publicly apologize to him for this statement or he would withdraw from the tournament. Only after the officials carefully explained to Big Bill about the little ins and outs of the First Amendment did he reluctantly agree to play on, whereupon he punished the audacious Norton in straight sets in the semifinals.

In search, in demand, of honor and sportsmanship, Tilden set off on a Don Quixote hunt. Purity was the goal, and all was black or white—no gray. When the United States whipped France in the 1925 Challenge Round by winning the first three matches, the Americans wanted to replace Billy Johnston in the final meaningless singles match the next day in order to give Vinnie Richards a chance to play. It was okay with Johnston, okay with Richards, okay with the French and everybody else. Nobody much even cared, for that matter. Tilden informed Dick Williams, the U.S. captain, that were the substitution carried out he would quit the team and never again play Davis Cup. It was, he said, against the spirit of the rules so to replace a man. It besmirched the Cup. No one could convince Tilden otherwise; Johnston played. There is not a person who ever knew Big Bill who does not remember him as excruciatingly honest. The family motto of "Truth and Liberty" lived with the man.

And yet, as a closet homosexual, he lived one great lie in shame for a lifetime. It appears quite certain that he set up such rigorous standards for tennis and for the rest of the world around him in an effort to try to somehow counter the massive ongoing deceit of himself, of his every day. The poor man: he believed, essentially, that he was a wrong call.

But the game would be pure. Even George Lott, who disliked Tilden and called him Tillie just to infuriate him, says, "I never once saw Tillie take a point that he believed did not belong to him." There were many times, if a call went wrongly in his favor and the linesman would not reverse his decision, when Tilden would then move to the center of the court, place his hands on the net and declare to the umpire in the chair, "I won't accept that point." If absolutely obliged to, if the umpire would not overrule the linesman, then Tilden would tend to things his way by throwing the next point or two, or a whole game, or even a whole set. In a pet, he once even threw a set in the Challenge Round.

"I'm not throwing anything for the gallery," he told a friend once. "I'm doing it for inside of me." Of course, ever honest and without false modesty, he expanded on that a bit more on another occasion. "All right, maybe if I weren't Tilden I wouldn't throw points," he said. "But I feel like I must compensate when there is an obvious error." He stopped at this point and let a small smile play over his face. "Especially since I'm going to beat the guy anyway."

Furthermore, the whole business was clouded because Tilden was a moral despot, and he expected the other players to throw points for him if he thought he had been wronged. If the umpire, the referee, the linesman, the fans, the press and the opponent all believed one way about a call at the other end of the court from Tilden, but he believed the other, he still expected the other player to go along with his judgment. He was the sole authority. Nothing made people more livid toward Tilden, on or off the court, than his habit of asking, "Would you like to correct your error?" He said that regularly.

In his tennis fiction, players were always faced more with unfathomable moral dilemmas than with forehands or serves. Typically, from "On a Line with the Net": "Had the umpire seen? He turned away with bated breath. He knew by all the ethics of the game he should speak and admit he had touched the net, and yet—" Everybody in Tilden stories was forever giving his word of honor. It was like filling out forms: name, address, phone number, word of honor. Scruples were always being tested. Balls would fly through a small hole in the net, over-age players would sneak into junior tournaments ("If the Old School won, it would be by low, under-handed means"), players would compete for the wrong reasons ("mug-hunters"), while consorting with low lifes and professionals, even while hypnotized. There were so many ethical conundrums in Tilden's fiction that a fellow seldom had time to concentrate on tennis: "He had not yet repaid his father, but at least he had kept his honor." In all his writings the only time Tilden countenances a breach of honor is when an older player, the ubiquitous and faultless Dick Thomas, feigns injury in order to help his younger chum make the Davis Cup team in his place, because the boy has licked his drinking problem, having given his word of honor, and should get the chance to help the U.S.A. beat foreigners. Here, of course, we had a classic insoluble conflict—patriotism vs. honor—so Tilden could wink at a little bit of hanky-panky on behalf of the old red, white and blue.

Big Bill firmly believed that the people who played tennis, especially the nephews of Uncle Sam, were morally superior to those who trafficked in other games. This little tract, which appeared in one of his earliest books, takes care of just about all his views on the subjects of his country and his game: "The spirit of the good sportsman is inherent in the American boy. He loves a fair deal and hates a crook. It is the fairness in the game that appeals to him, and it is for that reason that tennis is becoming the most popular of games."

Because he truly did place honor at the top of his list, Tilden was less vulnerable on the courts than other men. "Play tennis without fear of defeat and because it's fun or don't play it at all," he wrote. "There is no disgrace in defeat. . . . Champions are born in the labor of defeat." At Tilden's peak, Sam Hardy, who had been Davis Cup captain and was closer to Big Bill than most men, said, "He never makes a serious business of winning tournaments. To him, the fascination of playing is paramount, the victory a minor consideration. He is as excited and happy over a match that he has lost as over one he won. This accounts for many of his defects. It is the penalty he pays for his mercurial temperament, but then, without this temperament, he could never be, as he is, the most brilliant and daring player in the world."

And yet, as with everything else about the man, Tilden was a behavioral paradox on the courts too. On the one hand he was the most scrupulous sportsman, obsessed with fair play; but on the other, designing and irritating—from the moment he showed up with the armful of rackets, the polo coat (sometimes complete with silk muffler), and underneath it the white V-neck with the red and blue piping that became known generically simply enough as the Tilden sweater. As he approached the court, he would, with graceful disdain, throw one racket far out before him, a pearl before swine, soliciting a "rough" or "smooth" from the other player. For warm-up then, after carefully selecting a racket, plunking the strings like violins, he would proceed through his repertoire, showing off for the crowd at the expense of his poor opponent. The other player often appeared to intrude on the relationship between the crowd and Tilden. When it was about time to start, he would call out gaily, "I'm ready whenever you're exhausted, partner."

Any official who dared to disagree with Tilden called down his most studied wrath. He would turn and stare at the poor fellow, withering him before the crowd. It was really not necessary for him to say anything, although occasionally, for effect, he might inquire to the heavens, "Is there no justice?" Finally, to take this bow from his quiver, it was proposed at the 1928 USLTA convention that a no-glare rule be put on the books. Players would be forbidden to glare at linesmen. This sounds too good to be true, but the members who were there reported that the no-glare measure never came to a vote because Big Bill heard about the suggestion, made a special trip to the convention, stood up, voiced his opposition to the matter, and then glared at any member who favored it. One by one the proponents backed down.

So too could he be brutal against any opponent he personally disliked or took some passing grudge against. In 1920, when Tilden first reached his peak, he heard that Sir Norman Brookes, the nearly universally beloved former Wimbledon champion, had made the observation that he would rather play Tilden than Johnston. The next time they met, Big Bill thrashed Sir Norman 6–1, 6–2, before easing off to 6–4 in the last set, overcome with some compassion for the old chap. Bewildered at the intensity with which Tilden had administered his shellacking, Brookes asked Tilden afterward why he had been so unmerciful. "I heard you thought I was easier to face than Johnston," he snapped.

At various times many people heard him say, "I never lose to anybody I hate"—usually where Jean Borotra, the brash French show-off, was concerned. Borotra won Wimbledon twice, but he could never once beat Tilden on grass. An obscure younger American named Luke Williams, a player from Yale, earned the honor of antagonizing Tilden more than any other man—even more, it seems, than Borotra or George Lott. In the semifinals of the national clay courts in 1927, Tilden beat Williams love, love and love, a "triple bagel" in modern tennis parlance, and the most one-sided victory he ever ran off.

On another occasion, in Milan, Tilden squared off against the Italian Umberto de Morpurgo, who was another player Big Bill didn't especially care for. Tilden was peeved to start, and when he drove his first three serves into the top of the net, he really began to fume. Instead of serving another ball, though, Tilden stalked over to the umpire's stand and demanded that the net be measured.

The Italian officials refused to accommodate this request and ordered him to go back and serve. So Tilden said he was leaving, and they rushed out with a tape measure; the net was one centimeter too high. With that corrected, Tilden returned to the service line and gave Morpurgo a singular thrashing.

Lott especially rankled Tilden. Relative to the hoity-toity world of tennis, Lott was a rough-and-tumble type. He had been an excellent baseball player as well, with an offer from the Philadelphia A's; he liked to bet on sports and chase women. His good buddy was John Hennessey of Indianapolis. But where Lott was street smart, Hennessey was more country bumpkin, and Tilden was somewhat refreshed by his naïveté and put up with his antics better than he did Lott's. Then, in April of 1928, Hennessey stepped over the line.

Tilden had been made Davis Cup captain that year, and he brought Hennessey, six other candidates and himself down to Augusta, Georgia, to compete for positions in the upcoming zone matches held in Mexico City. The United States could have beaten the Mexicans with any two players picked out of a hat, but Tilden browbeat the USLTA into letting him set up a rugged "camp" for the team. Tilden was occupied, traveling with some repertory stage company, when asked to take over the team, so he could force a few concessions. Among other things, Tilden liked the idea of a team camp because he had just become enamored of little Junior Coen, and he wanted a chance to be with him and ease him onto the team, even though Coen was only fifteen.

The spartan bivouac turned out to be first-class accommodations at the Bon Air Vanderbilt, which was even better for little Coen's chances since, except for Tilden the teetotaler and the little teenager from Kansas, the other candidates for Mexico City were out running around at all hours.

Frank Shields, who was conceivably the most handsome athlete in history, not only came back early one morning drunk, but he also smashed up a car in the process. And the car was one he had borrowed from Captain Tilden. Furious, Tilden punished Shields by sending him out to play Hennessey all morning. Hennessey was the hottest player on the premises, but Tilden had set up an actual tournament to decide who qualified for the trip to Mexico City.

The day the tournament began, before any team members had been selected, Hennessey came down to breakfast and, skylarking, called over to Tilden, "Hey Bill, what's going to be our dress in Mexico City?"

Tilden sized up the wiseacre. "Welll," he said at length, drawing the word out. "If that's the way you're going to be, Mister Hennessey, I guess I'll have to change the draw and play you this afternoon myself."

Over lunch, with that confrontation staring him in the face, Hennessey struck on a plan that "might drive Tilden crazy." It was a cool April in Georgia, and many of the players had brought their college letter sweaters. Hennessey went to Wilmer Allison and borrowed his University of Texas sweater with the burnt-orange T. From John Van Ryn he borrowed the black and orange of Princeton and from Arnold Jones the Yale blue. Then he put the three sweaters on, one over the other, plus his usual coat and muffler, and hied off to face Big Bill. "I looked like Strangler Lewis," Hennessey says. "I couldn't raise my arm, I had so much merchandise."

There were two or three hundred people in attendance, there to see Tilden's big tournament begin. The captain watched with suspicion as the bulky Hennessey took off his coat, twanged his racket strings à la Tilden and picked one to warm up. He was wearing Arnold Jones's Y. Midway through the practice hit, Hennessey held up a hand, walked over to the side and took off the Yale sweater, revealing another, this one the big T. The crowd snickered appreciatively while Tilden began to fume. Then, just as Big Bill was to serve to open the match, Hennessey summoned a halt again, went back to the sideline and took off his Texas sweater, going down to the P and drawing even more applause and laughter with his striptease. Tilden was so furious that he spent the whole first game trying to slam balls at Hennessey, who won just by ducking nimbly.

He only played one game in the Princeton sweater before getting down to his regulation white shirt, but Tilden never really simmered down the whole match. Once, Hennessey pulled off a beautiful sweeping crosscourt forehand, slashing it on a dead run for a winner. "Wheee!" he called out with excitement.

Tilden came to the net and addressed him sternly across it. "I wish you wouldn't whee me," he said.

"Why not?" Hennessey asked.

"Because it just isn't done in international tennis," Tilden huffed, and then he turned and stormed back to the baseline. Hennessey beat him 8–6 in the fifth. John McGraw, the famous baseball manager of the Giants, was watching. He turned to his companion, William Fox, the movie producer, shook his head and said, "I've never seen such psychology in forty years of baseball."

Tilden wasted little time getting back at Hennessey. For the Mexico City matches, the captain had two of his boys along, Coen and Arnold Jones. Despite the fact that Hennessey's hot streak continued and he kept beating everybody in practice, Tilden included, Big Bill sent telegrams off to the USLTA suggesting that Jones was playing over Hennessey. Unluckily for Tilden, the team trainer, Bill O'Brien, happened to chance upon a reply from the USLTA to Tilden alluding to the situation. Instantly O'Brien figured out what sort of messages Tilden must be sending back to the States, and so he alerted friends of his in the USLTA.

Soon Tilden got the word to play Hennessey if Hennessey was winning. "Somebody's taking care of business that doesn't concern him," he harrumphed at a team meeting, but he had no choice but to play Hennessey in the second singles.

Tilden did work his buddy Jones in with him in the doubles, and later, against China, he even teamed up with Coen (who is still the youngest American ever to play Davis Cup), and in France for the Challenge Round he demànded that he and Frank Hunter play the doubles. Hennessey and Lott were the obvious choices, clear-cut winners in practice, but Tilden wanted his buddy with him in the spotlight. It was a frightful decision on two counts: not only were Tilden and Hunter more likely to lose than Hennessey and Lott (and they did), but the doubles wore Big Bill down so, he was less fit for the next day's singles too.

Hunter was perhaps the only contemporary in tennis to grow even reasonably close to Tilden; but for all that, Hunter was not so much a friend as he was just exceptionally capable of figuring out how to get along with Big Bill. The two men called each other the Smarties, and if Tilden got annoyed at Hunter, he would say, "Smarty, you give me that indescribable irk!"—promptly driving the other players up the wall.

Certainly the Smarties made a real odd couple. Hunter—direct, peppy and even somewhat flip today past eighty—is still partly active as a liquor executive in New York; before he lost millions in the 1929 crash, he was a newspaper publisher. A man's man, in every way, Hunter has shot big game and chased good-looking women all over the world. But if he was completely different from Tilden in many respects, he was just as strong-willed, and he could not be dominated by Big Bill, on or off the courts. Significantly, it was Hunter who went to Tilden one day and suggested they team together. Tilden was so flattered that someone past adolescence would actually want to play with him that it never occurred to him that the arrangement profited Hunter more than it did Tilden. Hunter was a fine player, with an outstanding forehand, but his game was limited and Tilden was crucial to his success.

Nonetheless, although Tilden was constantly after Hunter, scolding him for his dissolute life, he protected his partner carefully and would permit no one else to censure Hunter for the same things he chided him for. Similarly, Hunter made an effort to understand Tilden, and even to defend him if necessary. There was a time when the Davis Cup team was domiciled in London, and Hunter took up with Tallulah Bankhead, who was appearing in a play there ("Frank and I were *en rapport,* if you will excuse the euphemism," Tallulah noted somewhat later). She used to get mad at Tilden because he would get mad at Hunter for running around with Tallulah instead of preparing body and soul for the next match. She was going on one night, bitching about Tilden's bitching, when Hunter snapped at her, "Now look, Tallulah, I play tennis because I love the game. Tilden plays because it's his life."

So, whatever the huge personal differences, there was a genuine bond that joined the Smarties. And in Tilden's case, in his world of extremes, those who fell on the side of the angels were lavished with the greatest attention, devotion and loyalty.

In 1927 Big Bill's favorite antagonist, the USLTA, made the mistake of using Hunter to cross Tilden. The USLTA, led by its major-domo, Julian (Mike) Myrick, ordered the U.S. Davis Cup captain, Chuck Garland, to play Dick Williams with Tilden in the Challenge Round doubles against the French—notwithstanding the fact that Tilden and Williams were both left-court players and that Tilden and Hunter had already proved themselves that year as Wimbledon champions and were clearly the class doubles team of the country. When Tilden learned of the final decision on the morning of the match, he simply replied that he would play with Hunter or he would not play at all.

"Mr. Tilden, you will follow instructions," he was ordered.

"Gentlemen," Tilden announced, "I will be in the sitting room playing bridge, and when you have decided to name Mr. Hunter as my partner, come and inform me."

Periodically, as the time for the match drew nearer, the USLTA officials would approach the card table—with increasing timidity. At last, desperate, they pleaded with him. "You're interrupting my game," Tilden replied. The crowd was already settling into its seats when the USLTA finally gave in and told Tilden that the Smarties could play. "Fine," said Tilden. "I'll dress as soon as we finish this rubber." He and Hunter won in five sets.

In 1930 at Forest Hills Tilden refused to go on the court for his quarterfinal match against John Van Ryn because he maintained that all the hoopla that attended his playing would disturb Hunter. He and John Doeg were already well along their quarterfinal on the adjoining stadium court. Finally, the tournament chairman confronted Tilden with an ultimatum. "How long does it take you to dress into tennis clothes?" he asked.

"Fifteen minutes," Tilden replied, not quite sure what the man was getting at.

"You be back here on the court with Van Ryn in twenty minutes," the chairman said. Tilden complied with the order, but he sulked, making no real effort to return service in the first game, and losing the set without displaying any enthusiasm for the fray, and showing more interest in Hunter's losing effort. As soon as Hunter was beaten, Tilden turned attention to his own endeavor and quickly dispatched Van Ryn.

Besides Hunter, Tilden's other most famous doubles partner was Vincent Richards, with whom he won three U.S. championships, the first in 1918 when Richards was fifteen years old. Tilden took great delight in denigrating himself as a doubles player, but in fact he won five U.S. titles with three different partners, reached the finals with another, and again with Richards on another occasion. He also won four national indoors with three different partners, the 1927 Wimbledon with Hunter, and, with a variety of partners, he was 9–2 in Davis Cup doubles (and one of those he lost on purpose).

Tactically, in fact, Tilden was a superb doubles player. Since it is a game more of strategy, of angles and touch, all of which Tilden mastered, it should hardly be any surprise that he excelled at it. Lott, who is generally considered to be America's greatest doubles specialist of all time, attributes this position of eminence strictly to Tilden. "I learned how to win in doubles just watching Tilden hit," he says bluntly. "He could hit a drive, a lob and a dink shot all off the same motion—just like a good pitcher throwing a fast ball, curve and change-up the same way."

No, the only limits upon Tilden the doubles player were his personality and his ego. "You had to handle him properly," Hunter says. The trick, it seems, was that the partner should run the team, keep the team together, while all the time letting Tilden do pretty much what he wanted to— and make him think he was the captain. Tilden poached, took overheads (even though that was his weakest shot) and generally did as he pleased. No wonder only schoolboys could suffer him as a partner for long. Straightfaced, the USLTA yearbook once remarked of a match, "Sandy Wiener acquitted himself creditably when allowed to participate in the proceedings."

Quite predictably, Richards and Tilden grew apart as

Richards grew up. He was a strong personality himself, and he paid little or no attention to Tilden's suggestions about how he could improve his game. Then in 1922, as Richards really began to come into his own, he made the unfortunate mistake of beating Big Bill in a couple of matches during the winter. Tilden regularly played lackadaisically in this off-season competition, often as not because he was working more on the stage than on the courts. But falsely emboldened, Richards was led to venture a few rash predictions about how he had caught up with Big Bill. One can almost see Tilden reading this championship obituary of his in the paper, saying "Welll," and making some special plans for Mister Vinnie Richards.

That summer, instead of bothering to go to Wimbledon and defend his title, Tilden stayed in the States. Just a few days after Wimbledon was played, he met Richards in the finals of the Rhode Island State. This, in effect, was Tilden's Wimbledon 1922. He beat Richards 6–3, 6–1, 6–0. Richards played exceptionally well.

Having handled that necessary piece of business, Tilden teamed up again with Richards in the national doubles. In the finals at Longwood in Boston they beat the top Australian team of Gerald Patterson and Pat O'Hara Wood 4–6, 6–1, 6–3, 6–4, dealing with them comfortably near the end. With the match obviously in hand, Tilden began to amuse himself and to poach more than ever. At one point Big Bill practically moved his younger partner off the court to take an easy overhead and put it away with glory.

Three years before, in a similar situation, Tilden had knocked Richards cold, stealing an overhead from him and clubbing him on the skull in the process. That incident made such an impression upon Tilden that he used it as the focus of a short story years later. But now, at Longwood in 1922, Richards was infuriated that Tilden had upstaged him. While the crowd cheered Big Bill, Richards turned to him and said, "Bill, you do that again, and I'm going to hit you on the goddamn head."

Tilden was flabbergasted. It is safe to say that no one had ever talked to him that way on the court. Shaken and subdued, he finished out the match and then left for New York for the Challenge Round against Australia. The finals at Longwood against Patterson and O'Hara Wood had taken place on August 29, and less than a week later the same two teams squared off at Forest Hills. That was such a rout by the Australians—who polished off the Americans 6–3, 6–0, 6–4—that everybody immediately assumed that the Australians had played possum up in Boston in order to sucker the United States into playing Tilden and Richards again in the Davis Cup.

In fact, the Aussies were every bit as stunned at this inexplicable turn of events as everyone else. Richards was the only person who really knew what was going on. Years later he told friends that Tilden had gone out there that day to punish him for the incident at Longwood. The United States was up 2–0 in the singles when the match was played, and both Tilden and Johnston were a lock to cinch the victory the next day in the final two singles (which they did). Tilden threw the doubles to humiliate poor Richards, who was making his Davis Cup debut. In the three awful sets, Tilden made only seven earned points, while committing twenty-five errors outright. There was name-calling in the USLTA for months thereafter about the selection of Richards. He was not allowed to play doubles again for the United States for three more years.

For years thereafter, he and Richards were at odds, although Tilden came to Richards' professional debut in 1926, thereby providing some kind of an endorsement to the proceedings. And then, in the last desperate years,

Richards was there to help when Big Bill called on him, as was Hunter as well. Vinnie Richards was the last person he wrote to for charity. "Angel Child," Big Bill told Gloria Butler once, "if you have just three friends in your lifetime, that's an awful lot."

Chapter Five

"Any artist belongs to the country and to the world"

TILDEN was formed by three different egos on the court. The simplest was the competitor, heady and fierce—all the more so since he was invulnerable to any shame from defeat. Then there was the actor, vain and unequivocal, even picayune. Finally, and what most set him apart, there was the artist, which was perhaps not so much a whole other Tilden as it was a combination of the first two—but a sum greater than those parts.

Generally, athletes are not presumed to be artists by the public, nor do they view themselves as such. And probably they are right not to. The best of athletes are, in a literal sense, merely superhuman, or "natural athletes" as they are more prosaically known. They're gifted by God, and so they can just go out and do things, raw, better than other people—hit balls, run, jump, kick, whatever. Often in sports it is the least talented, the ones who have to work at it, who are actually the more artistic. For example, George Lott, with guile, change of pace, ploy, ingenuity, may well have been an artist at doubles, while even so attractive a performer as Bill Johnston, a much superior player, was only that: better at tennis. But not an artist.

Of course, what athletes do may be very beautiful indeed. Bobby Jones swinging a five-iron was a picture of grace, as Jack Dempsey was of power, as Babe Ruth of style. But in a curious way, while magnificent athletes such as these contribute something artistic, it is not so much that they are the artist as it is that they are another part of the artistic form. Great athletes are best viewed just as more of nature's wonders, like flowers, waterfalls or snow-capped mountains. It is wise always to keep athletes in perspective. Red Grange and Jesse Owens could run like the wind, that is for sure, but they were no more creative artists than was Man o' War.

But certainly, if any athlete can be an artist, then Tilden was—master and genius of his craft, and entertaining as well (which is not to be sneezed at). It was crucial to him too that the big people, the right people understood that he was an artist; even more important was it that he believed this himself. He possessed so little self-esteem otherwise.

Tilden always credited Mary Garden, the famous opera singer whom he knew well, with providing him with the concept of athlete-as-artist. "Now you listen to me, Bill, and then don't listen to anyone again," she said to him once when he was down. "You're a tennis artist and artists always know better than anyone else when they're right. If you believe in a certain way to play, you play that way no matter what anyone tells you. Once you lose faith in your own artistic judgment, you're lost. Win or lose, right or wrong, be true to your art."

Probably, though, he would have eventually reached these same conclusions by himself. For one thing, as he grew older it became increasingly necessary for him to justify his playing of a game. All the other players, which is to say the heterosexuals, were putting tennis on the back burner and going about the business of making a living and raising a family. But tennis, as Frank Hunter said, was Tilden's whole life. He turned to his fictional characters to defend what he was.

In his novel, *Glory's Net*, the hero, David Cooper, tells his wife, Mary, "I've played my last match. I'll never play again."

But she replies steadfastly, speaking for Tilden, "No, David, you must play. You owe it to your country, to the game, and to us. . . . You are an artist in your line. Any artist belongs to the country and to the world." Eventually Tilden also came to apply this privately as a rationalization of why he should have nothing to do with women: they took the artist's attention from his art.

While Tilden the athlete carried the sport of tennis to new levels of proficiency and originality, he required the additional profiles to stamp him as artist. He needed the actor to provide the drama and the competitor to extricate himself from the crises which the actor got him into. It all worked together to provide a virtuoso performance. At the time, René Lacoste wrote, "He seems to exercise a strange fascination over his opponents as well as his spectators. Tilden, even when beaten, always leaves an impression on the public mind that he was superior to the victor."

Without that audience he had trouble stirring himself. While obviously indulging in the usual Tildenic hyperbole, he nonetheless made the point best once with: "In practice I am no good at all. Half the kids I play with can beat me. I will be perfectly frank and honest: I love a crowd. It is the excitement of a tournament that inspires me and makes my game better." And if the crowd made him play better, it also encouraged him to play longer. "One thing for sure," Junior Coen says, chuckling, "when he got out on the court, that was his stage, and he didn't want to hurry off."

Against an outclassed opponent Tilden might just hit easy shots at the fellow, helping him along, or he might get the audience worked up by contesting patently good calls. "For heaven's sakes, Lev, are you blind?" he would scream at the highly respected umpire H. LeVan Richards. "Hell's bells, that ball was way out"—even though it was obviously in by inches. The crowd would boo and hoot at Tilden, and he would storm about in mock anger. But at the end of the match he would go up to Richards and say: "I'm sorry, Lev, I apologize. But I thought they really deserved a show, didn't you?"

This sort of burlesque would be much too tacky in something like the Davis Cup, though, so then Tilden would put on a more sophisticated act. In the 1924 Challenge Round, Tilden's singles opponents were Gerald Patterson, over the hill, and Patrick O'Hara Wood, no match for Big Bill on any day. Tilden decided, basically, not to bother playing them; there were better ways to reward his fans. As S. Wallis Merrihew, who was the editor of *American Lawn Tennis Magazine*, explained:

> Throughout the Patterson match, Tilden looked as if he were merely practicing strokes, or experimenting with them. He paid comparatively little attention to Patterson's shots. If they were good, as they not infrequently were, he let them go; or, if he could reach them, he would return them with interest. But it was his own shots he was thinking of most of the time, studying them as if he were in a laboratory and they were specimens.
>
> In three sets against O'Hara Wood, Tilden lost four games. He was in no hurry to finish; indeed, he seemed to like long rallies and plenty of them. Although O'Hara Wood won so few games, he played well and appeared to enjoy the match.

His favorite bow to showmanship was to purposely fall behind against a lesser opponent. There seems little doubt that he even amused himself and the crowd that way once in the Davis Cup, going down two sets to one against James Anderson of Australia in the 1922 Challenge Round. He did it regularly in smaller tournaments. Pouring a pitcher of water on his head (even on a cold day) was often the symbolic signal that he was ready to play in earnest and make his comeback.

Acting aside, Tilden also genuinely believed that it was often better to start modestly and then shock your opponent when you suddenly raised your game. He convinced Hunter to play that way, from behind, against Lott in the 1928 semifinals at Forest Hills. "Come on, Bill," Hunter said, aghast, "you just don't go around giving away sets in the national championships." Well, Tilden said, he did sometimes, so Hunter followed his advice, and after Lott won the first set, he whipped him three straight.

Nonetheless, Tilden was seldom fool enough to put show over substance. The competitor in him would not permit the actor to paint him into impossible corners. In fact, three of his most famous cliffhangers—two of which he won—which have generally been assumed to have been Tilden stage productions were all almost surely played straight. The first two took place in 1921, early in his prominence, and thus helped account for his tricky reputation. In both these cases, though, the real reason that he fell so far behind was because he was sick, but since he kept the seriousness of his illnesses to himself, other reasons had to be invented to explain how lesser men could threaten the great Tilden.

The first of these close calls came in the finals of the 1921 Wimbledon. He had sailed abroad that May on the *Mauretania* with Arnold Jones and his father. The voyage was smooth and Tilden won the French championship, clay court title of the world, hardly without breaking into a sweat, but he was a worn man. Except for a few weeks' respite from tennis during the winter, he had been traveling and playing crucial matches almost constantly for a year—in America, plus two trips to Europe and one to New Zealand. His resistance low, he had to have an operation to remove some boils after he won in Paris, and then as soon as he reached London he was required to move into a nursing home for three weeks in order to recuperate from what was delicately referred to as his "indisposition."

Over Tilden's protests, the Challenge Round was being retained for one more year at Wimbledon, so he had to play but one match to keep his title. Thus he was still in bed when the tournament began, and he didn't begin to play at all until five days before the final. He made his first public appearance in a mixed doubles match and appeared terribly weak. Except for such brief forays to the courts, he remained bedridden right up until the day when he ventured out to play the Challenge Round against Babe Norton, who had beaten Manuel Alonso to win the all-comers.

Norton, an irrepressible little South African, was already being characterized as the Peter Pan of the Centre Lagoon, and he was a popular favorite by the time he faced off against Tilden. Promptly, to the delight of the crowd, the little underdog took the first two sets from the invincible world champion and appeared a sure winner.

Here Tilden tried a whole new tack. He gave up his normal hard-hitting game and took to chops and slices. Quickly Norton found himself down 3–0 in the third set before he could catch on to this new approach, and so, foolishly, he gave the set away 6–1. With an exhausted sick man across the net, he should have forced every point. At the same time, the gallery came to life, booing Tilden for his chips and chops. The referee kept advising the crowd that the American was playing quite fairly and within the rules, but the elite in the stands would have none of that. It seemed to them that no gentleman would play lawn tennis so deviously. They kept booing Tilden lustily. He kept chipping and chopping. Norton fell completely apart from all the turmoil, and as Tilden himself noticed, "He simply threw away the fourth set from sheer nerves"—and at love. Now Tilden not only had the match deadlocked again, but he had won two sets with an expenditure of only thirteen games.

Norton steeled himself at this point, however, and while Tilden staggered about the court, the Peter Pan of the Centre Lagoon took a 5–4 lead, and then had 15–40 on Big Bill's serve—two match points. Tilden saved the first without incident, but at 30–40 he hit a ground stroke that nicked the chalk to stay in. Norton managed to return that shot, and Tilden's return was going way long, he says. Realizing this as soon as he hit the shot, Tilden ran up to the net to congratulate Norton on his victory. According to Tilden, when Norton saw him running up, he figured that Tilden would not be approaching the net to volley unless his approach was clearly in, so he played the ball that was going out, hit it out himself, and Tilden had deuce.

That crisis passed, Tilden quickly enough held serve, broke Norton's and held again for 7–5, set and match, the last Wimbledon ever played at its old site on Worple Road. Tilden then proceeded to the locker room, where he fainted dead away. He only passed out twice in his life: this time in 1921 and again thirty-two years later when he dropped dead. Nevertheless, the tale began to grow that, to make it interesting, Big Bill had let Babe Norton have the first two sets and then a couple of match points in the fifth.

Later that summer, on September 2, 1921, Tilden drew Zenzo Shimizu in the opening match of the Challenge

Round against Japan at Forest Hills. It was an excruciatingly hot and humid afternoon, Tilden was still somewhat weak from his European illness, and, to boot, he had a carbuncle on one foot. Tilden had little mobility, and every time he tried to move in, "the swarthy little son of Nippon," as the press knew Shimizu, would bomb away with lobs. Shimizu won the first two sets and was serving for the match at 5–4 in the third. At 30–all, two points from defeat, Tilden braced and earned the break, 5–all. Promptly he went back down 15–40 on his serve, but again he got off the hook, and then he broke Shimizu for the set 7–5.

During the intermission Tilden had the carbuncle lanced, he changed into dry clothes and came back out and routed Shimizu 6–2, 6–1. It appeared as if he had arranged the whole scenario. The legend grew.

Still, the most famous Tilden turnaround tale was not to take place until 1927, when he was thirty-four and back at Wimbledon for the first time since he defeated Babe Norton. Tilden and Hunter had toured all over Europe that spring, and at Wimbledon Big Bill just blitzed through to the semis, losing only one set in five matches. His opponent was Cochet, who was in his prime, but struggling; two days before, against Hunter, Cochet was down two sets to love before he wriggled away.

Tilden was now too old for any monkey business against top opponents. He no longer had the stamina to risk giving whole sets away indiscriminately. Against Cochet this day his plan was to come out swinging and try for a quick kill. It worked perfectly, as he won the first set 6–2, simply overwhelming Cochet. Tilden also took the second set by 6–4, but he was still clearly in charge, taking all the crucial points, and when the third set opened, Tilden somehow raised his game to yet a higher level and threatened to annihilate the poor Frenchman. Returning serve, Cochet

won only two points in three games. Serving, Tilden broke
him two of three times, to assume a 5–1 lead.

When he aced Cochet to bring it to that score, Tilden
threw back the other balls impatiently (he usually carried
three in his left hand as a matter of course) and moved
over to return serve and finish it off. Hunter departed the
players' section and hurried down to courtside to congratulate his pal. As Cochet prepared to serve, King
Alfonso of Spain and his entourage entered the stands and
without commotion took their seats in the royal box up
behind Tilden. He said later that he never even noticed
their arrival, but at the time some correspondents wrote
that Tilden did take note of the famous newcomers. Certainly he was such a bug on royalty that it seems unlikely
that Tilden would miss a king. There were a couple of
other times, documented, when he went all to pieces for a
few points against journeymen opponents just because a
duke arrived.

In any event, Cochet won the first point and Tilden the
second, and then, at 15–all, he hit three straight balls out.
They crossed over, and Tilden picked up his three balls and
prepared to ace out Cochet. The next time Tilden won a
point he was down 30–love at 5–all. Cochet had won seventeen straight points, and then the set 7–5.

From all this came the story that when Tilden saw King
Alfonso arrive he decided that the king should get his
money's worth of seeing Big Bill. Hence, so this tale goes,
Tilden decided that he would lose a few games before
finishing Cochet off. Where that hypothesis breaks down is
that Tilden would never play so poorly before royalty. Of
course he wanted them to see him, but not to see him
appear inept. Big Bill lose seventeen straight points on purpose before a king? Never!

It is possible, and logical, that he made no great effort to break Cochet at 5–1. That way the king would at least have the opportunity to see Tilden serve a game and, ideally, ace his way to victory. Whatever, once Tilden began to miss, it all got away from him.

There is no intermission at Wimbledon after the third set. Hunter, who had come down to congratulate Tilden a few minutes before, now started to shrink away awkwardly. Tilden spied him. "Goddamn those first two sets, Frank," he said. Hunter smiled helpfully; he didn't really know what Big Bill meant, although evidently it was some allusion to the fact that both of them had won the first two sets off Cochet. Hunter hurried away. "It was such a curious thing to say," he says now. Anyway, Tilden certainly didn't make any references to the king.

Cochet won the fourth set 6–4. The press reported that Tilden appeared "grisly." Cochet won the fifth set 6–3. In the locker room, as with Hunter, Tilden made no reference to royalty's arrival. To Al Laney he said cryptically, "Maybe you were right"—which was a reference to Laney's charge that Tilden could no longer call on his great stamina. "He said it," Laney wrote, "with what I thought was scorn, but in a voice that carried a certain hatred too."

Today Cochet has no more idea what happened than he did at that time. "Perhaps he was more tired than I," he volunteers, adding that it should not be forgotten that Tilden beat him in the Davis Cup the next time they played. Certainly it hardly seems to have fazed Big Bill. Indeed, on July 4, only three days after the Cochet collapse, Tilden and Hunter won their Wimbledon doubles championship over Cochet and Toto Brugnon after being down two sets to love and 3–5, and then 4–5 and 15–40.

Big Bill's annual confrontations in the Nationals with Little Bill were crucial to sustaining his reputation as a dramatist; one way or another, he always produced surprises against Johnston. For example, when they met in the quarterfinals of the 1921 championships at Germantown (seeding was introduced after this tournament), Big Bill was peeved because everyone claimed that he had won the year before only because of his big serve. "I'm going to see what I can do without aces," he announced beforehand. Before an overflow crowd of twelve thousand, he whipped Johnston in four sets with ground strokes, and then went on to take his second straight title.

The next year they met in the finals in what was named "a match for the Greek gods" a month before the tournament even began. In those days of amateur play, trophies were the major booty, and it was traditional in the lasting tournaments for cups to be retired by a three-time winner. Since Johnston and Tilden both had two legs on the current trophy going into the 1922 finals, it was certain to be removed from circulation. Little Bill especially yearned for it as the capstone to his career. Not only were his and Tilden's names inscribed twice on it, but Dick Williams', Lindley Murray's, Maurice McLoughlin's and Bill Larned's. Not till then, or to this day, has there ever been such a prize in American tennis as the cup that would be retired in 1922.

Tilden was unquestionably the favorite, but although he had won the last two national championships, he and Johnston were remarkably close overall. They had split ten matches evenly and were almost dead even in sets too; Tilden had won twenty, Johnston nineteen. So the little fellow had a good chance. Every seat was taken, and standing room three and four deep, twelve thousand jammed into the wooden stands at Germantown to see the match of Greek gods on September 16, 1922.

The diminutive deity, Wee Willie Winkie, rushed through the first two sets in splendor, his backhand the equal of his fabled forehand; 6–4 and 6–3 he won. Somehow Tilden checked him there, took a long lead in the third set, and Johnston let it ride out at 6–2. Tilden had been required to put a lot of effort into stemming Johnston, whereas Little Bill had coasted into the intermission. He prepared to come out rested and run Tilden off in the fourth set.

Rushing the net, slashing volleys away from the bigger man, working over his backhand, Johnston held his serve at 15, broke Tilden's at 30, and held his own again for 3–0. Germantown was Big Bill's own court, but the crowd was patently for Little Bill, and they roared as never before when the two men crossed over.

Sitting next to the umpire's stand was Mike Myrick, the powerful USLTA official who was invariably in charge of that organization, whether or not he happened to be president that particular year. Myrick and Tilden despised each other, and it occurred to Big Bill that the only possible reason Myrick might be sitting where he was would be to disturb him. As if to prove that to Tilden, Myrick smiled at him now with oily delight, offering false consolation. "Well, Bill," he said, "it's been a great match."

"It's damn well gonna be one," Tilden cracked back, and he stormed off onto the court. Poor Little Bill. As their Davis Cup captain, Sam Hardy, said of this juncture in the match, "With any other player, Johnston would have been free at that point. But he is never sure what Tilden will do. He is not a psychologist and he finds himself in opposition to an attack that is largely psychological."

Yet even with all that, Johnston played Tilden to deuce on his serve, and as they moved to close quarters, Little Bill pounded a hard volley to Big Bill's feet. Incredibly, Tilden reached down and reflexed a backhand half-volley lob that popped over Johnston's head and bounded home a winner in the corner. Johnston stood there aghast, unbelieving. The crowd was shocked to silence until one man stood up and bellowed, "He didn't make it! No, no! No man ever made that shot! He's a liar!" Then the place exploded. Johnston glanced up reflectively at the man who had screamed, almost as if to endorse that opinion, and then he turned and walked slowly back to return serve. He won six more points in the set and no more games. In the final set, Tilden only won 6–4, but always had the set in hand, exploiting Johnston's backhand, crushing it whenever he needed a point.

In the locker room Little Bill said, "Well, I'm glad we both played great tennis today."

"I was lucky to win," Big Bill said.

"No, I played the best I know how, Bill, but I still couldn't quite do it." And then, when Tilden moved away, Johnston dropped his head into his hands and to himself he muttered, "I can't beat him, I can't beat him, I just can't beat the son of a bitch."

Tilden carried the cup over to Auntie's, where she and Twin placed it in a prominent place in the living room.

No matter how many times Tilden kept on beating Johnston, though, Big Bill was so intensely disliked in most tennis circles that hopes for Little Bill always fluttered high. The 1924 Nationals brought a new epidemic of wishful thinking to Forest Hills. Tilden was embroiled in a big fuss with the USLTA that year, his time devoted to the theater was increasing, and he came to the finals with a desultory five-set win over Vinnie Richards. In contrast, Johnston was at perfect pitch, routing Gerald Patterson 6–2, 6–0, 6–0 in forty-two minutes in the other semi. The scuttlebutt ran that Tilden was out of shape, that he only beat Johnston because of his stamina, and that now Little Bill was ready to level sweet revenge.

"Billy's really out to get you," someone said to Tilden in the locker room after he edged Richards. He was standing before a mirror knotting his tie.

"So I've heard," he replied, looking into the mirror.

"There's a lot of money bet around against you."

"I've heard that too," Tilden said grimly, still concentrating on the tie.

So the next day Big Bill came into the warm-up slamming every ball. Nobody was ever again going to say that it was only a matter of conditioning. Little Bill never knew what hit him. "A Tilden rampant," wrote Allison Danzig in the *Times*. "Absolutely merciless. . . . Johnston was as helpless as an infant." Gerald Patterson, who had been destroyed by Johnston, put that in perspective: "Tilden is the only player in the world. . . . [The rest of us are] second graders." Tilden beat Johnston 6–1 in twelve minutes, then 9–7, 6–2, fifty-eight minutes in all. Fifty years later Al Laney wrote, "That was Tilden at his absolute peak, and I have not since seen the like of it."

Actually, most people in tennis came late to giving Tilden his proper due. He existed under a critical double standard, and he knew it well enough; but being short-changed that way did not really bother him, at least not in the traditional sense. He might get raving furious at someone for writing harshly of his playing, but he was not reacting because he was wounded by the criticism but because the writer was wrong, and it was his responsibility to apprise the misguided man of that fact. As an artist, Tilden simply could not be offended by those who were not artists themselves; in that way he neatly insulated himself from the public heat that any athlete normally must endure.

René Lacoste grasped this point early. Of all the men who played Tilden, Lacoste studied him the closest, read him the most carefully, because early on he concluded that the only way to beat Tilden was first to fathom the mind. Then maybe you could deal with the game. Lacoste kept books on Tilden, records and scouting reports, and like some mob hit man, hand on his gat, Lacoste took to carrying a racket with him at all times every day, fondling it, getting to know it better. Unlike Little Bill's, the next challenge to Tilden had to be total and sophisticated, for Lacoste perceived that he was not vulnerable to pressure and defeat like other athletes. "Tilden does not concern himself at all about the public," he explained to the French. "He does not seek approval of the public, but only the satisfaction of his own mind." In a sense, you couldn't even play him, so how could you possibly beat him? Big Bill never really played anyone but himself.

CHAPTER SIX

"I can't do that anymore with my keystone finger gone"

B Y all that should be, Big Bill Tilden's tennis career ended in October 1922. This was barely a month after he had defeated Johnston in the great five-set comeback in the Nationals. Although by now he was a figure of international renown, Tilden still lived with the two maiden ladies in Germantown and spent the autumn weekends bombing around the East Coast in his red Marmon roadster, playing free exhibitions just for the fun of it. He was, at the time, especially enamored of young Sandy Wiener, and always carried him along as his special doubles partner.

On Saturday, October 7, Tilden's little troupe headed way down into southern New Jersey to play an afternoon's matches in the country town of Bridgeton. Besides Wiener, the group also included an earlier Tilden protégé, Carl Fischer, and Wallace Johnson, essentially a chop artist and a top-ranking player from Philadelphia. In the second set of a singles match against Johnson, Tilden scurried back to try to retrieve an overhead smash. Understand the circumstances: the champion of the world, at the height of his powers, playing a meaningless exhibition in the middle of nowhere before a few hundred kibitzers. For that matter, he was even winning rather handily; he took the set 6–0. There was no need to try a desperation shot.

Johnson was not very powerful, so Tilden figured he might be able to catch up to the smash on the bounce. He ran all the way back to the wire fence that surrounded the courts, and flailed at the ball in a mad effort to reach it. In the process, he somehow nicked the middle finger on his right hand on a strand of the fence that stuck out. It did not hurt at all; indeed, it seems that it didn't even break the skin. Big Bill went back to playing tennis, laughing at his vain effort.

Tilden's constitution was vulnerable to the germ staphylococcus aureus. His problems with boils at Wimbledon and in the Challenge Round against Japan the year before were both related to this, and a year later he was to suffer a similar sort of infection on his left hand. It was the kind of petty nuisance that a shot of penicillin would take care of now, but in 1922 it could be quite serious. A U.S. senator, Edwin Vare, who presumably had received the very best of medical treatment, had died of the same thing only shortly before Tilden ran into the fence in Bridgeton. The germ worked upon Tilden's body all week without his knowing it, and the next Friday he piled Wiener and some other players back into the Marmon, and they drove all the way up to Connecticut, where they were to play some matches at the Taft School.

It was there that Big Bill first began to feel pain. While he fulfilled his commitment and played for the schoolboys, he also sought out the school doctor, who confined him to the Taft infirmary overnight. Sunday, in increasing pain, he drove his gang back to Philadelphia, and the next day he saw a doctor in town. The diagnosis was, apparently, somewhat tentative, and so, typically, Tilden made the least of it. He often played in pain, having been troubled by floating cartilage in his left knee for years. Later, in his first seven years as a pro, 1931–37, playing fifteen hundred matches of one-night stands, he missed only three from sickness or injury. Besides, having endured all the awful deaths in his family, he seemed to have something of a laissez-faire attitude toward medicine and its men.

Wednesday morning, October 18, however, he woke up early in such intense pain that even he recognized the increased seriousness of his condition. Auntie and Twin had him rushed to Germantown Hospital, where he was put under anesthesia. Dr. William Swartley, a family friend, sliced open the finger all the way from the tip to the second joint (that is, the mid-point of the finger, where it bends the most). This was done in an effort to halt the infection that had already occurred, and especially to prevent it spreading to the tendons. Tilden, aided by morphine, was soon anxious to get out. He had his little theater production of *Dulcy* scheduled to go into rehearsal soon, and more pressing, Saturday there was a crucial football game between his alma mater, Germantown Academy, and its traditional archrival, Penn Charter.

But on that day, Saturday the twenty-first, two weeks after the accident, things turned worse again, the finger swelled up to "the size of a small apple," he fell into really considerable pain, and Swartley hastened to make five more incisions. For the first time the full implications of the situation came home. A great many doctors in the hospital urged Swartley to amputate the whole finger and thereby all but eliminate the possibility that the infection would spread. It was clear now that if it did, Tilden could lose his whole hand, his arm, even his life.

Swartley came to Tilden's bed. "They want me to take the whole finger off, Bill," he said. "That way you get out of the hospital and take no chances. But of course, if I do . . . goodbye tennis."

Tilden nodded. "If you don't?"

"Well, we're still ahead of the poison now, and I think we'll stay ahead of it," Swartley said, "but we're taking a real chance any time we fool with a staph infection. I can't say, Bill. It's your hand, your tennis, your choice."

"How long will it take?" Tilden asked.

"No doctor can say."

Tilden barely paused. "Let's try to keep it," he said.

Initially that decision seemed wrong, for the infection almost immediately worsened. Boils developed elsewhere on his body and had to be lanced, and the finger itself grew more inflamed, gangrenous all the way down to the second joint. But Swartley nonetheless remained confident that the worst had passed and that nature would remove the infected area itself. "The terminal phalanx has become gangrenous, but the line of demarcation is plainly visible," he said. "The bones of the second joint are loosening, and within a few hours the diseased tissue will fall off. Already the nail and the tip have disappeared."

Sitting up in bed the next day, Tilden felt encouraged enough to welcome the press, and, with his finger resting on a hot-water bottle, he assured them all that he would keep playing, even if just for laughs. He almost seemed to look forward to his threatened new status. "Suppose my finger is crippled," he said. "Then I'll go out there and take what's coming to me. There's no reason why I shouldn't take a licking when the time comes."

If that sounds gratuitous, a brave front, the fact of the matter is that that is exactly how he took it—manfully, quite cheerfully—when, years later, lesser but younger players began to beat him regularly. And certainly Tilden was prepared for the worse. He had long, beautiful fingers, and he used them in the holding of a racket much more than most players do. Billy Johnston, for example, gripped the racket securely in his palm and would have been troubled only slightly by a missing tip of the middle finger. Tilden himself acknowledged that both his forehand and backhand drives would be but minimally affected by the partial loss of a finger, since his thumb and forefinger took the full force of these shots.

Nonetheless, he believed that every other shot of his would be severely diminished—especially his slices and volleys. Recuperating at Auntie's after he was released from the hospital on November 13, he said, "I will consider myself lucky to get in the top ten for 1923, and I mean it. You see, I make so many of these shots with my fingers. Sometimes, to get on the ball, I hold my racket almost with the tips of my fingers. You can readily see how I can't do that anymore with my keystone finger gone."

And worse was still to come. On December 13 Big Bill had to be rushed back to Germantown Hospital, where Dr. Swartley performed another operation, cutting the finger off to just above the second joint. The deteriorating situation forced him to take off this much more, but Tilden and Swartley were still gambling. Instead of playing it safe and removing all or nearly all of the finger, Swartley not only saved the second joint but even a small piece right above the joint. That left it just a bit more than a stump, which was probably the difference. It is possible that had they played the odds and taken off even so much as a quarter-inch more, maybe just an eighth of an inch more, his days as champion would have ended.

Tilden came out of this operation more optimistic than before. "The Davis Cup will be my ultimate goal for the year," he announced. "If I feel I'm good enough to make the team, I'll ask the committee to take my word for it. If I find that I am not, I will frankly say so." Generally, however, the opinion was that he would never again be a factor in tennis.

Why that did not become the case, why the loss did not

damage his game at all, why it did not ruin it—is impossible to tell. By all logic it should have. The racket turned more easily in his hand. The finger periodically pained him all his life, it often bled, and he had to tape it before most matches. Even then, it hurt him quite a bit to volley. Sometimes it bothered him so off the court that he had to shake hands left-handed to spare it. Most people soon forgot about the amputation and just assumed that this was another Tildenic affectation. He would always carry his rackets in his right hand so that it would appear a more natural, convenient gesture when he offered his left. The stump was a nasty-looking thing too, hardly any cosmetic bonanza, with a grisly indentation at the top, where Swartley had sewed up what was left. Tilden never seems to have taken any pains to conceal it, but the loss was seldom evident in public. It was barely mentioned again until years later when it helped the police identify the tall man who had been picked up for molesting a young hitchhiker.

Technically, Tilden only altered his grip slightly, placing the racket more diagonally across the palm, with his hand a little bit farther behind the handle in order to gain additional support. He went right back to business and practiced for the first time on December 29, 1922, hardly two weeks after the last operation. He was so pleasantly surprised with that performance that he went off to Chicago the next week and beat Frank Hunter in a regulation match 3–6, 7–5, 6–4. By February even the last of the skeptics were convinced that he was still the champion. In fact, 1923 was to be one of his very best years.

The only match he seems to have lost all year was to one of his favorite traveling companions, the courtly and handsome Manuel Alonso. The Spaniard beat Tilden in the finals of the Illinois championships, so when they met in the quarters at Forest Hills, Tilden felt that he had a score to settle. He ravaged Alonso 6–0, 6–0, 6–2, "easing up a little" in the last set, it was noted in the press. He worked this rout of one of the top players in the world almost strictly from the baseline, venturing to the net on but a handful of occasions. Alonso, past eighty today, hunched but still keen, with sharp blue eyes, sits in his Madrid apartment and shakes his head woefully at the clear memory of that awesome afternoon of long ago. Then, proudly, he beams. He considers it something of a compliment that Big Bill Tilden, at his peak, would have deigned to play so brilliantly against Manuel Alonso.

Tilden lost only one set in that entire Nationals, polishing off Johnston in the finals in fifty-seven minutes, 6–4, 6–1, 6–4. It was an especially symbolic Tilden exposition, because the Forest Hills Stadium, which is still used for the U.S. Open, was built that year for a quarter of a million dollars precisely so that people could see Big Bill play. He also won the U.S. doubles title that year, joining with Babe Norton as an impromptu pick-up partner. He won the national mixed doubles with Molla Mallory, and he captured the Davis Cup again over Australia singlehandedly. Johnston somehow lost the opening singles to James Anderson, and then after Tilden got the United States back into a tie with a straight-set win over John Hawkes, the USLTA inexplicably selected Dick Williams to play with Tilden in the doubles. Both always played the left-hand court. A loss would have put the United States down 2–1 in points, and indeed, Williams and Tilden were trailing 17–15, 11–13, 2–6 after three sets. At this point Big Bill just took charge from the unfamiliar right court and won the last two sets for America 6–3, 6–2. He remained furious with the USLTA, however, for putting together such a perfectly ridiculous doubles team, and when he received some bad calls in his favor the next day in his singles match against Anderson, Tilden punished the linesman and the USLTA by throwing a whole set 6–1, with disdain, before going on to win.

In 1924 there is no record that he lost a match at all, even though he wasted considerable of his energies arguing with the USLTA about his right to write about tennis for money. With no fields left to conquer, his interests began to shift even more to the theater. He turned thirty-two in February 1925, and he lost a few matches that winter while he was still out of shape. By the summer he was back in form, though, and, finding interest in a new challenge, he ran off fifty-seven consecutive winning games, one of those rare, unbelievable athletic feats—like Johnny Unitas throwing touchdown passes in forty-seven straight games or Joe DiMaggio hitting safely in fifty-six in a row—that simply cannot be exceeded in a reasonable universe no matter how long and loud we intone that records are made to be broken.

Tilden started his run of fifty-seven when he was down 3–4 to Alfred Chapin in the first set of the finals at Nassau, Long Island. He won the next three games for a 6–4 set, then swept Chapin away, love and love. On to Newport, where Tilden won his first-round two-set match at love. Apparently at this point somebody mentioned to him that he had won twenty-seven straight games and that he ought to try and run it up. Amused at this challenge—if only because there were precious few others left for him—Tilden rammed through his next two matches, two sets apiece, at love, and came up against his old protégé Carl Fischer, with fifty-one straight games in hand. He won the first set against Fischer at love too, but then at 30–all in the first game of the second set, Fischer says that Tilden received the most atrocious call against him, and, distracted, he lost the next point, the game and the record streak in the bargain. Then he came right back and ran off six straight more winning games. Fischer thinks that Tilden might well have gone on to seventy or eighty winning games at that point if he had not had the one game taken from him, because it was a fresh incentive for him to focus on.

If there was any possible benefit from the finger amputation, it would be a comment that it elicited from Tilden shortly before he had the final operation. He was candid at the moment, because he feared his career was over and there was no point in modesty or bravado. This remark illustrates how utterly supreme he was, *knew* he was himself, during his peak years. "The psychology of the thing is this," he said offhand. "In the last few years I have had the confidence in my ability to return every ball I could reach. *When I missed, I was surprised.*"

Largely because of Tilden's sad, shameful last years, which hastened the tennis establishment to reject him and to turn Big Bill into a non-person, younger fans and players today, and even members of the tennis press who never saw him in action, have no real recognition of Tilden the player. What popular image of his style still survives—that he was essentially a cannonball server pounding away—is completely at variance with the truth. In fact, Tilden had three different serves (as he had three varieties for nearly every stroke), and in his prime, even against his toughest opponents, he would employ the cannonball no more than once or twice a game. A lesser player might never have to see it, except perhaps at a score like love–30 or whenever Tilden wanted to finish out a game with a flourish.

By any standard, the Tilden cannonball was the most formidable weapon of the time, and, unlike most big serves, it was almost all velocity. Players somewhat younger than Tilden, who played against both him and Don Budge near their respective primes, generally agree that Budge's serve was much "heavier," with more drag. Budge used a massive sixteen-ounce racket, and he hit bombs that exploded on contact; his serve could rip the racket from a receiver's hand. Tilden's cannonball was really more of a bullet, and it did not maim receivers so much as it blazed by them. To add to the effect, he used a much lower toss than do modern players, so the thing appeared to come even faster, without warning.

Nonetheless, as fast and as deceptive as was Tilden's serve, if he had only had the cannonball, good players would have learned to stand far back, measure it, and, supplying their own pace, deliver Tilden's cannonballs back to him faster still. The reason they couldn't get in this groove was because Big Bill also hit an American twist serve, which arched in, ideally kicking high and away to the backhand, and a wicked slice serve, which pulled the ball the other way, into a slide, right to left.

He stretched up to hit his serves at a point nine feet six inches above the ground, and, more than most players, he tended to aim right down the middle, simply because the net is lower in the middle and the distance from the service line shorter. Tilden obtained a high percentage of successful first services—even on his cannonball, when he could pick his spots—and, like any good pitcher, he could move the ball around. "The velocity was tremendous," says Ellsworth Vines, whose own cannonball was likewise highly celebrated, "and he had a gift of making a slight adjustment just before the racket met the ball, so that he could blow it by you on the corner or smash it dead at you."

And yet the serve was but a part of Tilden's arsenal, and it is important to remember that his record was just as impressive on clay as on grass. He won seven U.S. clay court titles, six in a row, plus a bevy of victories on the Continental clay, an especially soft and slow surface which mutes the hard serve. The crux is this: Tilden applied whatever he had to when he had to. He won the 1925 Forest Hills final over Johnston when he had an injured shoulder, which he confided beforehand was "gone," and which prevented him from holding hardly more than half his service games in a long five-set match that lasted more than two hours. And yet, as always in these years, Tilden prevailed at the end—and despite being down a set and facing three set points against him in the second set.

This time, lacking a reliable serve, Tilden concentrated on ground strokes, slicing them so that the ball bounced barely at all; down low, Johnston's Western grip was least effective, and the constant reaching wore him down. And so Tilden forged ahead in the fifth set. Serving at 5–3, 40–15, he measured the service line, looked down at the little fellow at the other end, and from somewhere out of his gone shoulder brought home a vintage cannonball. The ball went into the corner straight down the middle. Little Bill lunged with his backhand, but he could not touch the ball with his racket. Big Bill had won his sixth straight national championship, and although of course they did not know it then, it was the last point that Big Bill and Little Bill ever played.

Johnston's Western forehand was his prized stroke, of course, but at his peak it is quite possible that Tilden's Eastern-grip forehand and backhand were *both* better strokes than Johnston's best. His backhand—the one he had created as an afterthought in Providence in the winter of 1919—was a marvel of flexibility. Tilden could hit it crosscourt or down the line with equal facility, and with as much speed as seemed advisable. As a player gets older, a backhand drive—reaching across the body—becomes more difficult to hit, and Tilden's wonderful backhand began to get away from him around 1930. At that point he fell back on his slice backhand, and many people think that for the next decade or so this back-up backhand was better than any in the game save Budge's.

During the 1920s Tilden's forehand drive seems to have been overlooked mostly because he obtained more pleasure

out of slicing a forehand. For the same sort of reasons he
was never an outstanding volleyer. "He had such fun doing
other things that he didn't like to volley," Sarah Palfrey
Danzig says. Tilden generally viewed serve-and-volley
types as dullards, barely one step up from USLTA officials,
and this prejudice kept him from perfecting his own net
game.

He loved to play against volleyers, though. The two
Frenchmen who caught up with him, Lacoste and Cochet,
reached him from the back court; Borotra, the star at the
net, never did. Richards, the great American volleyer, had
so little success with Big Bill that the joke was that newspapers kept a standing headline set in type: TILDEN
BEATS RICHARDS AGAIN. Tilden liked to tantalize volleyers, hitting the ball at them in the beginning of a match,
and then slowly, with excruciating patience, taking the
shots inch by inch away from them as the afternoon wore
on. Eventually they would have to stretch to volley, then
move and stretch to volley, and then move and stretch and
not reach the ball. Diabolically too he would lure volleyers
up to the net, where they wanted to be, with drop shots,
and then send them chasing right back to the baseline with
lobs. His matches with Borotra always went on at length,
as Big Bill stole little bits and pieces of him along the
way.

Generally, if Tilden took to volleying much himself, it
suggested that his opponent was playing well. Because he
could usually control a match from the baseline, his coming
to the net often indicated that he felt obligated to try something different. His own volleys were sure, but seldom
hard, and even less so after he lost the top of his finger.

Tilden's prevailing big-game image has obfuscated what
a superb touch player he was: the racket in the fingers, not
the hand. He dreamed up and then perfected the drop shot
as an offensive weapon. He could flick a drop shot so that

it just carried the net, and then didn't really bounce, but sort of nestled onto the turf. Tilden viewed the ball as "an individual, the third party in the match." He could rattle on for as long as anyone would care to listen about how much spin to use to answer each particular shot, how to achieve "the middle road of spin plus speed," and where exactly to place the racket upon the ball (southeast corner for a forehand, southwest for a backhand). Ideally, he hit a ball waist high, just as it began its descent, and, like snow-flakes, no Tilden shots were ever quite the same. "The great majority of players are not students of the game," he wrote. "It is the love of tennis that has led me to the point where I never hit a shot without conscious application of twist or the deliberate attempt to use none."

He was also an expert on footwork, even something of a bore, and with years of practice he learned to take a short mincing step just before he turned so that he would be in perfect position to hit the ball perfectly with the perfect spin by the perfect stroke in order to deliver it to the perfect place. "It was like seeing Nijinsky dance across the net," Alonso says. "I saw Nijinsky once, and he went across a whole stage in three jumps. Tilden was that way. He played a game that made you feel so *uncomfortable*. Do you know? That was the way. He knew exactly how to make it difficult for you, so that even if you played very well, when you came off the court you had the feeling that you had not done well at all."

John Hennessey says, "He made tennis players out of all of us. Even when he was no longer at his best, you had to improve just by playing with him. Looking back, some-times you say, I don't see why I couldn't beat the guy every time. But you see, you didn't even know what he was doing to you. Oh, could he move a guy around. You didn't even know it. He was fifteen or thirty a game better than us all. Bill was the making of all the players, right to this day."

Despite his contemplation of all the mechanics of tennis, it was the psychology of the game that Tilden most emphasized. Indeed, once he had honed his game to its ultimate level, and once he had brought it back to that level every summer, what were the strokes and the shots and the footwork but rote? Thus, from a certain point on, the bulk of his thought about the game was about the thought in the game. He even did a long and complicated analysis of what were the pivotal moments in any match: the key points in a game (the fourth one if both players have won a point; otherwise the third); key games (seventh above all, then fourth and ninth); and key sets (the first one in best two-of-three; win that, he said, and you'll win the match 80 per cent of the time; and the third set in best three-of-five).

Physically Tilden was the first complete player, and whether or not he is the best ever, he is unquestionably the finest all-round player in history. Also he was the most charismatic, the most publicized, the most exciting and dramatic, and even, with the cannonball, the most glamorous. And yet, if he had been none of these, not one, he would still be regarded as a paramount figure in the game, because it was his genius and that application which took the whole sport, kit and caboodle, from one level of sophistication way up to another. It would be as if Babe Ruth and John McGraw had resided in the same body, as if Vince Lombardi had quarterbacked the Packers on offense and played middle linebacker on defense while he also coached them and gave all the halftime commentaries on television. Tilden and tennis. Tilden was tennis, body and soul.

On top of everything else, he contributed a whole body of literature on the subject. His tennis fiction was forced and trite, but his writings about the playing of the game, however technical, read smoothly and even with a certain grace, notwithstanding something of an intrusive evangelical flavor that is reminiscent of Charles Atlas instructing young men in how to obtain biceps. *Match Play and Spin of the Ball*, written a half-century ago, is not only the seminal work on tennis but unquestionably still the ultimate authority as well. When the young John Newcombe won his first Wimbledon in 1967 someone asked him where he had originally learned to play the game. "Reading Bill Tilden's book," he said, and with some surprise, as if "Didn't everybody?" When Arthur Ashe and Stan Smith traveled on a State Department tour through Africa in 1970, they suddenly chanced upon a beautiful young teenage player in Dar es Salaam, Tanzania. They could not believe his form, his strokes, his understanding of tennis, for there was neither anyone around to teach him nor to play against him. It turned out that his father had brought "Tilden's book" with him from India and taught his son from it, working him for months in front of a mirror before permitting the boy to hit a ball, and then requiring him to play exactly as it was written in the book. The boy (who subsequently earned a tennis scholarship to an American college) was literally, to his limits, a Tilden image; it was like finding an Eskimo speaking perfect first-century Latin.

Since Tilden never stopped discovering new concepts of his game, it would be as unfair as impossible to try to present an all-purpose summary of his views. Basically, though, he believed that tennis should be played "as a defensive game with an offensive mental attitude." The main point, he wrote again and again, was to hit the ball back. "Nothing is so disconcerting or upsetting to a player as to miss. A magnificent shot, which beats him completely, doesn't cause a player much mental anguish, because, if he's a sportsman, he will admire it and not worry about it anymore. On the other hand, each time he sees an important shot of his own sail out of the court or into the net, a player becomes more nervous and less likely to win the match."

While he never did inscribe a tennis manifesto, Tilden did once give his nephew William T. Tilden III a list of thirteen points for playing the game. They were not instructional dogma (watch the ball, bend your knees, etc.), but neither, taken as a whole, did they add up to some grave philosophy, which they would have, no doubt, if Tilden had written them all out and published them. In that case, they would have surely been stuffy and dry, Polonius writing a Defense Department memo. But as it is, the thirteen points make a fascinating informal catalog, diverse, almost haphazard and arbitrary—and as intriguing for what he did not choose to mention as for what he did. In paraphrase:

1) Tennis is a game of errors (as above: don't miss).

2) Play to your opponent's strength. That way it is easiest to exploit his weakness at a crucial point. Also, keep in mind that if your opponent does have a weakness, everybody has concentrated on it for so long that he has developed compensations that may sucker you. For example, players with the weakest backhands are most adroit at running around their backhand and hitting a forehand down your throat.

3) Double faults are inexcusable. You should develop a second serve as difficult as the first.

4) Returning serve is just as important as serving, inasmuch as 50 per cent of all points begin that way for every player.

5) A good player never misses the easy ones. Remember that if you do miss a simple shot you should have made, you have really given your opponent two points—the difference between plus one and minus one. Within this context, Tilden once wrote about choking: "I believe that

the champion will miss just about as many shots as the second-class player, but he will miss them at different times. The champion seldom misses a shot he should make at a critical moment."

6) Play your hardest at 30–15 or 15–30.

7) Come into a match with alternative plans of attack. Tilden went on the court with as many as four different game plans, and sometimes ran through all four and came up with another while playing.

8) On the other hand, never change a winning game.

9) Make it easy on yourself. For example, if you want to serve wide to your opponent's backhand, well then, move closer to the sideline so that you can get a better angle. Never mind if that helps him figure out what you are doing. If he tries to outguess you, cross him up and hit one down the middle.

10) Play the odds in covering a court. Figure out where your opponent is most likely to return a shot and head there. This will save you a lot of steps. Tilden's nephew happened to mention the word "anticipation" at this point to show that he understood, whereupon his uncle promptly flew into a rage, calling him "hopeless," as he often did, and other things as well. "Anticipation," Big Bill roared, "is just a fancy word for guessing." He didn't guess, he said; he studied and learned. He thought that 98 per cent of tennis players were stupid.

11) Results before form. Be comfortable and don't try to hit the perfect stroke.

12) Vary the spin and pace of the balls you hit or your opponent will get in a groove no matter how well you are playing and beat you at your own game.

13) You must have a killer instinct, even though you must also be a sportsman.

But all these aside, Tilden himself won on sheer will more than for any other single reason. There is one passage from *Match Play and Spin of the Ball* which best seems to explain the thrust of his spirit. It accounts for everything he did on the court, from the moment he walked out there with his Tilden sweater, his rackets and his élan. "When two players start a match [he wrote], it is always a battle to see who will dominate and who will be pushed around. One player or the other will ultimately impress his tennis personality upon the other. The one who does will win, because by so doing he forces the recognition of impending defeat upon his opponent. One of the surest ways to achieve this state of affairs is to set your own tempo and hold it. Do it courteously, with all due regard for your opponent's right, but do it."

I'm ready whenever you're exhausted, partner!

CHAPTER SEVEN

"You are a parasite . . . a tennis gigolo"

AMONG the additional contributions that Tilden incidentally made to tennis was controversy. Before he came along, tennis was a genial family affair, but by the time he departed the amateurs, the whole game was in turmoil, in which it has remained to this day. Of course, given its ample quota of official dimwits, tennis would surely have located the path to self-destruction all by itself had not Big Bill been there to show the way. Nonetheless, let it not be said that he didn't do his fair share.

When Tilden came to prominence, tennis was still a country club diversion controlled by those few country clubbers who took the time to join committees and wear ribbons and issue orders. The players themselves were ciphers. Perhaps a third or more were women, who were expected to keep their place in all endeavors at that time. The remainder, the men, were collegians or recent graduates who played for a few years during the summer and then got married and went on to other gainful pursuits. As a consequence, a small cadre of older officials were the only ongoing guardians of the game, suffering the players as necessary evils.

Tilden thought this system unjust long before it affected

him much personally. He started sniping at the USLTA when he was a tennis reporter for the *Evening Ledger* in Philadelphia around 1915, when he was still an inconsequential local player. Then, when he became a prominent figure in the game, he rattled the USLTA even more by taking an active interest in the USLTA. This struck many tennis bigwigs as unfair of him, and indeed, subversive. Players were supposed to content themselves with playing.

Besides, Tilden was really quite an original, revolutionary thinker. Although generally conservative and traditionalist, even elitist, he was quite progressive and something of a rabble rouser when those traditions got in his way. But to give the devil his due, Tilden was suggesting things fifty years ago that are just now being changed, if at all. For example, as early as 1920 he suggested that the word "love" be dropped from the tennis lexicon. Although he much preferred grass courts, he recognized their maintenance impracticability if tennis were to grow, and so he proposed that some form of hard courts be made the universal theater of action. Although he was firmly against professionalism practically till the day he signed (when, typically, he became the most impassioned proponent of professional play), he was agitating for open competition, where amateurs and pros could face each other, as early as 1927. At the same time he staggered the establishment by arguing, at Yale, that college football players who fill such stadiums as, for instance, the Yale Bowl, should be paid for their special contribution to higher education. "I believe in the old hokum about the amateur sports theory—sports for sports' sake," he said. "But the economic pressure must be considered too. A man can get good money if he is a good waiter or a good musician, so why shouldn't he make good money if he is a good football player?" Almost half a century before a league of tennis teams got off the ground,

Tilden was advocating just such an idea.* Tilden was the
first to call for a change in the Davis Cup format, arguing
that it was too protracted, which is exactly what the
players are arguing fifty-two years later, as the Davis Cup
diminishes in prominence because it is too protracted. In
1921 he called for the end of Challenge Rounds at Wimbledon and in the Davis Cup as being grossly unfair in behalf
of the champion (which he was). Wimbledon changed its
policy the next year, the Davis Cup in 1972. For expressing
such mad opinions, the USLTA found Tilden a meddler
and a gadfly.

His antipathy toward the establishment only increased
as he became a more important player. "I have never
solved the puzzle," he said, "of why a man sane and wise in
his business and personal life should change to a stubborn
fanatic the moment he becomes an amateur sports official."
Tilden's special nemesis was Julian (Mike) Myrick, who, in
and out of the USLTA presidency, controlled just about
everything in American tennis but Big Bill Tilden. He was
pompous and arbitrary, and it was said that one word from
Myrick was enough to keep a lesser player off the circuit.
Because shamateurism was a way of life and there were no
contracts, even top tenners who were not independently
wealthy were at the mercy of Mike Myrick.

He and Tilden first came to real crossed swords at the
finals of the 1921 Nationals at Germantown. Tilden had
disposed of Little Bill in the quarterfinals, and for the
championship his opponent was Wallace Johnson, his fellow Philadelphian with the chop strokes. Tilden owned a
22–2 lifetime edge on Johnson, and even those two defeats
had come years before. The finals were scheduled for a
Saturday, but when it rained hard the night before, with

* World Team Tennis, which began in 1974, is often known by its
initials, WTT. These also happen to be Tilden's initials, but nobody in the
league has noted this felicitous coincidence.

more showers forecast, it was obvious that there would be a
postponement until Monday (blue laws prohibited Sunday
play in Philadelphia then). However, Myrick, who was the
tournament referee, figured that the soft, tricky sod provided Johnson with his one chance in a thousand to de-
throne Tilden, and he convinced the other officials to try
to get the match in on Saturday.

Outwardly unmoved, if seething inside, well aware of
what Myrick was up to, Tilden simply went out on the slip-
pery turf and played Johnson's own game. Like his opponent, he just chopped every ball. Without traction, it was
easier that way. This went on until the rain began to fall
and forced a delay. After twenty minutes Myrick called
them back on the court. Okay, Tilden went back to chopping. Johnson had a break at 8–7 when the rains began in
earnest again, but Myrick kept the match going in the hope
that Johnson could wrap up the set. Tilden broke right
back though, and with the rain coming down harder,
Myrick called it a day at 8–all. Presumably Tilden would
have chopped along to 100–all if Myrick had kept them
going.

Monday, in bright sunshine, Tilden came to the court
"with blood in his eye," according to Carl Fischer. Poor
Wallace Johnson was stationed across the net, but the
USLTA and Mike Myrick were Big Bill's oponents. On his
first serve he aced Johnson with the hardest cannonball he
could muster, and then, without even bothering to take off
his sweater, he beat him 6–1, 6–3, 6–1 in forty-two minutes.

In 1923, when the USLTA accused Tilden of taking
money for making instructional films, his ire was raised
again, and he suggested that he was being manhandled by
a double standard. "There is a definite penalty of suspicion
attached to superior ability," he declared, intimating, in the
bargain, that the USLTA was peopled by mediocrities. The
organization was not only buffaloed by his statements and

actions, but it was always on edge that the fact of his homosexuality would become public knowledge and deal tennis a mortal blow. Although no one can prove it, many have thought that the USLTA had him tailed for a while in the hopes of catching him in a compromising situation, so that the incriminating evidence could be used to blackmail him, to keep him in line.

Worst of all, from the USLTA's point of view, Tilden would just never go away; he was visible to the point of ubiquity. He would, for example, pay his way to USLTA meetings and raise hell about the proposed rankings, screaming that the suggested number six should be number eight, number eight seven, and so on—and how could the ranking committee possibly ignore the advice of the undefeated champion who had beaten the whole lot of them himself? Tilden took all the fun out of rankings. He not only beat everybody on the courts, but then he wanted to certify it on paper too. The USLTA tried to divert his interest by designating him as the official ranker of the junior players, but that was all very tricky because he invariably had favorites among the boys he was supposed to be dispassionately ranking.

But turnabout is fair play, and the USLTA was forever sticking its nose into business that it should have left to the players. The selection of the Davis Cup team was always a free-for-all, but since Tilden and Johnston simply could not be overlooked in the singles, this drew all the attention to the doubles. Hardly a year went by in which that decision failed to produce some controversy, and often nobody was sure who was going to play in the damn thing until the players walked on the court. Then, when the match got under way, committeemen would actually come down by the court and offer pointed suggestions to the players. When Tilden wouldn't do what the bigwigs suggested one year, the head poohbah declared that "Tilden chose to park his intelligence outside the stadium."

The especially ridiculous decision in 1923 to pair Williams and Tilden, two left-court players, produced intramural recriminations all winter. Actually, Tilden had been the one who had staved off disaster that day, but Williams was an agreeable sort and nobody in the USLTA wanted to insult him. Big Bill accused the Davis Cup committee of "star chamber methods" and threatened never to play again. It was a typical quarrel which neither side could win. The USLTA needed Tilden to bring victory and pay the bills, but it was always frightened that he would destroy the organization. Tilden needed the USLTA to play, but was convinced its members were unfair to him, if not indeed cheating him of his athletic birthright. "It drove Bill crazy," Hunter says. "He realized he was building stadiums and making money for other people, but he didn't know how to go about diverting that to himself."

The one thing Tilden did have was a platform. Off and on he had been a journalist since he left college—he listed "newspaperman" as his vocation on forms and questionnaires—and there was always some publishing syndicate ready to pay to print his views. Tilden made as much as $25,000 a year for several years during his heyday in the 1920s by writing special newspaper pieces. Much as star athletes are "color announcers" on television today, it was quite common at that time, when newspapers were the only mass communication, for the big names to have regular bylines. Of course, except for Tilden and a few other literate interlopers, almost all the stars had their pap cranked out by ghosts. Indeed, when Big Bill was first informed early in 1924 that he was violating amateur canons by writing for pay, his first response was brilliantly sharp and in character: that *he* was the honorable man, writing his own material; if anyone were to be punished it must be those who sank so low as to put their name upon something they did not write.

The USLTA had no response for that. The organization was on thin ice in the special case of Tilden, because, as he speedily pointed out, he had been writing for a living long before he gained any prominence in tennis. How could they deny him his life's work? In passing, he also noted that writing is "an honorable and recognized vocation," an assessment which did nothing to harm his position in the hearts of editorial-page writers. Nonetheless, on March 15, 1924, the USLTA gave Tilden a cursory hearing and then affirmed its original ruling: All players had to stop writing about tennis for remuneration or be banned, effective January 1, 1925.

Tilden, somewhat presaging the Duke of Windsor, announced, "I cannot give up my profession," and to leaven that declaration he soon signed a new contract calling for a weekly tennis commentary plus daily accounts of the 1924 Davis Cup, piecework which could net him $20,000 or more for the year. This abject effrontery staggered the USLTA. Despite all evidence to the contrary, for some reason the organization always seems to have routinely expected Tilden to bow supinely to its directives. A bewildered Holcombe Ward, president of the rules committee, said, "Our present champion is extremely versatile without doubt. He is not only a great tennis player, but he is an interesting writer, a lover of music, an actor, and I don't know what all else." Alas, pressed for a more complete inventory of the what all else, Ward responded by labeling Tilden "a bad influence."

This was a godsend for Tilden. Not only did it provide him with a magnificent opportunity to revel in some righteous indignation, but he had been searching desperately for any excuse that would get him out of having to go to the Olympics that summer. That was the last year that tennis was on the schedule. "If the committee considers me an evil influence," Tilden intoned gravely, making Ward's "bad" much badder, "then I cannot, with self-respect, represent this country on the Davis Cup or Olympic teams." Big Bill picked up a lot of support too. Tennis clubs had referendums on the issue, and several players, notably Vinnie Richards, who also wrote a lucrative newspaper column, backed Tilden. A Bill Tilden Fair Play Society was formed and a public effort begun to force USLTA officials to reveal what side benefits they accrued from tennis.

Tilden himself eventually proposed a compromise, that a player be allowed to write, although neither his name nor any titles be used. The USLTA wouldn't buy that, but a week later, June 13, Tilden was suddenly named to a special select committee to study the whole matter. Included with him were a number of other tennis people of opposing persuasions on the issue, as well as Devereaux Milburn, the polo star, Grantland Rice, the esteemed sports columnist, and Senator George Wharton Pepper. By August Tilden was back on the Davis Cup team, as if nothing had happened, which indeed it didn't until December, when the committee finally got around to deciding that a player could write about tennis so long as he did not *cover* an event he was participating in.

That compromise was fine with Big Bill, who followed it to the letter of the law. He would write his same old column about tennis in general, and then give out paid "interviews" at the tournaments he played in. A typical such example of this period, for instance, was an Associated Press article allegedly about Tilden. Actually, it consisted of a brief introductory paragraph, which served as the byline, and then seventeen paragraphs of Tilden "quotes." It did not take long for Myrick and the rest of the USLTA to realize they had been had, and by the summer of 1925, when Tilden gave out another syndicated "interview" for pay in St. Louis, he was threatened again with being barred. Big Bill, playing dumb (a rare role for him to submit to), said there must be some misunderstanding, and he agreed to attend a meeting in New York to straighten everything out. By now the USLTA was getting apoplectic on the subject of Tilden. The *minutes* of this meeting go on for 117 pages, and from all of this the upshot was that Tilden said he was sorry and wouldn't do it again, and the USLTA said better not or you'll be suspended. Those chants chanted, Tilden went right on doing exactly as he pleased, content in the knowledge that the USLTA needed him more than the other way around. "Writing," he declared archly, "is a matter of taste, not amateurism."

Finally, in July of 1928, when Tilden was in his decline and out of the country, the USLTA decided to go for his jugular. At Wimbledon Tilden had written a number of articles for the Christy Walsh Syndicate. They appeared in more than one hundred newspapers, including the *World* in New York, without making so much as a stir, until the California USLTA head, Dr. Sumner Hardy, had a fit about the July 3 piece that ran in the San Francisco *Chronicle* under the headline TILDEN REVIEWS FIRST WEEK'S PLAY ON TENNIS COURTS AT WIMBLEDON. Since Tilden stayed in the tournament for several more days before Lacoste beat him in the semifinals (thereby putting a huge depression into the gate for the finals), Dr. Hardy maintained that the articles were "too current." Grown men prepared to assemble and ponder that possibility.

Unbeknownst, Tilden moved on to Paris. He was not only the star of the Davis Cup team, as always, but this year the USLTA had made him captain as well. In Paris the Americans were to face the Italians, with the winner to play France in the Challenge Round. Naturally the Americans were odds-on against the Italians, and in anticipation of a showdown between the Musketeers and "Le Grand Bill," a whole new stadium had been built at Roland Garros. Ticket sales were rocketing along on July 17 when a special USLTA meeting was convened in New York, and it was quickly decided to ban Captain Tilden for violating Paragraph 4, Section B, the "Amateur Writer Rule" that he had helped author himself. For the USLTA it was a perfect move. The U.S. team didn't have much chance of beating the French anyway, and as the visiting team, it wasn't going to cost the USLTA that much money.

On July 19 at the Hotel Carlton in Paris, where the draw for the Italian matches was being held, someone noticed that Tilden was not present. "Tilden is no longer captain of the team," said Joseph Wear, a Davis Cup committeeman who had himself just learned the news. Pandemonium followed Wear's statement and shortly thereafter, when Tilden entered the room in an obvious emotional state, the assembled press rose and cheered him. De Morpurgo, the Italian star, embraced him. "I'm sorry, Bill," he said. "This takes all the fun out of it."

Tilden at last managed to raise his hand to still the tumult, but he was so carried away himself at being a certified international martyr that before he began to read his prepared remarks, he cried out, "I refute all charges! We will win the Davis Cup! I hereby apply for the job of training all Davis Cup members for the grueling matches ahead!" Electrified and unable to restrain itself again, the press once more rose as a body and cheered Tilden. Then, face pale, lips trembling, Big Bill read his statement. When he was finished, the Musketeers all gathered around and commiserated with him.

Despite his personal antipathy to Tilden, it was George Lott who immediately began a move to get the whole U.S. team to go on protest strike. The walkout surely would have worked too, except that Tilden himself pleaded with

Lott not to let Uncle Sam down. Wear, the Davis Cup committeeman and Tilden's last-second replacement as captain, did resign in protest from the USLTA. Lacoste announced that he would not defend his Forest Hills title, even though, with a third victory, he could retire the trophy. For that matter, the Crocodile did not even want to go through with the Challenge Round. "We would rather lose the Davis Cup than retain it where there may be some excuse in the absence of Tilden," he said. The press reported that despondent Frenchmen were mumbling "pauvre Beeg Beel" all over Paris. Ticket sales, which had passed a million francs, stopped dead, and then, worse, people started coming in to get their money back. The few hundred fans who bothered to attend the U.S.–Italian matches expended most of their energy craning their necks for Tilden, who watched as a mournful spectator, alone, high up in the stands.

In Amsterdam, in the midst of the 1928 Olympics, a number of the best-known amateurs stopped writing their usual paid columns about the games to use their space to bemoan the fate of Tilden. So too did the remaining U.S. Davis Cup players in dispatches to their newspaper employers. In America the news of the suspension took over the front-page lead, driving the assassination of Mexico's president-elect and a search for lost Arctic aviators to less prominent positions. If we can believe it, even President Coolidge wanted to know what the hell was the USLTA up to now. USLTA President Samuel H. Collom, who had been en route, unaware of the suspension, was so appalled at the response he found in Paris that he called up Myrick and the other ringleaders in New York and argued with them for two hours, running up a $1950 phone bill.

Despite this plea from President Collom, as well as advisory opinions from Joseph Wear and similar counsel from both USLTA men on the scene, the bigwigs in New York would not lift the suspension. The USLTA was then utterly flabbergasted to discover that the ill-bred American public sided with Tilden. Indeed, the incident put such a lasting dent into the psyche of the organization that, incredible as this may sound, when the USLTA produced its official encyclopedia in 1973, forty-five years later, it actually wrote, for history, that it would have preferred its own team to have lost to Italy so that the USLTA could have escaped all the subsequent unpleasantness: "It was unfortunate that the team did not lose to Italy, and then the whole matter never would have arisen."

But, too bad for the USLTA, its team did win, and the whole affair was soon getting out of hand. The French, caught in the middle, were neither amused nor understanding. They had a whole big new stadium to pay for. Besides, until the USLTA made an issue of tennis players writing, it had never occurred to any other nationalities that there was anything wrong with it. Ticket refund demands kept coming in at a faster clip, so at last the French tennis officials turned to their government, which approached the U.S. ambassador in Paris, Myron Herrick. Meanwhile, in Washington, the French ambassador made his presence felt. Herrick did not act unilaterally, but whether or not Coolidge got into the act personally is not known for certain. He may very well have, because he really didn't have much else to do that summer, and the Tilden affair was the closest thing going at the time to a real international crisis.

In any event, egged on by Washington, Herrick ironed out a deal with the USLTA whereby "in the interest of international good feeling," the USLTA would permit Tilden to play in Paris and then spank him when he returned home. The suspension was lifted hardly twenty-four hours before the Challenge Round was to begin, and Tilden didn't himself learn of his reprieve until he arrived at the draw. As soon as that was concluded, with Tilden matched

against Lacoste in the opener the next day, Big Bill hurried
to the courts to practice with Junior Coen; it was the first
time in days, literally, that he had played. "He was practically hysterical," Coen says. "He couldn't hit a damn thing,
so finally he just stormed off."

Against Lacoste, Tilden was posted as a 2–1 underdog.
The Crocodile was the defending American champion and
had just won Wimbledon as well; he was the acknowledged heir to Big Bill, best player in the world. Not only
that, but Lacoste had defeated Tilden in their last four
meetings, he had him now on his home courts, his surface,
and before a manic Gallic crowd; moreover, Tilden was
lacking practice and was terribly distracted and emotionally spent by the controversy of the past week. On top of all
that, play began in the teeth of a swirling wind that kicked
up the red dust and even started a small grandstand fire.
Tilden lost the first set 6–1, and this was no possum act; he
was aimless and disoriented, playing as hopelessly as he
had the day before against Coen in practice.

Somehow, at this point, Tilden steeled himself for the
challenge and threw his usual regular game out of the win-
dow. Instead, he started slicing every ball, this way and
that. As steady as Lacoste was, and that was his suit, Tilden outsteadied him. If Tilden could not beat Lacoste as
Tilden, then he would beat Lacoste as Lacoste. On the
slow clay, with long, enervating rallies, the old man won in
five sets. He was thirty-five now, and he was somehow yet
to win both Forest Hills and Wimbledon again, and while
this was not his finest tennis, in many respects it was his
best and most remarkable match of all. The other Americans, so familiar with the agonies of the mind that afflicted
Tilden that week, watched the victory in disbelief. Lott
was so excited when Big Bill won the final point that he
jumped out of the stands, and in doing so lost an expensive
bracelet he had just bought for his girl. Still in awe at what

he watched that afternoon in Paris, he calls it "a display of
versatility that has never been equaled."

In the locker room Lacoste slumped, confused and de-
spairing, and cried. "Two years ago I knew at last how to
beat him," he said. "Now, on my own court, he beats me. I
never knew how the ball would come off the court, he con-
cealed it so well. I had to wait to see how much it was
spinning—and sometimes it didn't spin at all. Is he not the
greatest player of all time?"

Tilden was too old by now to sustain this kind of performance, however, and on the next successive days he lost in
the doubles with Hunter and then his singles match to
Cochet; so the Davis Cup stayed in France, as everyone had
assumed it would. Then, in August, also as everyone had
assumed, the USLTA prepared once again to try to suspend Big Bill. He was granted a trial on August 24 in New
York. "Trial is a very amusing word," he told the press, and
he told the USLTA that he couldn't even be bothered to
attend, as he had other fish to fry. Exactly, as a matter of
fact, he was engaged doing "tennis monologues" near Boston at the Waltham Vaudeville Theatre.

The USLTA's special committee of eighteen assembled
without the defendant at eight o'clock on the appointed
night at the Hotel Vanderbilt. Mike Myrick opened the
meeting with this charge: "If Tilden is removed [tonight]
it is going to be one of the biggest things that has ever
happened in tennis . . . and we must have reasons so that
everyone will understand our actions. We have got to treat
Tilden not as Tilden but as anybody else." Six hours later
the eighteen voted to suspend Tilden "indefinitely." Unoffi-
cially, "indefinitely" meant at least through Forest Hills and
then for as long as necessary until Tilden would eat some
crow. He really never did, either. "They are calling me a
liar," he cried at first, pointing out that he had traveled ten
thousand miles, paying more than two thousand dollars of

his own expenses to captain the Davis Cup team this year. "I am far more amateur in spirit than some of the men who have run tennis for years with one eye on the gate, while exploiting me for their advancement," he remarked later. Those members of the press who sided with the USLTA he called "Bolsheviks." But the USLTA got thirty-four other countries to uphold its ban and twice turned down Tilden's requests for reinstatement.

Steadfastly, if for no evident good reasons, he refused to take the sensible way out and turn pro. "I will have nothing to do with professional tennis," he declared, adding somewhat snobbishly, "I hope everybody knows me better than that." Well, certainly he had been consistent in this view all along. As early as 1920, after he won his first championship, he had turned down Arthur Hammerstein's offer of $25,000. In 1924, when the writing flap first broke, he turned down Tex Rickard, and then, in 1926, when Cash and Carry Pyle signed up Suzanne Lenglen and Vinnie Richards, Tilden rejected an offer to work the top of the bill against Richards.

The younger man had already signed, venturing the observation that he didn't see why he, as well as the USLTA, couldn't make some money out of tennis. Tilden hardly gave Pyle a hearing, even though the promoter guaranteed him $25,000 for a six-month tour. "It would have to be doubled," Big Bill replied idly.

"All right, it is doubled," Pyle snapped back. Fifty thousand dollars was a great sum of money in 1926. Only Babe Ruth made more among salaried athletes, and no other athlete earned probably even half fifty thousand. But Tilden turned down Pyle quickly enough again.

"Mr. Tilden," Cash and Carry said, "I think you are a damn fool."

"Mr. Pyle," Big Bill replied, "I think you are right."

But money simply was not the object and Tilden would

not lower himself to turn pro. The USLTA was itself so
relieved that he did not join the Lenglen-Richards troupe
that for once the organization actually decided that he was
on the side of the angels, and when Tilden's new Broadway
show, *They All Want Something*, opened that fall, the
USLTA put the arm on its New York area members and
made them go buy tickets to see it.

This reconciliation was short-lived, however, if only because finally the USLTA members had to see him act. The
disputes began to flower again, culminating in the suspension of 1928. At this point too, while Tilden continued to
speak out ardently on behalf of amateurism, even he was
beginning to realize that the ideal was far separated from
the fact. While he would not express these new views, he
did insert them in his fiction. In his novel, *Glory's Net*,
which was almost surely written during his suspension (if,
indeed, not inspired by it as well), Mary, the wife, says this
to David, the champion: "You are a kept man. You are a
parasite. . . . Can you give business value for the money
you receive? No, you give nothing. Economically, you are
just the same as a kept woman. You are paid for someone
else's pleasure and to be exploited at their wishes. . . .
David, you are a tennis gigolo."

And David himself later pondered the same thing. "A
wave of loneliness swept David," Tilden wrote. "Why the
hell was everyone else in the world happy except him?
. . . What was he doing to justify his existence?" Even
the crassness of professionalism began to pale alongside the
dishonor of shamateurism. What would Teddy Roosevelt
have done?

By February of 1929, when he was ranked number one in
the country for the ninth consecutive year, the USLTA was
ready to lift Tilden's suspension. While he would not
apologize publicly, the organization, nobody's fool, was
able to divine that he was properly "chastened in spirit."

And then, barely a month after he was reinstated, the USLTA began advertising extensively that henceforth, William T. Tilden II, banned by the USLTA for writing tennis articles, would soon be writing exclusive tennis articles for the official USLTA publication. Even Big Bill must have recognized that the situation was simply ludicrous by now.

CHAPTER EIGHT

"The Lord never meant my face for a hero!"

QUITE possibly what might have pleased Tilden most about dying was that he received an obituary in *Variety,* which, while making note of his affiliation with tennis, identified him as a "quondam actor and playwright." Since *Variety* dismissed both Aly Khan and Prince Rainier as "non-pros" when they were connected to show biz through marriage, Tilden was getting, at last, some acceptance from the community where he craved that the most. He was brave enough to have sometimes confided to friends that his stage failures hurt him more than any tennis defeat.

It would not have surprised anyone who saw Tilden act to learn that he came to the theater by default. His first love was music (save for jazz, which "I cannot stomach"), but he had no ability whatsoever as a musician. Nor could he paint. He did have some success as a writer, but not where he wanted it, in fiction, creating.* His best writing was as a journalist or as a technical tennis authority, and the further

* Sadly, the closest Tilden ever came to eminence in fiction was in another writer's book. In Vladimir Nabokov's *Lolita,* the nymphet takes tennis lessons from a great former player who has "a harem of ball boys." The wrinkled old coach's name is Ned Litam. Backwards, Ned Litam spells "Ma Tilden."

afield he got from that area of professional expertise the
more inept he was. Tilden's attempts at humor were always
forced, his people shallow and their actions contrived.
Much the same could also be said of his acting.

Al Laney of the *Herald Tribune* recalls, "As a writer
yourself, you could always get a story out of him because
he was so fertile with ideas. But the trouble was, he could
be so vehement, with the most ill-considered opinions. He
took everything whimsically; I mean literally: by whim. He
was even what you could call a violent man, if not in the
physical sense. I remember once in the spring of 'twenty-
seven at the Carlton Hotel in Paris, he took after me for
something I had written, and at first he really scared hell
out of me, but he made such a scene, screaming, over-
dramatizing, throwing his arms about, the whole business,
that after a while it became one of those things where you
begin to get embarrassed *for* the person causing all the
commotion."

Somehow, that seems to be the best and fairest description of what Tilden was like acting. "Why yes," Laney says.
"The trouble was, that in his acting, he accentuated all the
objectionable things in him."

People who excel in one public enterprise often seem
especially at a loss elsewhere; one to a customer. Tilden
always thought that the critics were as unfair to him as
they were unkind—disposing of him too quickly with lines
like "for an actor, he's a pretty good tennis player," that
sort of thing. But, if anything, in Tilden's case the professional critics seem to have treated him more sympatheti-
cally than did his friends, most of whom scrunch up their
faces at the mere memory of him on stage.

Tilden made it worse by taking it all so seriously. If he
could have merely indulged himself in acting as a vanity, as
a sideline, as athletes through the years from John L. Sullivan to O. J. Simpson have, it would have been a bric-a-brac

everyone could have genially accepted. But, of course, Tilden immediately became an authority on the subject. When his first play opened on Broadway to the most overwhelming critical disapproval, Tilden would not accept the verdict even when the theater threw the show out in the cold after two weeks. Thereupon, Tilden scouted all over Broadway before he finally found one vacant theater, the Mayfair on Forty-fourth Street. It only had three hundred seats, and the owners didn't want Tilden's bomb there either, but he was persistent. So at last they told Tilden he could have the Mayfair for rent of $1800 a week, a record at the time for "a little theater." Determined to stay on the boards at any price and vindicate himself and the play, Tilden took the deal even though the play could not have broken even if it had sold out every seat for every performance.

In one way or another, all his life he displayed an inclination to act—reading stories to his younger friends as a child, in neighborhood theater in Germantown, on the courts, in his melodramatic disputes with the USLTA, whatever. Also he overacted all his life. Frank Hunter says he put $2500 (the maximum Tilden would allow one individual to invest) into Big Bill's *Dracula,* and that Tilden obtained full backing for that show remarkably quickly because everyone figured that was one role where even Tilden couldn't overact. But apparently he did. "He played four Draculas at one time," Hunter says, adding that he played most of the other parts as well, as it was his habit to learn all the roles and prompt the actors who didn't keep up to his ordained pace.

The most agreeable criticism of Tilden was that he bore a forced resemblance to Alfred Lunt. This pleased Tilden. He played a couple of Lunt roles (like *Clarence,* in which he first appeared on Broadway in 1923 at the Lyceum Theatre in a one-night charity performance), and he did nothing to discourage the similarity even after Alexander Woollcott wrote, "Mr. Tilden goes in quite a bit for shy eccentricity on the stage and so rolls his eyes and writhes his lower jaw as to suggest that shortly before the birth of his dramatic ambitions he was badly frightened by Alfred Lunt."

As much as Tilden liked being on the stage, he appears to have liked the idea just as much. Almost from the moment he achieved a certain prominence in tennis, reports began to pop up that he soon would be signing such-and-such a contract to appear on the stage or in films, and he did nothing to discourage any of these tidbits. None of these putative artistic deals seems to have worked out, however, until 1924, when he broke into big time show business with his own movie production. It was entitled *Hands of Hope*.

This silent screenplay, written by Tilden and, coincidentally, starring Tilden, also featured an actress named Marjorie Daw and a child actor named Bill Quinn, who were respectively his favorite actress and child actor. Tilden's childhood buddy Roy Coffin helped him to finance the production, and together they scared up $75,000, a lot of it from members of the Germantown Cricket Club. Coffin's cousin, a New York stockbroker, signed on for the balance.

The saga revolved around a struggling young artist in Greenwich Village (played by Tilden) who falls in love with a wealthy society girl. For a crucial dance scene Tilden used his tennis contacts to requisition an estate on Long Island, and he and Coffin got a lot of their old pals from Philadelphia to pack their black ties and come up as extras. In the process of filming under the bright lights, a quantity of bootleg booze was consumed, and then the next morning when the extras woke up and opened their eyes a number

*Tilden's mother, Selina Hey.
She was called Linie.*

*His father, William T.
Tilden, Sr. A prominent
Philadelphia businessman
and clubman, he was active
in the Republican party.*

A photograph of the coming world champion, possibly taken about the time of his first national finals, in 1918, when he was 25, or even earlier.

Big Bill with Gerald Patterson, the great Australasian player, whom he defeated in the Challenge Round at Wimbledon in 1920 for his first major title. Note that the racquet handles in this picture and subsequent ones are bare wood. Leather grips were not added until the 1930s.

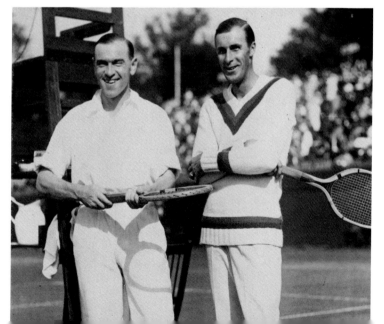

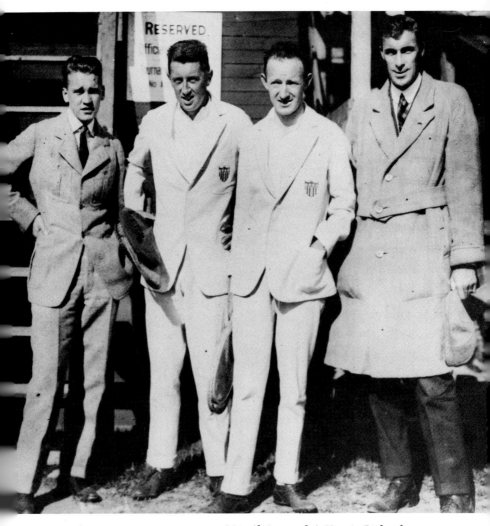

The U.S. Davis Cup team of 1922: (left to right) Vinnie Richards, Dick Williams, Little Bill Johnston, and Tilden. They are congregated at the Longwood Cricket Club, near Boston, where Big Bill and the 19-year-old Richards won their third national doubles title. Richards snapped at Big Bill once during the match, and so to put his young partner back in his place, Tilden threw their Challenge Round doubles match against Australasia the next week, knowing that victory in that match was not necessary to win the Davis Cup. Shortly after that, Tilden beat Little Bill in five sets in their most famous U.S. Singles final, "the match for Greek gods."

Big Bill alone with his first love. "If I had to give up tennis or music," he said, "I would give up tennis."

Big Bill and his other love—acting. He especially favored parts with uniforms, and this rather fetching pose, in 1922 in Philadelphia, was almost surely for the title role in the Booth Tarkington play entitled Clarence, in which he made his Broadway debut in a one-night charity performance.

On a trip to Hollywood in 1923, Tilden and the Spanish star Manuel Alonso (far right) played with Charlie Chaplin and Douglas Fairbanks, Sr. Tilden adored actors, and Chaplin remained a special friend for life; a few days before his death, in 1953, Big Bill played his last tennis on Chaplin's private court.

In a posed shot, possibly taken at Germantown Academy, which both attended, Tilden watched his favorite protégé of the 1920s, Sandy Wiener. Tilden came back to coach at his alma mater when Wiener was there, and the young boy was Big Bill's doubles partner in the match late in 1922 when Tilden scratched his middle finger on the right hand, got it infected, and had to have part of it amputated.

William T. Tilden II in 1923, at the age of 30, at the height of his powers and midway through his life.

"Now you listen to me, Bill. You're a tennis artist, and artists always know better than anyone else when they're right. If you believe in a certain way to play, you play that way no matter what anyone tells you. Once you lose faith in your own artistic judgment, you're lost. Win or lose, right or wrong, be true to your art." —Mary Garden, the opera singer, a close friend of Tilden's

In the amateur days, the biggest honor was to "retire" a tournament trophy with three wins. With his 1925 victory in the U.S. championships, Tilden did it a second time. This trophy is now on display in Los Angeles in the living room of Mrs. Marrion Anderson, the executrix of his will. The more famous challenge cup, which he retired in 1922, is in the possession of Mrs. Anderson's son Arthur, who was Tilden's last protégé.

"When he came out and started trotting down the stairs, it was the
laird taking possession of his empire. Even if you were going to beat
him, you knew you were only a subject."—Jean Borotra, of France's
Four Musketeers

In Mexico City in April 1928, Tilden (third from left), captain of the
Davis Cup team, poses with teammates John Hennessey, Wilmer
Allison and Junior Coen, Big Bill's favorite little protégé that year.
Coen, only 15 years old, was picked by Captain Tilden to play doubles
against China in the next round, and is still the youngest U.S. Davis
Cupper in history.

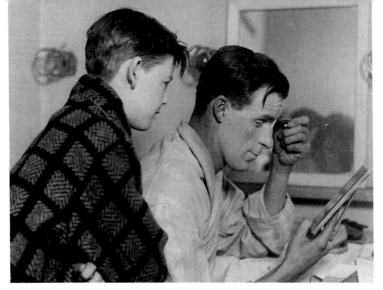

With his favorite child actor, Little Bill Quinn, Tilden makes up in 1926 for his role in a short-lived Broadway offering entitled Don Q Jr. *"Tilden keeps his amateur standing," one theater critic wrote.*

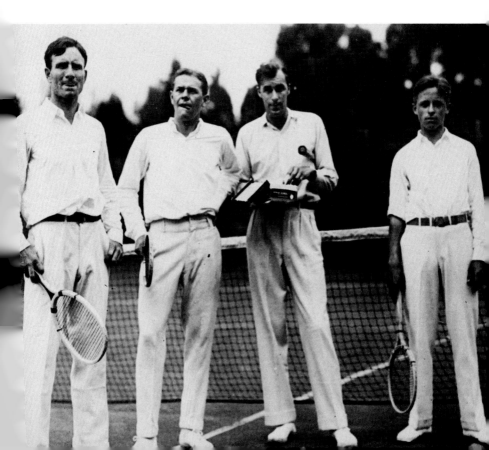

Two of the Four Musketeers—Henri Cochet, whose game Tilden greatly admired, and Jean Borotra, whose personality he detested—prepare to play "The Smartys"—Tilden and his pal Frank Hunter—in the 1928 Challenge Round at Roland Garros. The Frenchmen won in five sets.

Tilden and René Lacoste before one of their classic matches. Theirs was a relationship primarily of great mutual respect rather than affection. Tilden described "the Crocodile" as "detached, solid, phlegmatic, analytical, subtle, shrewd."

In 1930 in Berlin—"I would rather play there than in any city in the world"—Big Bill relaxes with some ball boys.

Tilden walks into Centre Court with his oponent, Wilmer Allison, for his farewell Wimbledon appearance in 1930. At age 37, he became—and still is—the oldest man to play through to win the championship. He won in straight sets, "beaming throughout."

Backstage at a play entitled I'm Wise, *watching British actor Huntley Wright apply makeup. The date is lost, but was probably sometime in the 1930s; place, Southsea, England.*

Tilden, the pro, age 42, and still playing superbly, sailing for matches abroad.

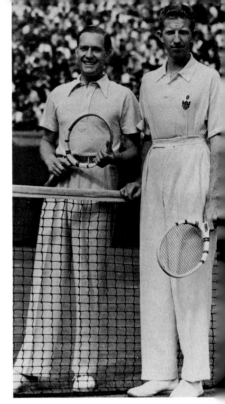

Baron Gottfried von Cramm of Germany (left) and Don Budge of the U.S. pose at the net before their 1937 Forest Hills final. Tilden liked Budge and toured with him later, but he and von Cramm were especially close, and Tilden had coached the German Davis Cup team that year. The Germans lost only because Budge beat von Cramm in a match that Tilden called "the greatest ever played."

September 1939, and the European war brings the pros back to the states: Budge, Ellsworth Vines, Lester Stoefen and Tilden. Big Bill was never to go abroad again.

The benefit match for war bonds that Tilden was boosting in this picture took place in New York on his fifty-second birthday, February 10, 1945.

Vinnie Richards was a great benefactor of Tilden's in Bill's indigent last years. This photograph, taken in 1945, also provides a fairly good look at the grisly amputation job done on Big Bill's right-hand middle finger in 1922.

Proud of his slimness, when he gave up the long white ducks, he went to rather short shorts. "Those legs," said Gussie Moran in admiration. "Grable should have had such legs."

of them couldn't see anything. Everybody thought that a bunch of Germantown's finest had gone blind from bad whiskey. As it turned out, though, they had somehow only been temporarily blinded by a delayed reaction to the klieg lights.

When the movie opened there were, as Frank Deacon recalls, "a lot of long faces" in Germantown, but this was evidently more a response to the art than to the ledger. Roy Coffin maintains that this was at least one Tilden theatrical adventure that broke even. Coffin says that it might even have made money but for some intricate film distribution controversy that spilled over and affected *Hands of Hope* so that it could only be played in the little nickel-dime cinemas.

Later that year, 1924, Tilden signed a contract with somebody named Worthy Pictures, Inc., to appear in films written by somebody named Ella Wheeler Wilcox. Apparently that dog just didn't hunt, and no more was heard of it. Nor did he ever play a starring role for a King Vidor picture, as it was announced that he would in 1927. Evidently, except for a few instructional tennis films, his only other cinematic contribution came in 1927 in a period piece on the Gay Nineties. This was a silent film entitled *The Music Master*, which starred Neil Hamilton, a New Hampshire factory worker recently turned matinee idol, who had only shortly before been the first screen Gatsby. Against the handsome Hamilton, Tilden played Joles, the comic butler. "I should only do character roles and heavies," Big Bill said. "The Lord never meant my face for a hero!"

Moving right along. The Great White Way! Tilden's Broadway debut was in a dreadful melodrama that kept changing its name, if not quite fast enough to outdistance critical sentries. It was written by one Bernard Schubert and opened out of town under the title of *The Kid Himself.*

Tilden played a supporting role to the kid, who was played by the ubiquitous young Bill Quinn. Marjorie Daw, old Miss Reliable, was also roped into this effort as the romantic lead opposite Tilden, but she kept her wits about her sufficiently to quietly depart the cast long before it reached Broadway. Tilden was panned, even from the first night in Wilkes-Barre, where the local critic wrote, "Last night at the Irving Theatre another example of misplaced ambition was in evidence." With due perception, the Wilkes-Barre critic even commented in passing that Tilden seemed particularly lost in the love scenes. Undismayed, and with a new leading lady, Juana Nelson, taking Miss Daw's place, *The Kid Himself* shuffled on to Washington, Wilmington and Stamford. *Variety*, by definition a trade paper which must occasionally avert one eye from the stage and cast it upon the box office potential, opined that Big Bill's name value gave the play a chance. Moreover, noting Tilden's resemblance to Lunt, the Washington *Variety* correspondent even thought that Tilden was "doing right nobly . . . he makes good" in the part.

That one good notice notwithstanding, the show came into New York retitled *Don Q Jr.*, and Tilden was so nervous before the opening on January 27, 1926, that the same man who gorged himself before tennis matches could manage to down only an egg and milk mixture—and he almost threw that back up. *Don Q Jr.* was pilloried by almost all of the New York critics, although many of them also came out of the fray defiled, having been unable to resist using tennis jargon, squeezing it into their reviews like toothpaste back into the tube. The *Herald Tribune* returned serve best, assuring its readers that Tilden "keeps his amateur standing." The *Morning Telegraph* ran a large headline, TILDEN IS STILL TENNIS CHAMP, while underneath reporting that he "lost in straight sets." The *Post* scored it "love–fifteen." In the *World*, Alexander

Woollcott had the best time of all, a real field day. Taking off from the advertisements, which proclaimed that Big Bill Tilden and Little Bill Quinn were starring, he wrote, "Its quality as entertainment was cautiously inspected for this journal by Medium-Sized Franklin P. Adams and Great Big 'Normous Alexander Woollcott. They found it not so good, not by a long shot."

At his most charitable, Woollcott called *Don Q Jr.* "a tottering comedy . . . about a fine manly tough little newsboy who says 'Aw chee' a good deal but has a heart of gold." The direction he found downright "deplorable" and Tilden "pretty bad," which was fair enough, since Tilden himself later admitted that he was "incredibly bad in that show." At the time, however, he was quite pleased with his performance, and on opening night, upon the conclusion of the show, he came to the front of the stage to address the audience, which included a number of tennis players, many of whom had backed the production. They cheered wildly, encouraging the bemused Woollcott to observe, "They all seemed to be having a grand time, and I have no doubt they found it agreeable to see Mr. Tilden do anything imperfectly."

It was this dreadful production, unloved by all others, that Tilden kept alive as long as he could—changing the name again (to *That Smith Boy*) and paying an outrageous rent to keep it in view. After a couple of more weeks, however, even he had to give up the ghost, whereupon he retreated back into the safer haven of tennis. Immediately, on February 19, he was upset by Jean Borotra in straight sets in the quarterfinals of the national indoors: 13–11, 6–3. It was the first time since 1919 that Tilden had suffered a defeat in any national singles tourney, and the first time since 1917 that he had failed to reach the semis of any singles tournament he played in. A week later, in a special international match, he lost 6–4, 8–6, 6–3 to René Lacoste, his first defeat in best-of-five since 1919, and his first international defeat ever in singles. Then, moving outdoors and down South, he lost twice to Vinnie Richards in March and April; and in June in New Haven, where he was appearing nights in a play at Yale, he lost to Alfred Chapin, who wasn't even ranked in the U.S. top ten.

While these defeats rather astonished people, nobody appears to have attached much lasting significance to them. "It was not Tilden that I beat today," Borotra volunteered graciously. "He did not play in his real form." And after the second defeat to Richards, Allison Danzig wrote in the *Times*, "Tilden can go on being defeated almost day after day, but it will change few expectations as to what he will do in the national championships." Instead, there was a real tendency to attribute the losses to his increased stage exertions. Initially it was suggested that the switch from stage lights to tennis lights had been too radical an adjustment for Big Bill, but then, when he kept losing outdoors as well, it was ventured further that the emotional concentration (and the disappointment) with *The Kid Himself/Don Q Jr./That Smith Boy* had unsettled him for tennis.

It was later that summer of 1926 that Lacoste and Cochet, both coming to their prime, at last beat Tilden in a Davis Cup match and at Forest Hills—although on both occasions Tilden was injured. Nonetheless, notwithstanding advancing age and a debilitating injury, it is certainly significant that Big Bill was not defeated in top-level competition until the year when he began to seriously divide his attention between tennis and acting. Although the brutal failure of his January Broadway bomb may have well been behind him by the time he suffered his shocking September defeats in 1926, the fact is that by then he was already preparing to go back on the boards in a few more weeks.

This show seems to have been his all-time personal favorite: a comedy by Courtney Savage entitled *They All Want Something.* Tilden bruited it about proudly that the game Mr. Savage had written the play especially for Little Bill Quinn and him; with the playwright's taste inclining toward that level, it should come as no surprise that the *Times* found *They All Want Something* "elementary school entertainment" when it opened at Wallack's Theatre on October 12, 1926. The plot, such as it was, concerned a wealthy heir, played by Tilden, who is for some obscure reason posing as a tramp when he gets hired as a butler. At a party, a famous author is supposed to appear, and when he doesn't show up, the heir-turned-tramp-turned-butler is pressed into service to masquerade as the author. It sums up the quality of the script to learn that one of the biggest laughs in the play comes when someone asks Tilden, posing as the author, if he has ever played tennis.

The reason that Tilden could eventually admit so blithely that he had been "incredibly bad" in *Don Q Jr.* was that he thought he was a regular knockout this time around, in *They All Want Something.* Since he had transformed himself from the ugly duckling in tennis, he assumed he could do the same in acting. Alas, the view was a singularly private one, and no dispassionate critics ever noted any improvement in his thespian graces. "He strikes a good many poses and manages to play about half of his scenes directly to the audience, enacting the role with none of the vitality that he shows on the courts," the New York *Times* critic wrote this time. But Tilden was positively gaga about *They All Want Something.* He pumped more good money into it in a lost cause, and then he worked desperately for the next few years to get it produced in London.

He was never again to make it back as a star on Broadway, but he worked the hinterlands like a real trouper; at one time he was starring in one stock company, directing what he could in a second, and preparing to organize a third. *Dracula,* in which he believes he drew his best notices, was a steady favorite; plus the usual Lunt specialties such as *Clarence* and *Dulcy.* And let us not forget *The Poor Nut, Interference, Is Zat So?* and *The Buzzard,* a mystery written by Courtney Savage of *They All Want Something* fame. It was *The Buzzard* that Tilden reluctantly tore himself away from in 1928 to take over the captaincy of the Davis Cup team; by then he had declared that he wished to make theater "my life's work."

Indeed, he did wrestle with it to the end, forever trying to write and act in plays, usually ones that he backed himself. He did not confine his efforts to the legitimate theater, but surfaced as a cabaret performer at the Trocadero Restaurant in London in November 1929, where he unleashed monologues about tennis upon a discriminating public. Some years later Big Bill dressed up this act and brought it stateside for what was called his "vaudeville debut" by *Variety.* "Offering needs building and will then have possibilities," the newpaper decided, but it just didn't seem to build, and no more was heard from it. Nor did anything develop in 1935 after Universal signed Tilden to appear in a film entitled *The Amateur Racquet.*

In something of the same vein, he also started a new magazine in Chicago in 1934. It was named *Racquet,* and its editor and publisher quit after one issue; so Tilden, who had started off modestly enough as associate editor, took over and moved the whole operation to New York. He contributed comment, instruction, a melodramatic serial entitled "Love Means Nothing," and a great deal of doggerel, such as "The Tree, by Joy Killer," which began "I think that I shall never see/A tennis court without a tree." A takeoff on "The Midnight Ride of Paul Revere" was called

"The Forehand Drive of Paul Sorere." Tilden also put together a banal little poetic tennis alphabet, e.g., "B is for Borotra, Bounding and Bright . . ." And so on. The magazine, like the plays, had a pathetically short run.

But Tilden kept coming back for more in the arts. While he passionately adored tennis, was obsessed by it and played it virtually every day of his adult life, he also was clearly befuddled and even a bit embarrassed that he had succeeded so in such a sweaty endeavor. He longed to make it in something more orthodox, and however much he succeeded as a tennis actor and a tennis artist, he could have been truly satisfied only with the real McCoy. It was one more sadness in his life that he became greatest in the world at something he was not altogether proud of.

In our technical, sophisticated world, athletic proficiency is highly prized only so long as it is just a sideline. Of course, because of the vast sums of money that an athlete can make nowadays, the pursuit upon the ball fields is accepted as more honorable than it was in Tilden's day. Nonetheless, then and now, an athlete always begs one leading question of himself: *What will you do when you grow up?* Tilden had the idea that if he could make it at something in the grown-up world, that would somehow dignify, legitimize, his playing the games. It obviously bothered him that he was not only a homosexual among heterosexuals, but that he was also a child among adults.

For the family, his niece, Miriam Ambrose, writes, "We are still a bit vague as to why he chose tennis. . . . If he had lived in a different environment, no doubt he would have applied himself to something else; but we might be mistaken if we assumed that he would have been less successful. His primary aim was to excel. . . . [Twin, his maiden cousin] went along, hoping to the end that mastering a game would be a steppingstone to a more significant accomplishment, given his spark of genius and talent. That hope was to some extent shared by the family—*wrongly*, as I see it now. We ought to have been satisfied with what he did, which in itself was surpassing."

And, of course, sadder still, he should have been satisfied himself.

CHAPTER NINE

"I'll beat you yet, Rainy!"

W HEN it came time at last to lose, Tilden could not have ordered up a better lot of protagonists than the Four Musketeers. Colorful, compact, clever men of enough distance and intrigue, they contrasted neatly to Big Bill and made as good a corporate foil as Little Bill had ever been an individual one. Besides, Tilden needed them. Since he had determined not to quit at his peak, since he felt an obligation to go out with his boots on, somebody had to beat him—and how much more satisfying that that be a bunch of faraway young Lilliputians than some blond reasonable facsimile from Southern California.

Indeed, the way it worked out, Tilden was a whale of a loser. Nobody ever won like Big Bill Tilden, but then again, nobody ever lost like him either. Ironically, while he is the most notable player in the history of his sport, many of his most momentous matches were defeats. Of course, a major reason for this is that once he had taken the measure of Bill Johnston there was no one to offer him any real competition until he had gone over the hill and met the Frenchmen scrambling up. René Lacoste, Henri Cochet, Jean Borotra, and in the trench warfare of the Davis Cup, Toto Brugnon, the doubles specialist: it appeared as if they were ganging

up on him, which indeed they were. It was a curious de-
nouement; he was not *dethroned,* as they always say of
fading champions, but instead he merely seemed to let
others rule at his pleasure. Suddenly, when Tilden played,
there was a whole new priority: first just that he was playing, then the result. "When he came out and started trotting down the stairs," Borotra says, "it was the laird taking
possession of his empire. Even if you were going to beat
him, you knew you were only a subject."

But if no one man succeeded Tilden, the three singles
stars of the Musketeers were, by any standard, players of
the first water. Lacoste, Cochet and Borotra all won Wimbledon twice—six years running for France. They all three
won their own national championship at least two times
apiece, plus Forest Hills a total of four times, and Borotra
even won the Australian title once. Appropriately, each in
turn first borrowed small pieces from Big Bill's invincibility,
and then, as a group, took it all away. In February 1926 it
was Borotra who gave Tilden his first defeat of any consequence since 1919 when he beat him in the U.S. indoors.
Next, Lacoste became the first man ever to beat him in the
Davis Cup, and, following, Cochet knocked him out at
Forest Hills. The next year, with Brugnon, they schemed to
wear him down by their numbers so that they could bring
the Davis Cup to France. As soon as they arrived back in
Paris, Lacoste advised the French people, "At Philadelphia
Tilden could not be beaten by one player; he was beaten
by a team."

Tilden added to this luster in defeat with his own generosity and graciousness. He often said, for example, that the
finest tennis he ever played was in the 1927 finals at Forest
Hills when Lacoste beat him, thereby patently suggesting
that his very best was not so good as another man's. Overall, Tilden was an even greater fan of Cochet's, called him a
tennis "genius" and characterized his ability to hit the ball

on the rise as revolutionary. "Cochet plays a tennis I don't know," he said.

Yet as much as Tilden praised the French players, and they him, he really didn't care much for the country, for France. England, the land of his forefathers, was like a second home, and Germany he came to adore, but as fond as his public acceptance was in France, he thought the people false and notably inefficient as well. (For a man who depended so on room service, the latter was of no small consequence.) Insofar as tennis was concerned, he especially despised the French crowds, which he found emotionally rank and phony. In his antipathy, only Borotra stood higher, and ultimately he melded the two hates by deciding that the whole country was nothing but a personification of the Bounding Basque. "Borotra [Tilden wrote] was what passes for 'typically' French. That is to say, he had all the charm, warmth, glamour and insincerity which is Paris."

Borotra, as are all the Musketeers, is still alive, and even today he admits to friends sadly that it has always disappointed him that "Bill didn't like me." Even that understates the case, for Tilden despised him more than any other world-class player of his acquaintance, possibly only excluding Helen Wills, whom he called "the coldest, most self-centered, most ruthless champion ever known to tennis." Tilden was easier on Borotra, classifying him only as "a charlatan, the greatest faker in tennis history." In a way, too, that was something of a compliment, for what really infuriated Tilden about Borotra was that the Basque was an actor, just like Tilden, and Big Bill was of the opinion that there was only room for one actor in big-time tennis. Borotra happened to be a very good actor too. The crowds loved him. A consummate gamesman, he was never better at appearing to be a sportsman than when he was actually working a con against his poor opponent.

After his defeat to Borotra in the 1926 indoors, Tilden never lost to him again, although he had a number of close calls. Once he beat him at Wimbledon despite the fact that he had thrown his sacroiliac out in the previous match, and had been walking around nearly bent double the day before he had to face Borotra. His final victory over the Basque was in the semifinals at Wimbledon in 1930, when Big Bill boasted that he would beat him with lobs. This sort of tacky bragging, à la Muhammad Ali, was altogether out of character for Tilden; he disliked Borotra that much. But he did beat him, and he beat him with lobs. Borotra's strength was his net game; his service was just a device to get him in close, and despite having grown up on the *en-tout-cas* clay surface, which is slow and encourages baseline rallies, Borotra had nowhere near the ground strokes of his confreres.

The valedictory Borotra-Tilden confrontation at Wimbledon in 1930 was archetypal of their meetings. Borotra emerged with what was described as an "immense bath towel," which immediately delighted the crowd and incensed Tilden. After pausing to wipe himself off with this huge towel, Borotra won the first set at love. But Big Bill was only belling the cat. The whole set, he was hitting lobs that made Borotra go back and reach for overheads, as tiring an exercise as there is in the game. Eventually Borotra ran out of gas, and Tilden won in five sets.

The year before at Wimbledon Borotra directed his bamboozle at Tilden's vanity. From the first, every time the two players changed courts after the odd games, Borotra would gush compliments at Big Bill as they passed each other by the umpire's chair. "Oh Beel," he would cry, "your forehand down ze line—*magnifique!* I cannot even pretend to stay on ze same court wiz you this day." Delighted, puffed up with praise, Tilden was encouraged to go out and try to live up to Borotra's assessment. He would attempt impossible shots, shoot for the lines. Not until he lost the first set did Tilden see that Borotra was killing him with kindness. Thereupon when he changed courts, Tilden would go around the other end of the net in order to escape the Circe. Undaunted by this response, Borotra began to hesitate after the odd game, waiting to see in which direction Tilden would head, and then he would rush to meet him there and hand out his compliments. Finally Tilden solved the dilemma by walking straight to the center of the net and, with his long legs, scissoring over it. Borotra didn't win another set.

Nothing that Borotra ever did on the courts infuriated Tilden, however, as much as a genuine thoughtful assistance he once provided. In 1927, when Lindbergh flew the Atlantic, Tilden was in Paris playing some casual international matches against the Musketeers, sort of a Grapefruit League Davis Cup. Mary Garden, his friend, was also in Paris, and after Lindbergh landed, the American Embassy called her up and invited her to sing the National Anthem at a reception for the young hero. Unfortunately, Miss Garden did not know the words, but since she went to the tennis matches that day, she asked Big Bill, the superpatriot. Alas, he didn't know the words either, so he set off to inquire of other American players. None were of any more help, but Borotra, who happened to be a superb linguist, chanced along just as Tilden was explaining Miss Garden's plight to another no more helpful Yankee Doodle Dandy. Borotra walked over to Tilden, asked him to take his pen out, and began reciting: "Oh say can you see . . ." right on, word for word, through to "home of the brave." As long as he lived, Tilden never got over that, that a foreigner . . .!

Cochet was the only one of the Musketeers who turned pro, so he and Tilden had the most extended rivalry, but although they were acquaintances and admirers of long

standing, they were never close. They exchanged autographs once: "To Bill, who taught me all I know about the
game of tennis." "To Henri, who beat my best." Taciturn
and rather uncomplicated, Cochet came from modest circumstances, and, unlike Tilden and Lacoste, students of
the game who practiced all the time, he was a natural athlete who tended to be somewhat lazy. Cochet had a weak
serve, he seldom bothered to lob, and he had a backhand
which Tilden characterized as "a little too cramped and
defensive." But he had perfect balance to his game, equal
parts offense and defense, and he was lightning quick, with
snap wrists, so that he could dart in and, with his short
wristy backswing, take shots early and zing them back, cutting off the angles in the bargain. This procedure so mesmerized Tilden that it wasn't really until they both reached
the pros that Big Bill learned how to adjust to it.

Lacoste was cultured and wealthy even before he
stumbled upon the agreeable knowledge that people would
pay large sums for crocodiles stitched upon their shirts.
Therefore, even though he was a full decade younger than
Tilden, their shared upper-class backgrounds made them
friends of a sort—although for some reason, as if he'd just
come in from Lubbock, Texas, Tilden always pronounced
René as "Rainy." Theirs was a relationship primarily of respect rather than affection. Like Tilden, Lacoste had
mastered the game by dint of sheer industry, and his whole
personality reflected this. Tilden once used six adjectives in
a row to describe Lacoste, and not one of them was very
tender: "detached, solid, phlegmatic, analytical, subtle,
shrewd." Lacoste always carried a racket, he kept detailed
scouting reports on opponents, and although he was three
years Cochet's junior, seven years Borotra's, and ten years
Brugnon's, he was the leader of the French team. Not until
the Crocodile's game crystallized against Tilden was victory for France at hand.

The Musketeers also received support and advice from one special quarter: Suzanne Lenglen. The Maid Marvel had dominated tennis among women as had Tilden among men, so she provided her countrymen with a certain stature in tennis simply because they came from the same land as she. Although Mme. Lenglen signed on with Cash and Carry Pyle and toured the United States, she had no great affection for tennis in America. On her only trip as an amateur to the States, she lost a controversial match at Forest Hills, quitting in the middle, claiming illness, for which she was castigated by the disappointed press and fans. Also, Tilden had made a fool of her once.

Big Bill didn't care much for women players to start with. He would hack around with his little favorites in mixed doubles, but he made it plain that he was slumming. He even expressed the belief that no man should bother to instruct women at tennis, but leave that wasted task to others of the sex. And generally, he simply never took the proficiency of female players seriously; for one thing, he was of the opinion that women's arms fitted into their sockets strangely. So, on one of his first trips to France, when Tilden heard that the Maid Marvel herself was watching him practice, he set a trap for her and began playing poorly. Sure enough, she took the bait, came down on the court, introduced herself and asked if they could not hit a few together. Tilden graciously welcomed her onto the court and continued to play sloppily, and at about three-quarter speed. Completely trapped by now, the Maid Marvel grew so emboldened that she asked Big Bill if they might not play a few games. Gee, if you'd really like to, he said. She shrank off the court a few minutes later, beaten 6–o, hardly having won a point.

So it was with some measure of revenge that Mme. Lenglen helped conspire with the Musketeers to beat Tilden. It was she who convinced Lacoste that the way to succeed was to make Big Bill hit the cannonball—keep after him, make him run and give him the angles for a time, but wear him down and force him to use the big serve over and over to shorten points. "If you don't make him use that cannonball," she told Lacoste, "he'll be sixty before you beat him." Lacoste checked out her theories with his own research and discovered that if Tilden was allowed to pick his spots, he could get his cannonball in 80 per cent of the time—and would win almost all those points. So at last they had the key piece to the puzzle.

The French had first burst upon the scene at Wimbledon in 1924, when Borotra beat Lacoste in the final; previously no Frenchman had even attained the last round. The Australians beat the Musketeers in the Davis Cup Interzone, though; and in the real world championship, the one at Forest Hills that Tilden played in, Lacoste was the only Frenchman to enter, and he went out in the quarters to Little Bill Johnston, who was in turn slaughtered by Tilden. But the challenge was building. Lacoste reversed the Wimbledon final the next July against Borotra, and this time the French beat the Australians for the right to play the United States at Germantown in the Challenge Round.

Nobody gave the visitors a chance, and, in fact, they lost 5–0, but that score was deceptive; with some luck, the French actually could have won. Tilden was forced to the limit in the opening match, the first time in years, since the Shimizu match, that he had been challenged. Borotra was his opponent here, and took the first set 6–4. Then Tilden won the second 6–0, but fell apart again as Borotra began to stab him with volleys, now deep, now to the sides. Desperate, Tilden tried to play in his stocking feet, and then in spikes; he tried to chop Borotra, but to little avail. The Frenchman won the third set 6–2, and was serving for the match at 6–5 in the fourth. Tilden broke him at 15, won the set 9–7, and then the deciding set 6–4.

As close a call as that was, Tilden came even nearer to defeat two days later against Lacoste. Curiously, the Crocodile had disappointed in the Australian interzone matches. He was routed in straight sets by Vinnie Richards at Forest Hills; and in the first day's play in the Challenge Round, Johnston had crushed him. But Lacoste measured himself by Tilden, and whenever he played him his game found new definition. This time too Tilden was certainly not up. The Davis Cup was already settled, 3–0 for America, Lacoste had played poorly in the United States, and besides, he was never a very prepossessing player. So he came out on court and promptly beat the big man 6–3 in the first set, 12–10 in the second, and led 4–0 in the third, with his own serve upcoming.

Tilden didn't know what had hit him. He was stumbling around the court and actually muttering to himself. People heard him keep saying, "If I can just get my head above water." Everything he hit, Lacoste hit back. Worse, like the tar baby, he never responded with any emotion. Lacoste didn't even seem to sweat; at the end of five-set matches, he would be immaculate. "The monotonous regularity with which that unsmiling, drab, almost dull man returned the best I could hit often filled me with a wild desire to throw my racket at him," Tilden said once.

While this match lacked any real pressure or importance, inasmuch as the Cup had already been decided, as a personal exercise in courage it may have been Big Bill's greatest accomplishment. Down two sets and 4–0 in the third to the Wimbledon champion, only two games away from his first major defeat in six years, he broke Lacoste on guts— going for broke with placements—then poured a pitcher of ice water over his head on the sideline, went back out and aced his way to 4–2, and finally caught him at 5–all. Even then he had to endure four match points at 5–6 before he took the set at 8–6.

Lacoste was not undone, however. He went right back on top 3–0 in the fourth set, but again Tilden rebounded, and, playing in his stocking feet once more, he won 7–5. That broke the Crocodile's back, and Tilden won the match 6–2 in the fifth going away, giving up only three points in the last four games. The five sets took two hours and forty minutes, but Lacoste walked off the court looking fresh and unmoved; in his dispassionate mind he was already sifting his mistakes in order to prepare a tailor-made plan to beat Tilden in 1926. He decided that he must mix up the length and pace of his shots better, he must do a better job of keeping the bigger man away from the net, and that he must have something in reserve for a crunch. What Lacoste settled on was a slice serve that would carry Tilden off the court and away from the attack; he would throw that in as a surprise just when Big Bill made his move. Tilden himself had such success in long matches because he squirreled little tidbits away. "How did we finally beat Tilden?" Cochet asks now. "We were younger, and ahh," he says with a smile, "we had Tilden to learn from."

Despite all his special efforts, Lacoste still would not have beaten Tilden in the 1926 Davis Cup had not Big Bill injured himself midway through the match. Although almost no one knew it, Tilden had played with a weak left knee since it slipped out in a match at the Wilmington Country Club in 1915. After he injured it more seriously in the match against Lacoste (technically, he tore the semilunar cartilage in the knee), he could never reach peak again. Stretched and strained through the years, the knee joint was very unstable, but at that time the chances of correcting it with surgery were slim. Should an operation have failed, the knee would have been left permanently stiff. So, all through his career and often after the 1926 Lacoste match, Tilden played in considerable pain, but without a word. Carl Fischer, an osteopath, says that the loose cartilage would make the muscle have a clonic spasm, and there were times when the knee could be heard vibrating—and from some distance. "It sounded just like a purring cat," Fischer says. "I've never heard or felt anything like it, before or since."

Anyway, when Tilden did tear the cartilage against Lacoste, it was the fifth match of a Challenge Round that was already decided, 4–0 for the United States. The two men had split the first two sets and stood at 6–all in the third, Tilden serving at 40–30. Lacoste made a short return and Tilden rushed up diagonally, stopping quick to make a drop shot. That is when the knee went out. Since the whole business was meaningless at this point, he should have defaulted on the spot and rested the knee for two or three weeks. Instead, he not only played out the match but he began play at Forest Hills only two days later. The knee had no chance to heal. As soon as he hurt it, he limped back to serve, whereupon he double-faulted the game away, and then Lacoste took the set 8–6.

This was the occasion when Dick Williams, the team captain, was out on a side court somewhere playing a friendly pick-up game of doubles. Tilden felt he better go on, so he had the knee taped during the intermission, and after a slow start in the fourth set he came back with vengeance. Down 4–2 and 40–15 to Lacoste's serve, he brought the crowd to a fever pitch, rallying to obtain a set point for 7–5. But he failed to win it, and was too hurt to keep after the steady little man. Still, Tilden went out only in drawn-out agony. Lacoste won 8–6 after his third deuce, second match point, hitting a perfect drive deep into the corner. Limping, all form gone, in pain, Tilden staggered after the ball, reached and then dove, somehow managing to get his backhand on the ball, but only enough to send it fluttering back to Lacoste at the net. He tapped it back into an empty court. Appropriately, Big Bill was lying wounded, face down on the ground, when at last he was conquered.

The French were beside themselves. Here they had lost the Challenge Round 4–1, they had only manged to beat a thirty-four-year-old lame man in a meaningless match, but *they had beaten him.* All the extenuating circumstances aside, that was the point. Years later, John Kieran was to call that match "the first leaf of autumn," and Tilden himself realized that he was in deeper than ever before. "I was a sap," he admitted later. "This was one of the finest tennis players and tennis brains I have ever encountered, and I underestimated him. I saw too late that Lacoste had figured a way to beat me. I saw that this small youngster had developed that slice serve just for the purpose of using it against me in the important games. This disturbed me a lot because I recognized it as very sound tactically, and it made me wonder what else this fellow might have up his sleeve."

Within the week, Tilden had lost again too, this time to Cochet in the quarterfinals at Forest Hills. Black Thursday that day was called. Besides Tilden losing, Johnston was beaten by Borotra and Williams by Lacoste. The guard was changing; that same week Jack Dempsey lost his championship to Gene Tunney, and Bobby Jones was defeated in the golf National Amateur. At least Tilden carried Cochet five sets, a feat in itself, considering his knee. He even led 6–5 in the fifth, but in sight of victory he gave out; 8–6 for Cochet. For the first time since 1917 Tilden would not be in his country's national finals; for the first time since 1920 he would not win them.

The next year, 1927, Cochet and Lacoste beat Tilden in all three of the major national championships, the most famous of these being the bizarre collapse before Cochet at Wimbledon. But, in fact, all three championship defeats were close, and all could have easily gone to Tilden. Certainly he began the season in spectacular fashion. He had ice skated all winter to build up his knee, and with the spring he took off on a tear through Europe with Frank Hunter, following a victory trail through Germany, the Netherlands and Belgium.

Tilden then came on to Paris, clubbed Lacoste and Borotra in some exhibition team matches, and not only looked invincible in the early rounds of the French championships, but captivated the Parisians by throwing points magniloquently and crying "Gee!"—for which the fans demanded a translation. Big Bill ripped through Cochet in the semis, encouraging the vanquished to pronounce Tilden "stronger than ever." And for the finals against Lacoste, thousands of fans had to be turned away. The more agile of these climbed trees to watch. It was an insufferably hot and humid day, and the match took more than three hours—five sets of sixty-one games. Tilden could have claimed the championship after the third set, when Lacoste suffered cramps, but Big Bill would not accept victory on those terms, and he gave his younger opponent a full half-hour to recover. Lacoste had to be assisted from the court and given a massage. On another occasion, in the midst of a game, Lacoste lurched for the net post and held on to it for a couple of minutes, regaining his breath, as Tilden stood by patiently, granting him as much time as he wished. In the broiling sun, even the linesmen wilted, and Cochet was pressed into duty to call one of the service lines.

Lacoste won the fourth set 6–3 to tie the match, and the final set began with the two men trading games without incident. Then, in the eighth game, a visiting American who was umpiring called a foot fault on Tilden, infuriating him. The next game he served, Big Bill began by calling exaggerated attention to his feet—"Which foot, Muhr?" he yelled sarcastically to the umpire—and then he served four good old-fashioned cannonballs at Lacoste. The first the

Crocodile punched back weakly into the net. The next three he couldn't even touch with his racket. The place exploded. "Oh, he was a pip," Frank Hunter says. "And you know, that may have been his best match of all. He really won the thing twice. He gave Lacoste the extra rest, and then that serve."

That came with Tilden serving match point at 9–8. Big Bill reached back and fired home a cannonball ace, Lacoste nodded his head in admiration, and the two exhausted men moved to the net to shake hands. Suddenly Cochet, sitting in as linesman, raised his hand and called the ball long. Tilden and Lacoste looked in shock over at Cochet, and then, without a word, they moved back and took up their positions for the second ball. "It was clearly a good serve," Hunter says, "but Bill never thought that Cochet stole it from him. Neither did I. Henri just didn't see the ball. It came in so fast it took the line with it." But whatever the motives and the circumstances, it was the end for Tilden this day. Once again he had gone so far, and there was no more for him to summon. Enervated and perhaps unsettled by Cochet's call, he never won another game, double-faulting the match away 11–9.

At the end of the summer, in the final at Forest Hills, Lacoste beat Tilden again. It was in straight sets too, but scores of 11–9, 6–3, 11–9, a match that Tilden sometimes cited as the best he ever played. The three sets lasted an hour and fifty-three minutes, as Lacoste meticulously retrieved every ball. On the slower *en-tout-cas* surface in France the two had rallies that lasted for as much as forty-two returns, and even on the fast grass at Forest Hills most points took half a dozen or more returns. Theirs was neither a defensive baseline exchange nor dreary pittypat but a probing, testing game, a fencing match quite unlike anything played today. Lacoste might start in a step or so at one juncture, then decide better of it and go back and hit another four or five shots, searching for an infinitesimally better opening. Tilden always worked the corners, changing speeds. Points were stitched, patterns.

Manuel Alonso compares Lacoste to an artillery piece. It might take a while to get on target, firing a few for effect, but then he would raise or lower his sights accordingly and remain zeroed in for as long as was necessary. It was the ideal game to employ against Tilden because it took the best advantage of his age and his knee. "I know how to beat this guy," Tilden said before the Forest Hills final to a friend, "but I don't know if I'm capable of it. You've got to make Rainy hit every ball himself. He uses your pace. But I just don't know if I can chop everything."

In his mid-thirties now, no longer indefatigable, Tilden had evolved a certain strategy of economy of energy. He no longer could afford the luxury of fiddling around for the first set. He had to go right out and pocket it. If he got ahead in the second set, fine, he would pursue that seriously, but if not, he would coast through the second and prepare himself for a major effort in the third. A rest period (except at Wimbledon) would follow, giving Tilden a second wind, so that he would make an all-out effort to finish things off in the fourth set.

Against Lacoste at Forest Hills, he should have carried out his plan perfectly, but the knockout punch was gone. This day, as so often in these years, he could drive his opponent to the brink, as ever, but he could not shove him off. In the first set, which Lacoste was ultimately to win in twenty games, Tilden had it won in fourteen. He was up 7–6, 40–love, serving, and lost five straight points. In the second set he was ahead a break, 3–1, and then lost five straight games. In the third set he had Lacoste 5–2 and two set points. The next year, 1928, at Wimbledon, Tilden and Lacoste staged something of a duplication of Forest Hills. This time they met in the semifinals, and Tilden, brilliant in patches, led two sets to one, with game point for 4–1 in the fourth. Suddenly, at that instant, Big Bill Tilden vanished. He double-faulted once, then again, lost the game, the set, and then the match, winning only nineteen more points. "It's a worthy ending of a great career," the London *Daily Telegraph* wrote, if somewhat prematurely. Tilden, never daunted, just shouted afterwards to Lacoste, "I'll beat you yet, Rainy!"

Big Bill did too—a month later in the famous Davis Cup match after his suspension was lifted. He also was to win Forest Hills one more time, and Wimbledon too in a final burst, but by now the scepter had passed. The most important defeat of them all had come at Germantown late in the summer of 1927 in the Challenge Round against the Musketeers.

This was the third straight finals for the French, and they came carefully prepared. Johnston, they decided, was through—and they were right; he retired a few weeks later. But with Richards turned pro by now, the Americans had no choice but to use Little Bill in the second singles. That, the French figured, guaranteed them two points. To win then they only had to take Tilden once in his three matches, singles or doubles. Therefore they planned a war of attrition, replacing Borotra in the singles with Cochet, and then using Borotra and Brugnon as the doubles team, so that Cochet and Lacoste could devote all their energies to singles. By contrast, the Americans not only had to use Tilden, age thirty-four, in both singles and doubles, three days running, but, as was their custom, the USLTA officials managed to botch up the obvious doubles selection of Tilden and Hunter, so there was much emotional spillage before Big Bill finally forced them to play it his way.

The matches went just as the French had figured. Lacoste drew Little Bill in the opener, and gave him only seven games in three sets. Thus, when Tilden hit the courts against Cochet, he not only realized that he had to win, but that he had to do it fairly expeditiously if he was to have any reserve for the second and third days' work. Using his second-set rest plan, Tilden went ahead 6–4, 2–6, 6–2, but he fell behind 6–5 in the fourth. Tilden could not afford to be carried five sets against the younger man. His cannonball was fading. Cochet had started out by receiving it far back of the baseline. By the second set he had his toes on the line, now he was even a bit in advance of it and drawing a bead on some of Tilden's hardest serves. So now, with his own service coming up, for the first time in his life Tilden took what he called a "stimulant," that is, some spirits of ammonia. He served a love game to tie the set at 6–all, broke Cochet at 30, and then served out again at love, booming home a cannonball ace to close him out. It was a split, one-up, after the first day.

The following afternoon, in the doubles, Tilden was never more influential, even supreme when that was required of him, but, nonetheless, Borotra and Brugnon were fighting two battles, and they won one of them. Their first goal, obviously, was to win, but second, failing that, they sought to keep the old man occupied for as long as possible. In that they succeeded, carrying him five strenuous sets, lobbing much of the afternoon, sending him back and forth from the net. In defeat the picadors had done their job, and now Lacoste would get Tilden in the fourth match, the first singles of the final day.

A Lacoste win would only serve to bring France even at 2–all, but it was a foregone conclusion that Cochet would dispatch Johnston in the concluding match, so that, effectively, Lacoste vs. Tilden was for the Davis Cup. Big Bill was thirty-four, the Crocodile twenty-three; the American had played nine sets over the past two days, the Frenchman but three, and with a rest day after that modest exertion. Tilden realized that he had to win quickly were he to win at all. He came out firing the hard serve, which is what the Musketeers wanted, and he came out shooting for the lines, for winners. His only chance was to burn Lacoste off the court with a flash fire.

By contrast the imperturbable Lacoste calmly set out to keep everything in play. In the first set, which told the tale, Lacoste did not win a single earned point. Every point in the set was determined by Tilden—his errors or his placements, and there were many more of the former. Lacoste won 6–3. This meant Big Bill had to throw everything into the second set. He did, and he won 6–4, but the effort depleted him. Lacoste took the last two sets 6–3 and 6–2. Overall in the match, Tilden made nine aces and Lacoste but one, Tilden made thirty-three placements and Lacoste twenty-two, but Tilden made one hundred errors and Lacoste forty-nine.

There were 15,186 fans jammed into the temporary wooden stands at Germantown, and although that was his home club, even there Tilden had generally long been considered the heavy. But now, as he strode from the court, alone, head bowed in defeat, his long legs reaching out over the land he had crossed all his life, the people began to rise and cheer him. It was not for his match so much; he had not played that well. The cheers were for him. And many began to cry for him too. Tilden, totally unfamiliar with this expression, was for once completely at a loss as an actor. At last he thought to raise his hands above his head, like a boxing champ, and the crowd hurled down another tumultuous roar for him.

Lacoste was so emotionally spent by the whole experience, by the approaching fulfillment of this great quest for France, that when he watched the final match, sitting in hot sunshine, he had to wear two sweaters and an overcoat against a nervous chill. Tilden came and sat by his side, and together they watched Cochet play Johnston. The

American somehow won the second set to tie the match, but by the third the people could see that it was all getting away from him, and that there was nothing he could do.

Relentlessly Cochet moved in, closing upon the dream. Johnston had no place to hide. "God bless you, Little Bill," a woman called down near the end, and more people began to cry again, this time for the pitiful tiny figure. At the end, when Little Bill knocked a forehand into the net, Cochet hurled his racket thirty feet into the air. Mrs. Cochet began to cry and continued for half an hour. In Paris the people poured into the streets crying "Victory at last!" A place for the Cup was designated in the Louvre. In the stands at Germantown, Lacoste, still in some shock and his heavy clothes, rose with Tilden, and solemnly they turned to each other and shook hands. Thus, after seven years, did the Cup go abroad.

CHAPTER TEN

"All they can do is beat him, they cannot ever be his equal"

TILDEN won his last major tournament at Wimbledon on July 9, 1930, ten years and six days after he had defeated Gerald Patterson to win his first. In that full span of the 1920s no man who reached the final at either Wimbledon or Forest Hills ever again attained that distinction. It was as if Tilden were a chapter and closed it for them all by his leaving. He turned professional on the final day of 1930.

His departing Wimbledon was a relatively easy victory. The young Texan, Wilmer Allison, took care of Cochet in the semis, while Tilden was dealing with Borotra, and then he dismissed Allison in straight sets in the finals. His cannonball was on, and, most agreeably, King George and Queen Mary honored Tilden by their witness. She wore a salmon pink gown. Delighted with this audience, Tilden wrapped things up in barely an hour, "beaming throughout." He was thirty-seven years and five months old. When Ken Rosewall reached the 1974 Wimbledon final against Jimmy Connors when he was well into his fortieth year, it was pointed out to him that he could now succeed Tilden as the oldest man ever to play through to victory. With a shy smile, almost embarrassed at this information, Rosewall replied in a way so becoming, "Ahh, but that was Tilden."

And, of course, Connors routed him, so Tilden remains the oldest champion.

Big Bill had also won his seventh U.S. title the year before, 1929, coming back from two-sets-to-one deficits in both the semis, against John Doeg, and in the finals against Frank Hunter. Despite his age, he was never more active, playing almost compulsively. He celebrated the arrival of the new decade, the 1930s, by playing an indoor doubles match in France on the night of December 31, 1929. By July of 1930 he had already accumulated thirteen singles trophies, thirteen doubles and nine mixed for the year. With Junior Coen as his doubles partner, a German favorite named Celia Aussem his mixed, he marched through Europe playing wherever a tournament was thrown up. Risking amateur excommunication, he even ventured to play the pro champion, Karel Kozeluh of Czechoslovakia, beating him 6–4, 6–4 at Beaulieu on the Riviera. Besides Wimbledon, he also won the championships of Germany, Austria, Italy and the Netherlands, although losing to Cochet in the French finals.

After a typical, predictable dispute with the USLTA over his newspaper writing, Tilden agreed to play in the Challenge Round against France only five days before the matches opened in Paris—"against my wishes and despite my better judgment," he added. The next day he turned an ankle, and he was still limping when he squared off against Borotra in the opening match of his eleventh consecutive Challenge Round. Immobilized by the ankle, Tilden lost the first set 6–2 and was down 2–5 in the second as well. Then, magically, he began to move about, and while Borotra looked on aghast, he won five straight games, and then the next two sets. A couple days later, though, Cochet beat Tilden in four sets, his last Davis Cup match.

Even Tilden could see that the tennis world was a set piece by now. Without another exceptional player there was no conceivable way for the United States to regain the Cup. Against the best competition, Tilden had grown too old to win two singles matches in three days, let alone help take the doubles too. (As it was, right after he retired, the United States couldn't even qualify for the Challenge Round. It wasn't until 1937, when Budge came into his prime, that America could recover the Cup.) On the other hand, once Tilden had won again at Forest Hills, avenging the USLTA for his 1928 suspension, and then after he capped his European cavalcade of 1930 with yet one more Wimbledon triumph, there remained nothing for him to accomplish personally.

Frustrated by the reductions of age, appearing more effeminate in his gestures, he became testier, even petty, on the court. Once on the Riviera, in a match of no consequence, the umpire, an Englishman, finally just got up and departed when Tilden kept on fussing. At Orange, New Jersey, he rudely informed the tournament chairman that Big Bill Tilden was not accustomed to competing on grass that had the texture of a "cow pasture," and had to be coaxed back onto the court. Another time, when he bridled and went "uh uh," wagging a finger at Junior Coen, cautioning the boy not to overreach his doubles responsibility, John Hennessey, on the other side of the net, waggled his finger and said "uh uh" to his partner. Promptly Tilden stalked off the court in the middle of the match and refused to return. At Rye, New York, when he was playing quite valiantly with a twisted muscle in his right leg, he decided that the crowd was granting him insufficient credit for guts. At last, down 1–6, 0–4 and 15–all to Cliff Sutter, Tilden shrieked, "I think I've had enough of this gallery," and, picking up his rackets, departed the premises.

Besides, he was lonely in the amateurs; there was no one left for him to pal around with. Hunter had business to tend to, and Junior Coen was going to college. Tilden had no fondness for the upcoming younger American players, and, save perhaps for Sidney Wood, thought the whole lot of them halfwits. The chance for Open tennis, which had so nearly been voted in on several occasions, evaporated, and his tedious rows with the USLTA were apparently never going to cease. It was time that Big Bill played strictly for Big Bill.

Germany, wide open, with a high level of tolerance for homosexuality, obviously influenced his more independent bent. He had enjoyed an instant love affair with that free-wheeling society, and as late as 1938, when Hitler was in the saddle, ready to march, Tilden said, "I became, and still am, the most ardent admirer of the German people. I would rather play in Berlin than any city in the world." He had first played there in 1927. Crowds waited for him at the boat train, he was feted with a dinner at the Red and White Club, most fashionable in the city, and he received a standing ovation the next day merely for umpiring a match—with even more of the same when he played, toying with Germany's best. Tilden admired the way the ball boys stood at attention, the way the crowds responded so dutifully, and the way, when there was rumored to be a Communist demonstration, a police phalanx stood ready to guard him on the courts.

Gottfried von Cramm, eighteen years younger, did not meet Tilden on this initial visit to Berlin, but they became friends within a few years, and, according to the Baron, "I was immediately accepted as an integral member of the entourage of the Berlin complement, which he, the king, assembled in all the world's tennis centers." Von Cramm, born in 1910, a man of impeccable lineage and demonstrable honor, now has luminous white hair and luminous blue eyes, with the handsome face and courtly manner that Tilden so admired. Sitting in his Hamburg penthouse, he remembers:

"Berlin Bill loved. Even for a few years after the Nazis took over, it was unique, cosmopolitan, tolerant—a dynamic momentum that could not be killed with one stroke. And Bill basked in the adoration, paid him more abundantly here than in any other center. He felt attuned to the limitless range of attractions, the mood which appealed to a voracious liver, as he was."

Tilden always took a suite at the Eden Hotel, for a time as chic and sophisticated as any in the world. Evenings would begin for Big Bill at the Eden Roof. Pleasantly tolerant in the way of that city, he laughed and quaffed ice water, while his companions downed cocktails. Then, proceeding gaily through a series of boîtes, his party would end raucously at four or five in the morning in some underworld dive on a side street off the Kurfürstendamm.

Eventually Tilden was hired as coach of the German Davis Cup team, and when the Germans came up against the Americans in the interzone final at Wimbledon in 1937, it was clear that Tilden's heart also resided with his paycheck. Great Britain was the defender of the Cup, but Fred Perry had become a professional, leaving the English team without a stalwart, at the mercy of whichever country won the interzone—the Germans with von Cramm, or the Americans with Budge. The team score stood at 2–all when these two faced off against each other in what has been accepted as the most exciting, if indeed not the very best, match of all time. Hitler himself telephoned von Cramm in the locker room just as he prepared to go out onto Centre Court, and his subsequent defeat by Budge this day no doubt left him particularly vulnerable in view of his anti-Nazi feelings, so before long he was arrested on morals charges and, later, ordered to the Russian front as an enlisted man.

Tilden, in the stands, applauded loudly for von Cramm throughout, and when the German took a 4–1 lead over

Budge in the fifth set, Big Bill rose and called to Henner Henkel, the other German singles player, who was seated some rows above. When Tilden caught Henkel's attention, he put the thumb and forefinger of his right hand together, forming a circle, the smug sign of success. Sitting between Tilden and Henkel was an American show-biz contingent which included actor Paul Lukas, Jack Benny and Ed Sullivan. When the feisty Sullivan spotted such an anti-American display, he leaped up, and, struggling to remove his coat and come down and slug Tilden, he hollered, "Why you dirty son of a bitch!" Regrettably for devotees of the sweet science, Lukas and Benny grabbed Sullivan and forestalled the impending fisticuffs. Tilden merely settled a sneer on the columnist and sat back down, whereupon Budge promptly fought back to win 8–6. But then, ever typically, Tilden was one of the first to reach Budge in the locker room, to congratulate him warmly, and, says Budge, it was Tilden who was then the first to declare to Budge and all others that the match had been the greatest ever played.

In many ways, the German social experience was revealing for Tilden, broadening his own attitudes toward homosexuality, fueling new fires of independence. Certainly his decision, at last, to turn pro had very little to do with money. Indeed, his official reason for becoming professional was to make some instructional movies for MGM; he hadn't even bothered yet to mount a tour, and he took pains to assure the USLTA that "I shall never teach professionally." That seemed very important to him at the time; he still looked upon teaching professionals as servants. Before he announced the final decision, though, he wanted desperately to win one more Forest Hills, an eighth. Back in the days before the Challenge Round was abolished in the U.S. Nationals, William Larned had won seven American championships, and even though Larned himself had long since publicly acknowledged that Tilden played in a higher league than he had ever even visited, Big Bill wanted the eighth title for the record.

Sadly, he came a cropper in the semifinals against John Doeg, who chose this day to present a full-court game to go with his big serve. Doeg made twenty-eight aces, twelve in the final set, while Tilden was able to break him but twice in twenty-nine service games. Doeg's forehand, always so undependable, held steady. Moreover, Big Bill was tired from playing four hard sets the day before against Van Ryn, and in the fifth game of the second set against Doeg he fell and scraped his leg. He played gamely thereafter with a limp and a huge strawberry on his thigh. After dropping the first two sets, Tilden did win the third at 6–3, but in the fourth, Doeg's thunder serves kept Tilden pinned back, struggling each time just to hold his own to stay even. Frustrated, he grew irritable and started bickering. The crowd got on him.

Alphonso Smith, one of his old protégés, was watching, and he says that when Doeg finally called out, "Oh for God's sake, Bill, let's play tennis," Tilden slumped, hurt. "The fight seemed to go out of him," Smith says. He lost 12–10, the first time he had been beaten by a countryman in a U.S. championship since 1919. Tilden played eighty matches in his nation's championships, at least one every year since 1916, except for 1928, when he was suspended. He won seventy-three, lost seven. He won 203 sets and lost 59, with 1591 games won to 975 lost.

As far as the USLTA was concerned, nothing ever became Big Bill so much as his leaving. Whereas Vinnie Richards had been vilified as an unpatriotic ingrate when he turned pro, the organization gracefully acknowledged that Tilden had good reasons for moving on, and sent him ahead with its blessings. The USLTA's official 1931 annual found additional evidence for canonization. "Principals of schools, and even boards of education," it wrote, "were quick to place their auditoriums at [Tilden's] service, as they recognized the educational and moral value of his lectures." For his part in this mutal charade of good riddance, Tilden clasped the USLTA to his bosom, concluding his official retirement letter by "wishing the game of amateur tennis and the United States Lawn Tennis Association all success in the future and thanking you for many courtesies to me." It had a good beat, and you could dance to it.

And so, after declaring unequivocally, unceasingly, that he never would turn pro, Tilden turned pro. Not only that, but the man who had once written, "Above all, it is amateur sports that appeals to the American people. . . . If it was good enough for Teddy Roosevelt, it is good enough for me, and it should be good enough for all true Americans"—that man instantly became the Pied Piper of professionalism. Much more than ever in the amateurs, Tilden was the whole show. Professional tournaments had no following whatsoever, being scrutinized dubiously by putative ticket buyers and downright charily by members of the press. There were no other pro superstars. Thus Tilden's first tours were nothing more than triumphal processions, and thereafter the world-conquering amateur champions were shoved out on the stage, mere ingenues, to appear opposite the old idol.

Tilden made his professional playing debut early in 1931 against Kozeluh, the recognized pro champion, in Madison Square Garden. A crowd of 13,500 paid a gate of $36,000 to watch Tilden mop up the Czech at his leisure. Then the Tilden Tennis Tour hit the road: Baltimore, Boston, Cincinnati, Youngstown, Columbus, Detroit, the Windy City, Omaha, Los Angeles and on and on. Tilden played Kozeluh, while Frank Hunter and Emmet Pare came along for the preliminary, what the tennis pros came to call "the animal acts." Tilden drove the promoter crazy by winning all the time. He was a refugee from boxing, where it was customary to keep things close, but Big Bill won the first sixteen matches against Kozeluh and ended up with a 63–13 edge, inspiring a horrible epidemic of BIG BILL CANCELS CZECH headlines, coast to coast. Tilden broke off in the middle of the Kozeluh tour in order to play a shorter series against Vinnie Richards. He won all ten matches, restoring a proper sense of *déja vu* from the 1920s, and then he picked up again with Kozeluh. In Paris they drew fifteen thousand in two nights; they then attracted the largest crowd ever in Brussels, and went on to a packed house in Amsterdam and a number of glorious dates in Germany.

Having demolished Kozeluh and Richards, Tilden needed a new foil for 1932, but the best he could manage was someone named Hans Nusslein, with other household names such as Roman Najuch, Bruce Barnes and Hubert Burke playing the animal acts. Not even a whole world mad to see Big Bill perform could fall for this bill, however, and Tilden lost some money and declared that he would play his "farewell match" in New York in January 1933. That worked so well that he kept hyping farewell matches regularly in the years that followed. Then Cochet was finally convinced to turn pro, whereupon Tilden went to Paris and smashed him 6–3, 6–4, 6–2 in fifty-five minutes in his professional debut there in September of 1933.

Better yet, since he was another American, Ellsworth Vines, a handsome young Wimbledon and Forest Hills champion, was being polished up for Tilden. On January 10, 1934, a turnaway crowd of sixteen thousand—much of it in black tie—paying a heavy five-dollar Depression top, showed up at the Garden to see Big Bill and the new blood. Allison Danzig noted in the *Times* that Vines's form was "far superior to his showing as an amateur." Tilden clobbered him 8–6, 6–3, 6–2 in an hour and five minutes. Vines was twenty-two, Tilden a month short of forty-one.

Playing one-night stands was too grueling for the old man, though, and Vines regrouped and won the first part of the tour 11–9. Then Tilden gave Vines a night off and returned to New York, where he beat Cochet in his U.S. debut in five sets for a $20,000 gate. Prime and rested for one match, Big Bill was still supreme. Then back again with Vines: seventy-three towns all told, 350,000 spectators. "I was at the top of my game," says Vines, who subsequently turned golf pro, "and he was a little slower each night. He was more irascible all the time too, gave the umpires hell. But he still had that big dynamic serve, he was still in top shape, and he still played the mental game of tennis to the hilt."

As Tilden wore down from the travel pace, Vines went on to win 47–26, and then for a time the two Americans joined as a team to play a series of Davis Cup–type matches against Cochet and a lesser Frenchman, Martin Plaa. Every year there had to be a new gimmick. In 1935 George Lott and Lester Stoefen, alleged as the best doubles team in creation, were hauled out of the amateurs to stand against Tilden and Vines, while a couple of second-rate women players were put on the undercard.

And soon it was time for another farewell. "My tennis days are over," he wrote. "The aged net star, that Patriarch of United States tennis, bids official farewell to international play. However, that rising youngster, William T. Tilden II, the individual himself, in person not a picture, will still in leisure moments miss his passing shots, volleys and smashes with even greater regularity than usual." Actually, he was just biding his time until Fred Perry could ripen on the vine and turn pro. Tilden called Perry "the world's worst good player," and leaving Western civilization to chew on that, he took off on an exotic playing tour of India, Malaya, Java, Japan and Egypt, where he coached for the Cairo Tennis Association. Despite all his fervent

promises to the USLTA and other spiritual heirs of Teddy
Roosevelt, he had begun taking lucre to coach as early as
1934, when an unnamed millionaire paid a thousand dollars a lesson to him.

The tours were undoubtedly profitable, even if Tilden
was an atrocious businessman and so fair and generous that
he often refunded guarantee money to promoters who did
not make their nut. Budge, who campaigned against Tilden
in 1941, remembers an evening in Elizabeth, New Jersey,
when Tilden entered the hall, quickly surveyed it and went
promptly to the microphone. The gym was so small that
the court fit snugly, with little room for the players to
maneuver past the baselines. Jack Harris, the promoter,
was hard of hearing and couldn't make out what Tilden
was saying, so he asked Budge. "Oh, Bill's just telling them
they can have their money back," Budge said. Harris
swooned.

Budge made more than $100,000 (paying only $5200 in
taxes) his first year on the tour, which was about as much
as Vines had grossed his first year. Although Lott says he
lost most of his money betting on other sports events, he
took in about $50,000 on his first tour. And Lott was no big
name. Tilden had to guarantee each new star a big cut—up
to 50 per cent of the net—but he still commanded plenty
for himself. The deal was like a treasure map that had been
torn in half; the public was anxious to see the new pro star,
but only if it could see him against Tilden. Whoever
played, whoever won, Tilden was still the draw. As Al
Laney wrote at that time in the *Herald Tribune*, "All they
can do is beat him, they cannot ever be his equal."

In 1937 Tilden was forty-four, and Fred Perry, that year's
new pro, had only recently debuted in New York against
Vines, who was the "official" professional champion, but
Tilden scheduled Perry himself a few weeks later and
pulled in sixteen thousand to the Garden for another heavy

payday. At that time it was estimated that Big Bill had netted $500,000 (in Depression dollars) since turning pro hardly six years before; and, given the Budge, Vines and Lott figures for comparison, that holds up as a perfectly reasonable guess. In terms of actual buying power, Tilden seems to have made as much money as the highest-paid modern athletes. He also must have worked exceptionally hard at spending it, because it was all gone soon enough.

CHAPTER ELEVEN

"Please boo me all you will between points"

C OMPARED to modern conditions, Tilden's frenetic one-night-stand tours were antediluvian, but so long as he could play, the circumstances were of no consequence to him. "He just loved tennis," Budge says. "The last time we toured, 'forty-one, he was almost fifty, and I beat him something like 55–6, but let me tell you: he loved it and he tried like hell every game. One time I asked him: 'Bill, what will you do when you can't play tennis anymore?' He just looked at me and said: 'Hmmmph. Kill myself.'"

The tour set a wearing pace, but it seemed to faze Tilden much less than the younger players. In a new town they would spend the day catching up on sleep or idling about. Tilden would immediately go to the arena, seek out the electrician and have him arrange the lighting to his specifications. He would simulate hitting overheads to get it exactly right. And, if the background at court level was not to his satisfaction, he was quite likely to go out and buy some green burlap and have it tacked up.

Depending on the weather and the distance involved, the tour moved by train or automobile, the players usually departing for the next city as soon as they finished the night's matches. The court itself was trucked about. It was a heavy sailcloth canvas named Dandux, which came in two halves, each weighing nine hundred pounds; with block and tackle, it required three hours to put the court down. Besides the players and the truckers, two other principals were usually traveling regulars on any Tilden tour. One was the road manager, there to keep an eye on the box office, because as vague as Big Bill was about business, it was easy for the local promoter to take him to the cleaners. As a tour guide, he also usually failed to trouble himself with petty little geographical nuances. It was nothing for him to schedule, say, Portland one night, San Diego the next and then San Francisco. "He just loved to play," says Vines, who seems to have been especially exasperated by Tilden executive decisions. "It didn't mean a damn to Bill whether we had to drive all night or ride a train all night to get to the next match. All he wanted to do was to be out on the court."

Before every match he would go through his repertoire for the fans, showing them the full spectrum of his classic strokes. Once the match was under way, he exhibited as wide a range of emotions; there was always a great deal of glaring and much grandiose point-throwing, depending on which way Tilden decided the linesman had erred.

Once Lott served an ace which Tilden, alone in the arena, understood to be a fault, so he went over to the offending linesman, who happened to be a petrified young man. "How was that, boy?" he demanded of him.

"Out!" the kid replied, changing his decision immediately.

Satisfied now that justice had been tended to, Tilden returned to the baseline, but when he looked up to receive serve, he discovered Lott over by the umpire's chair enjoying a drink of water. "Come on, let's go," Tilden hollered. Lott responded by picking up a comb and casually, patiently attending to his hair.

"Come on!" Tilden screamed again.

"Can't," Lott replied. He was really setting him up.

"Can't?"

"Too noisy, Bill."

"Noisy? What d'ya mean?" Tilden asked.

"I can't concentrate until that linesman's teeth stop chattering," Lott said. Tilden fumed the rest of the match.

Increasingly, it took little to upset his tolerance; he began, in pique, to quit all the time. As ever, he ruled. At a tournament in Brooklyn, when Tilden was informed that a tired opponent wanted a postponement of their match, he declared imperiously, "There are three things I'm prepared to do. I'll accept a default, I'll give a default, or I'll play the match." He and his opponent were instantly under way. Perhaps nothing infuriated him more than Lott's mimicry, but as Tilden grew older and more crotchety, even a player like Vines, the most level of men, came to task for alleged sinister behavior—quick serving, for example. "I won't stand for it. This tour is over," Tilden would announce, but it would all be forgotten the next morning, and on to the next match.

In Montreal once, when he was touring against Budge, a linesman made a succession of bad calls, almost all in Tilden's favor. Budge was undisputed champion then, for which Tilden sarcastically referred to him as "Mister God," but now, although he was the benefactor of these injustices, Big Bill came forward and demanded the linesman's removal. For this the crowd got on Tilden and began booing him regularly, even during the playing of points. At last, in the middle of a game, Tilden held up his hand to stop play, went to the umpire and took his microphone. "I knew he was glib enough to get out of it, but I sure didn't know how," Budge says.

"Ladies and gentlemen," Tilden began, "I believe you will observe the British way of letting a man defend himself before you condemn him. It is you, not I, who suffer

the most from these bad calls. Mr. Budge is now the greatest player in the game, and you have paid good money to
watch me try to put up a match against him. If I am to be
disturbed by bad calls, I cannot play my best, and if you
razz me or boo me during a point, you will only make it
more difficult for me. Please boo me all you will between
points. I have endured that all my life and am quite used to
it, but if you wish to obtain the most for your money, hold
off while I try to play the best player in the world. Thank
you."

There followed not a sound in the place.

Besides the road manager, the other extra person traveling with the Tilden troupe was a ball boy; he was selected
by Big Bill and went along with him. For the first time in
his life he was coming out of the closet—although, as
always, his homosexual interest lay only with teenage boys.
While there is no evidence that Tilden ever was black-
mailed, some unfortunate incidents were hushed up on the
road, some polite warnings given. Vines remembers that
there were a number of cities that the Tilden tennis tour
prudently avoided returning to, even though the gate
might have been exceptionally good the time before.

Most of the ball boys were from Europe, usually Germany. If traveling on the highway, Tilden and his boy
would ride together in his big blue Buick, letting everybody else pile into the other one or two cars. On the train
Tilden and the kid would share a compartment. Lott
remembers one morning when the players were sitting in
the observation car and Tilden came dashing in, distraught.
He said he was going to throw himself off the rear of the
train. Certainly this was only a generous portion of his
dramatic hyperbole, but the others jumped up and grabbed
him. "Not because we really cared whether Tillie jumped
or not," Lott says, "but just because the son of a bitch was
our bread and butter."

Finally they managed to calm him down and ask him what was the matter. "Fritzi's locked me out of the compartment," Tilden said, nearly in tears.

A few days later at a hotel he came into the lobby where a few of the players were killing time. This time he was all smiles. "Fritzi did the cutest thing this morning," he said.

"What?" someone asked, hardly looking up from his newspaper.

"Before I woke up, he took four hundred dollars and went out and bought himself a watch," Tilden said.

Such antics were not, however, always greeted with pleasure by Big Bill. His nephew says that on one occasion when Fritzi took some valuable item from Tilden, he wanted to turn the boy over to the local police and had to be talked out of that action by the other players, who were frightened that the publicity might damage the tour. Why a kid would have to bother stealing from Tilden is difficult to understand in the first place, since he bestowed upon his favorites practically anything their hearts desired. Vines remembers him once giving a boy a wristwatch that cost $1500 and on other occasions fashionable clothes—whole suits, jackets, expensive polo overcoats, like his own.

When Tilden did not have his own special ball boy traveling with him, he sought out new ones along the way —and not necessarily for sex, just for companionship. He was more comfortable with children. Sterling Lord, the New York literary agent, remembers the day Big Bill came to his home town, Burlington, Iowa. His father was promoting the afternoon's matches at the country club, where Tilden met young Lord, and they spent the whole morning together in the lounge talking tennis. After the matches Tilden drove the boy to his hotel in his big Buick. Alone in his room, Tilden never made a pass of any kind, just talked some more and then gave him a racket inscribed "To Ster, From Bill."

At a high school clinic in Indianapolis, Tilden spotted a little teenager named Allan Solomon, blond and cute. "How would you like to work for me?" he asked, and the excited little kid became a ball boy at that evening's matches downtown. Tilden carried him on to Chicago, and later, when Solomon went to school at Northwestern, Tilden would call him up whenever the tour came into the Chicago area and press him back into service as a ball boy. Solomon, who is now a businessman in St. Petersburg, Florida, says that Tilden never once made any sort of advance toward him, but would pay for his own room, buy him large meals, and sit and talk to him for hours. He remembers that Tilden seems to have had a list of other young friends, ball boys, scattered all over the country.

He was more alone than ever. Although still famous wherever he went—at least for endorsing Camel cigarettes in national magazines—he was only a name now, a memory that would not fade. He wandered in tennis, because there was no place else to go. The old house in Germantown lay vacant, his aunt dead, his cousin moved to England, and his old contemporaries were all gone from the game, to suburbs and board rooms and even, poor Little Bill, to an early grave. The boys, his boys, became his only real love, and his refuge as well.

The money just went—on the kids, on the suites, on picking up every tab that lay on the table. Anyway, none of it went on income taxes, because as slight as they were at this time, Tilden seems to have simply ignored paying them altogether. One day it all just ran out. On November 16, 1938, the Algonquin announced that it was seeking $2329 in unpaid back rent, and then the government asked for its too. Vinnie Richards came to the rescue. He paid the Algonquin bill and then went down to Washington and got the government to settle for something like a dime on the dollar. Then Richards set up some dates for a new tour and went over to London, where Tilden was holed up, unable to return to America and his creditors. Richards advanced him some money against his guarantee—and perhaps as much as several thousand dollars. Whatever, a week after Richards returned to the States, Tilden cabled him that he didn't have the money for a ticket home.

Occasionally in this period, Tilden also began to allude to his homosexuality in conversation, actually speaking of it, even passionately in defense of it. This man of sheer honor and wrathful righteousness was at last coming to grips with this strange thing within him that society considered illegal and sinful and inhuman. But if his walk and some hand movements were becoming increasingly effeminate, he was still no less the competitor, no less the star. It was, as ever, Tilden and tennis.

In June of 1939, with the war blowing in the winds, Tilden, age forty-six, was included when a new tour kicked off in London, at Wembley, and when he played, Al Laney, his old nemesis, was there, moved to write almost lyrically:

> The old guy was terrific . . . the star of the show. There can be no doubt about Tilden being the greatest star of all time, and you can name any sport you like. Before Budge was born, Tilden was a great player [and] the fire is still there, and the cunning and the showmanship. . . . He came to play Budge, the greatest player of the day, for the first time, with the air of a master about to give a lesson to a promising pupil. He strode majestically onto the court and made you feel, in spite of yourself, a bit sorry for Budge. . . . All through the match, it was Tilden you were watching, and not Budge. When it was over, he strode off the court as if he were the victor. . . .
>
> [And then] he was out there giving twenty years to Vines and beating him, outhitting the hardest hitter in

the game. Yes, outhitting Vines. He won 6–3, 10–8, and when he came safely past match point with as hard a forehand drive to the corner as any player ever made, they nearly tore the house down. They shouted and stamped on the floor and told him there was no one like him and never had been. They were right about that, too, and it was sweet music to the old gentleman's ears.

Tilden has made more money out of tennis in his time than anyone else, but they say he is broke now, willing to play anywhere for anything from fifty bucks up. So they're taking him along on this tour. They should be glad he's going along because they're lucky to have him. The old guy is not through yet by a long shot.

But he was, really. The tour ended soon enough. There were two weeks of air raid scares in London, so they were going to go to South Africa and resume action there, but nothing was safe anymore. The ship the players canceled off of at the last minute was blown up and sunk en route. Tilden came back to America, where there were to be very few more glory days, and many more sad ones, so that, in the end, much of his accomplishment was lost and much of his memory clouded. Tilden's niece, Miriam Ambrose, the daughter of his brother, Herbert, has written a lovely encomium entitled "My Father's Brother." It talks of love and faith and days long gone, and it also includes these thoughts:

> In essence, none of us really begin on the date of our birth, the forces that contrive us having long been present; nor do we exactly complete ourselves at the hour of our death, leaving, as we do, lingering impressions that fade slowly from people's minds. Something

of Uncle Bill was evolving in our predecessors from a time nobody can pinpoint, and his having moved through our midst stimulated emotions and reactions in us that are still engaging. His fame accentuated his ramifications, reminding others who never even saw him in life of things that he did; so his passage has not yet reached its end. . . .

In our [family's] view not much of what is generally known about him actually inspired his superlative tennis, which was the reason for his fame. He perfected his talent before he was heard of. Somewhere in the past, in his home, his school, among the people who nurtured him lies the key to the complexities that enabled him to do just one thing better than anyone else could do it.

What did make this strange great man?

Part Two

CHAPTER TWELVE

"The only child of William T. and Linie H. Tilden"

O N both sides, the forebears of William Tatem Tilden II were British. His mother was Selina Hey, called Linie, born in Philadelphia, one of four daughters of David and Selina Hey, who came to the United States in the middle of the nineteenth century from Dewsbury in Yorkshire. Mr. Hey began a wool-importing business that soon prospered, so Selina grew up quite comfortably. Despite their affluence the Heys were not ostentatious but solid religious people who took things seriously.

The Tildens, as all Tildens in the world, came from County Kent, that southeasternmost part of the British Isles. The postfix *den* is a Saxon word, equivalent to dale or dell, meaning "deep wooded valleys," of which there were many in Kent, inland from the English Channel. Tilden, with a variety of first-syllable spellings—Tylden, Telden, Tillden, as well as Tilden—is an ancient and distinguished line. One married the first Norman Earl of Chester, a nephew of William the Conqueror. Somewhat later, "Sir Richard Tylden assumed the cross and accompanied King Richard to ye Holy Land." There was a William Tylden at least as early as 1346, and the family was so large and important in Kent that Tilden became something of a place name as well; a will registered in April of 1492, some months before Columbus sailed, refers to certain bequeathed lands "in Marden, on the den of Tilden." The family crest is a battle-ax entwined with a snake.

Despite the deep roots in Kent, Tildens were early Americans. Joseph Tilden, a well-to-do London merchant, did not come over on the *Mayflower*, but, in a sense, he went one better: he helped fit out the ship and furnished some capital for the Pilgrims. Joseph's brother Thomas was, it seems, the first Tilden to arrive on American soil, landing in 1623 in Plymouth on the *Ann*, "allotted shares for three persons" (himself, a wife and a child?), but Thomas' track soon fades, so that the prime Tilden source in America is another brother, Nathaniel. A former mayor of Tentenden, Kent, a man of substance, Nathaniel Tilden sailed from Sandwich for the Bay Colony in 1634 aboard the ship *Hercules* with his wife, Lydia, seven children and seven servants. Within a year he was a ruling elder in the Scituate settlement in Massachusetts.

The Tildens eventually divided, generally, into three different American lines. The northernmost branch struck up from Massachusetts into Canada, largely to Nova Scotia. Tilden is a well-known commercial name in the Dominion, Tilden Rent-A-Car being the Canadian equivalent to Hertz. The family's middle branch, centering on New York State, produced Samuel Tilden, born in 1814 in New Lebanon, New York, near the Massachusetts line, who served as governor of New York and was awarded the Democratic presidential nomination in 1876, only to win the popular vote but to be cheated out of the White House by carpetbag politics in the only certified presidential vote fraud in U.S. history. The building of the New York Public Library was funded with the two million dollars that Samuel Tilden left for that purpose.

It was the third, southern branch of the Tildens, residing

for the most part in Delaware and Maryland, that produced Big Bill. His father, the first William Tatem Tilden,
was born in St. Georges, Delaware, where the Chesapeake
and Delaware Canal runs now. When William T. Tilden
Sr.'s father, a doctor, died, his mother, Williamina Tatem
Tilden, picked up and brought her only child to Philadelphia. A determined woman, Williamina Tilden was
searching for greater opportunity in the big city for herself,
greater future for her boy. Mother and son found an apartment, he enrolled at Central High and also began working
as an office boy for a shipping concern. A bright lad, he
moved over to the Reading Railroad as a clerk, and then to
David Hey's woolen firm, working his way up to a position
of some responsibility after he graduated from Central
High.

William T. Tilden Sr. was an impressive young man, nice-
looking, ambitious, obviously capable; and, indeed, it was
not so much a case of his marrying the boss's daughter as it
was of the boss making sure that one of his daughters
latched on to this fine specimen. With that purpose upper-
most in his mind, Mr. Hey invited the young man to lunch
one Sunday after church in April of 1879. Young Tilden
was twenty-four and still lived with his mother. This was a
potential social bonanza for the widow and her son, and
she planned to make the most of it. She polished his shoes,
pressed his worn-out suit, and, according to a tale still told
in the family, instructed him not to keep his hands in his
pockets.

So prepared, he set out for the big house on Eighth
Street, undeterred by a spring shower which forced him
briefly to cover along the way. When the sun came out, the
rain glistened on the fresh daffodils, and he was very nearly
confident by the time he reached the Heys' house and
walked up the steps to ring the bell. It was Linie who
opened the door for him, and she never let her sisters take

the prize away from her. They were married only a few months later that year, on a clear autumn Thursday, November 6, 1879; and soon thereafter Mr. Hey proudly accepted his bright new son-in-law as a business partner as well.

By that spring Linie was pregnant, and the first child, Elizabeth Hey, was born in October. Hardly a year after that, the prospering Mr. Tilden was given his son and heir, Harry Bower, and in June of 1883, a third healthy child, named for her grandmother, Williamina Tatem, was born. The Tildens by then had moved into a comfortable three-story red-brick end house at 5308 Germantown Avenue, next to Trinity Lutheran Church, a fine address on a cobblestoned thoroughfare with a trolley line that carried Mr. Tilden downtown every day to his office at 254 North Front Street. Other of the right Philadelphians had begun to notice this impressive young man who cut such a fine figure, who never ventured out without a fresh carnation in his lapel. Despite his public school education and the onus of being saddled with the most pre-eminent Democratic name of that era, he began to be accepted in all the best clubs and to gain some voice in Republican party affairs.

Linie Tilden, her family complete, had a housekeeper to free her from everyday drudgery, so she could concentrate her full efforts upon bringing up her three children to be cultured and kind, as she was, to support her husband, and to apply herself to her music, which she adored. They bought a piano for the parlor, and she played it often. The Tildens had only the fullest, happiest life ahead.

Williamina, the baby, died first, on Saturday, November 29, 1884, age seventeen months. She was buried out of the house that Monday, in the first raw winter cold, a hearse clattering out Germantown Avenue to the edge of the city, Ivy Hill Cemetery, where Mr. Tilden had hastily purchased a family plot. The cause of death was listed as "membranous croup," almost certainly because the parents did not want to admit what they surely realized, that the diphtheria epidemic had reached 5308 Germantown. In 1884 it was still six years before the diphtheria antitoxin was found, and the disease could spread like wildfire among children, especially in the same house; it moved by direct contact. The fever came first, with headaches, then a sore throat that swelled as the toxins coursed through the pained little body.

Elizabeth, the oldest, fell next. Just past her fourth birthday, she died on December 9 and was buried the day after. Again it was hymns played on Linie's piano in the parlor, and then another sad procession moved from the house to Ivy Hill, and another tiny coffin was lowered into the cold ground. Mr. Tilden still had his son left, but Harry had already become feverish; and even as they buried their second, they kept a death watch for their third. The little boy lived, in agony, only three more days and was buried on December 15, a Monday, just short of his third birthday, and only three weeks since the first of all the healthy children had so much as cried with fever. This time, for those who would make one more long trek to Ivy Hill, the death notice also added, in a pitiful updating, that Harry was "the only child of William T. and Linie H. Tilden." By then he was; their whole family was wiped out.

Bill Tilden was not to be born for another nine years. But for these sad events of 1884, he almost surely would not have been born at all. Because of them, his whole being and personality were greatly affected. It is not any exaggeration to say that much of the way that Bill Tilden was to be was determined for him years before he was born.

In the immediate time after the tragedy, his parents tried their best to carry on. But it was never the same again. There was never any more real lightness in their house.

Later in the winter, when the shock at least had worn off, Mr. Tilden took Linie to Atlantic City, which would be today rather like going to a fancy Caribbean resort. Soon thereafter Linie was pregnant once more, and with the birth of her fourth child, Herbert Marmaduke, at least William Sr. had replaced the son he had lost. When, six years later, Linie realized she was having another baby, she longed for a girl to replace the two daughters that had been taken from her. But it was another boy, born on a cold Saturday morning, February 10, 1894, and this child she named after her husband, William Tatem Tilden Jr., and she called him Junior. The name was the father's, but the boy was the mother's.

CHAPTER THIRTEEN

"Master Junior! Master Junior!"

JUNIOR Tilden grew up spoiled, in a comfort that approached opulence. In today's buying power, Mr. Tilden had an income in excess of $100,000, and his youngest child was born in a huge new house that the family had just moved into at 5015 McKean Avenue in Germantown. It was a stately red gabled mansion named Overleigh, so large that it now contains eight apartments. The grounds were gloriously kept with magnificent shrubbery, the house decorously appointed in the finest Victorian style of the time. Mrs. Tilden had her piano placed in a second-floor drawing room that she used; Mr. Tilden ordered a huge mahogany wardrobe specially made to hold all his suits, and a huge copper-lined tub to hold himself. The Tildens were known, even among neighbors of relative affluence, for being somewhat extravagant. They never bothered to save leftover food; what remained even of the largest roast would be sent home with grateful servants—"the help" they were always called—rather than be kept for next day's luncheon or snacks.

Germantown, which is now a racially mixed fringe neighborhood, declining all the time, was, before the turn of the century, a most fashionable Philadelphia enclave, perhaps the most elite of all after the Pennsylvania Railroad put a line in, with a commuter station, in 1884. The area drew its name from the original dominant ethnic population; when Germantown Academy, which Tilden was to attend, first opened in 1760, there were two head-masters—one English-speaking, one German-speaking—and even more than a century later, when young Junior was growing up, the Teutonic influence lingered. Pennsylvania Dutch farmers would journey into Germantown twice a week from the rich surrounding countryside to sell their produce in the farmers' market, and the richer kids often had a German governess; that was something of a status symbol.

Curiously, the Tildens, who usually had three of "the help" (at a salary of about three dollars a week each), preferred mulattoes. Nobody knows why, but they always had not only light-skinned servants but handsome ones as well. Alice Longaker, who grew up two doors down, says, "It was almost as if the Tildens had said, 'Send us the best-looking ones you've got.'" The Tildens' excepted, most of the help in the area came from nearby Pulaskitown, which, notwithstanding the Polish name, was in fact a predominantly Irish shanty village. Every Christmas, in an annual exercise of working Christianity and social consciousness, Mrs. Tilden and the other matrons of Germantown would take food baskets and hand-me-downs to the poor Irish.

In the summer the ladies would gather at backyard pavilions that were called summer houses; cooled by wells underneath, they would take their tea there. Or they would go over to the Germantown Cricket Club—always called Mannheim in the vernacular for the street it fronted on—sip large ten-cent lemonades and watch the young members play cricket. The Tilden house on McKean Avenue was just a few yards from Mannheim Avenue, and then but another block or so to the main clubhouse, which had been designed by Stanford White's firm. Because little pitchers have big ears, a completely separate and quite ample children's clubhouse had also been constructed.

The upstairs porch of the main clubhouse was the place to eat. It overlooked the cricket pitch. Cricket had been introduced into Germantown by the English hosiery weavers who had settled in the area, and despite the fact that the rest of America came to celebrate baseball as the national pastime, cricket remained the primary sport at Mannheim right up into the 1920s. It was altogether another world out there when Junior Tilden was growing up.

Indeed, although Germantown was within the Philadelphia city limits, and although the city was beginning to rush into modern urbanity, the setting for Junior's childhood was rural, the feeling of quainter and more gracious times past. Many of the residents still kept cows, storing the milk in the wells underneath the ladies' summer houses, and stables abounded, as they did at the Tildens'. (So did outdoor privies, for the help.) The gentlemen would ride to the hounds on Saturdays along the Wissahicken Creek; and weekdays, at the Queen Lane station, a certain amount of chaos always prevailed at commuter hours as the coachmen strained to still the startled horses as the steam trains came puffing in. Pony carts were not uncommon with the wealthier children. Herbert Tilden had his own horse and buggy.

From birth, though, Junior Tilden was catered to and guarded even more than the other society children of Germantown. The neighbors soon learned to expect one of the Tilden help to cry, "Master Junior! Master Junior!" at the first sign of dusk. He was assumed to be sickly and was held out of school. On one occasion, when he was around five or six years old, he woke up in the middle of the night and started crying for a toy he had seen in a shopwindow. Presently Mrs. Tilden woke the coachman and dispatched him to the residence of the proprietor of the toy shop, who was himself awakened. He went downstairs to his store, sold the toy to the coachman, who brought it home to Master Junior. Placated, the little boy went back to sleep.

Mr. Tilden did not involve himself in such episodes. He left the rearing of his youngest child strictly to his wife. A striking gray-eyed man, well dressed at all times, with a full mustache, he bore considerable resemblance to the modern actor Keenan Wynn. William Tilden Sr. was a perfect gentleman, a successful businessman, a hearty clubman, an elder in the Presbyterian Church, a popular after-dinner speaker, a pillar of the city of Philadelphia. Three times he was president of the Union League, the most prestigious Republican sanctum, a place still so haughty and aloof that even today an unintroduced visitor, no matter how polite and well dressed, will be quickly and rudely escorted from the premises, even though he may only wish to glance at the portrait of William T. Tilden Sr.

Mr. Tilden did not ever completely outdistance the memory of his childhood indigence; he was a man of more show than were his peers, who had been born to money. Besides the rich clothes and the carnations, he was a sucker for motor cars, as soon as they came along. Some stables were converted to garages, and the finest limousines always stood at Overleigh. Alice Longaker remembers that on one occasion her husband, Norman, who was an automobile salesman, was stuck with a flashy model he couldn't move. Finally he managed to unload it on Mr. Tilden by suggesting to him, "People will see this automobile and say right away, 'Here comes William Tilden.'"

With the wool business an ongoing success, Junior's father also turned to other pursuits, some big-kill investments and politics, where he was a natural. He was a man's man who loved to meet people and get into the midst of things. Alice Tatnall Franklin, a childhood acquaintance of

Junior, provides the best summary of his father: "He was an old-fashioned gentleman, but also the sort who quite often wouldn't show up at home on time for dinner."

Mr. Tilden grew in stature. He entertained Presidents Teddy Roosevelt and William Howard Taft at Overleigh, and began to cast his eyes upon high office for himself. While he neglected the upbringing of his own child, he certainly never denied the fact of his own public school heritage, and he was for sixteen years a member of the Philadelphia Board of Education. In that capacity he became known as the "Father of Fireproof Schools," and when he died years later the school flags were hung at half-staff and his obituary made page one, the lead story in the afternoon *Bulletin* (drawing much more attention in Philadelphia than, subsequently, did the death of his world-famous son). The Tilden Middle School at Sixty-sixth Street and Elmwood Avenue in Philadelphia is named in honor of William T. Tilden Sr., not his son, Big Bill.

By contrast with her ebullient husband, Linie Tilden seldom ventured far from Overleigh. She attended to her music (and she truly was quite an accomplished pianist), but that is not to suggest that she was some wispy, ethereal type. Rather, *"Trés formidable,"* says her granddaughter, Miriam Ambrose, with a smile. Mrs. Tilden was of average height, if somewhat slight, and she left the impression upon those who remember her that she was worried or unhappy. But she was a thoughtful woman and seems to have carried on the traditional Yorkshire characteristics that marked the Heys. "The folk up there are sensitive and passionate but dourly self-disciplined," Rex Bellamy of the London *Times* has written. "They have no respect for those who flaunt their emotions or opinions. They are good listeners rather than ready talkers. But they have a knack of identifying the nub of an argument—and then sticking to their opinions with a bluntness that can be brusque. A tough, hardy breed. Not the kind to push around." So Linie Tilden. And so too, then, her younger son.

All in all, Overleigh seems to have been a house where there was little expression of love and gaiety but where there was much respect and a fair amount of understanding. And always, like a grim drop cloth, the memories of 1884 overlaid the life that went ahead. That could be sensed even into the next generation. Miriam Ambrose, Herbert's oldest child, remembers: "It was seldom spoken of; we were simply told that it had happened a long time ago. . . . But the impression of grief was conveyed by members of the family, in fleeting glances, in sudden silent moments of despair that could not be controlled. We were told that Grandmother never quite regained the balance of her emotions afterward, and one sensed an insecurity of feeling for all that was held dear in Grandfather."

One lasting, if quite understandable, result of the tragedy was that Linie became obsessively health conscious. Her husband had been sufficiently involved in the upbringing of Herbert to insulate the older boy from her excessive protection, but Junior had no such counterbalance. While there is no evidence that he suffered anything more than the usual mild childhood diseases (plus possibly some minor bladder difficulty once), his mother decided he was infirm and ordained him so. Soon everybody in Germantown understood that Junior Tilden was somehow weak and different. This childhood impression was so strong that the completely contradictory facts of his life have never erased the early memories from the minds of those contemporaries still living. Josephine Reeves Walton, a close neighbor, shakes her head and says, "It's amazing that he became this great athlete. June was so very sickly. None of us could imagine that he would ever become this wonderful athlete."

Certainly the notion of sickliness was heightened by the

fact that he was kept out of school. This was not altogether uncommon at that time in Germantown, but mostly it was the girls, little ladies, who were held out of the hurly-burly of real school and placed in the more genteel atmosphere of a house known as Miss Knight's School. There, in a small cottage down McKean, the three Misses Knight provided lessons for the most unassured of Germantown's children. But Mrs. Tilden didn't believe that her Junior was even up to that experience. She kept him at home all day and had him tutored at her skirts. His earliest memory was of himself sitting reverently beside his mother as she played the piano, and although he almost never spoke a word of his childhood when he grew older, Tilden would always volunteer how much he adored his mother, how "I worshipped her."

Nor, in a very real sense, did he ever stop honoring her. Among the vast catalog of communicable ills that Linie Tilden feared her baby boy might someday contract were venereal diseases. From an early age the only sex training Tilden ever received was that women could give him a disease. Even his homosexual experiences were to be surface in nature, and he was ashamed that anyone would think him capable of some more fulfilling involvement. Physically, he simply never was able to accept another body, male or female, and, in extension, that made it so difficult for him to get close in any way to people, especially to his peers. More than any man, Bill Tilden diverted his sex drive to the arena, to a clean, bright place.

While far subordinate to the role his mother played in Tilden's childhood, his brother, Herbert, was a second major force, as he became something of a father substitute. Seven years older than Junior, tall, broad-shouldered, more handsome and outgoing, even cocky, Herbert was a natural idol for his younger brother. It was Herbert, who was himself good enough to win the national intercollegiate doubles and play number one at Germantown Cricket Club, who inspired Junior's interest in tennis and helped teach him the game.

But probably it was simpler things about Herbert that Junior envied most. Herbert was normal. Herbert got along with girls and was engaged to a very pretty one while he was still at Penn. Herbert interested his father; they were friends. After graduation he took a job as assistant secretary-treasurer of the woolen firm, which was now known as the William T. Tilden Co. Jack Beard, who lived in Germantown, remembers that all the neighborhood kids liked to watch Herbert play tennis because he was so entertaining and expressive, ranting and railing at himself and the vagaries of fate—but carrying on easily, antic, not studied as his brother was to be. Herbert even preferred a little liquid sustenance while playing, and often took a cool pitcher of martinis with him to the court. "Get me a lemonade," he called to a friend between games in one match. "And for God's sake, put some whiskey in it too," he added in a stage whisper, smiling broadly. Herbert Tilden was the sort of fellow a kid brother adores.

From an early age, Junior seems to have regretted the fact that he himself had no one to be an older brother or a father to. In his fiction, which is so revealing of the true man, and which Tilden obviously used as an avenue of self-disclosure, the relationships that dominate are older brother/younger brother, older friend/younger friend (particularly with the Dick Thomas character), and father/son. They form the core of the close, genuine human feelings he writes of, whereas husbands and wives and good friends of the same sex and age have only the most stilted, contrived relationships.

The idealized young male friends, who appear in a number of his short stories, are Frank Russell "and his chum and room-mate" Ray Mitchell; they play together on the

Yale varsity. In *Glory's Net*, his novel, much of the plot revolves around a brother theme, in which Tilden seems to have alternately cast himself as the younger brother he was and as the older one he would have liked to be. (The younger brother's name is Billy, the only time Tilden borrowed his own name for a major character.)

His stories where the drama focuses on a father/son relationship are all poignant, and all forced too. In "On a Line with the Net," Dave Morton is out there playing for his dad, who lost an arm at Château-Thierry. "The Pinch-Quitter" stars Edward Morris Jr., son of former champion Edward Morris Sr., who now lies dying after an automobile accident. "The Drive from the Sideline" is especially autobiographical, since it concerns a tennis player whose first love is music, but it is also a mystic story of sorts inasmuch as the player wins at tennis only after he has been hypnotized by his father.

Tilden succeeded in one quest in his life in that he became famous and was the child who brought honor to his beloved mother, a woman who had suffered so much agony because of her other children—children Big Bill replaced. He paid off a debt. But he could never find the son who could both love him and succeed him as champion, as he had loved Herbert and eventually surpassed him as a player. He searched unsuccessfully all his life for that son figure, and because he never found him, Tilden died a failed man in that one sense.

From the earliest, June played the older brother role. One of his first friends was a contemporary, Curtis Coggins, who lived just down McKean. Tilden loved to go around to his house and play, largely because Mrs. Coggins would then gather the two boys about her and read them adventure tales. *The Last of the Mohicans* was June's favorite. Thereafter, however, his friends were all younger, and he made them his coterie. "June even established his own nobility," Frank Deacon, a younger neighbor, recalls. "He was the king, of course. Jo Dodge was the queen. I believe I was a marquis, and Roy Coffin was a duke. It went all the way down to Judith Jennings, who was the court cat."

James Mapes Dodge, the inventor of the link belt, owned a mansion across the street from Overleigh, with a skating pond and a small house beside it where the children could warm themselves. Junior, always in a distinctive tassel cap, spent many winter hours on the Dodge pond, often playing hockey (with girls used as goalies, since their bloomers served well for stopping pucks). Then afterwards Junior would assemble all his younger friends in someone's house, where they would sit around a fire and drink hot chocolate. After a while, Junior would draw the curtains and begin to entertain with poetry and ghost stories. Previewing his professional acting summit, Dracula seems to have been his best performance, although he perhaps exhibited greater dramatic leeway when portraying several of the more nefarious villains from Sherlock Holmes. In the poetry section "The Wreck of the Hesperus," "The Highwayman" and the works of Robert Service were featured. June's recitals were so effective for the younger children that it seems that on a few occasions he was invited to appear at birthday parties, in the same capacity as a magician or a Punch-and-Judy show. "Oh, June could scare hell out of us." Frank Deacon laughs, still remembering those frightening evenings when he had to cut back home through the shadowy Cricket Club grounds after listening to a session of June Tilden's best ghost stories.

Junior gave his younger friends presents and attended their dancing classes at the club. He was a good dancer himself and always learned the newest dance before anyone else (the half 'n' half seems to have been his prize). So, he would go over to the ballroom and sit in the balcony, watching Mrs. Brooks conduct Mrs. Brooks's Dancing Classes. Eventually she noticed the thin older boy, and it became her custom to invite him to come down and blow the whistle for the Paul Jones, which always climaxed the day's dancing activity.

He also helped the younger children with their tennis games. "He was the kindest person," Josephine Reeves Walton says. "June taught everybody in the neighborhood." Tilden did play at a number of sports—skating, touch football, some soccer, and a local hybrid of cricket called tip 'n' go—but he never considered these games anything but pastimes. Tennis was the only sport he ever took seriously, and increasingly, as he got older, it grew more important to him. Music was always his overriding passion —even as champion he declared, "If I had to give up tennis or music, I would give up tennis"—but he could only express himself in tennis. Music was but an appreciation, no matter how deep, not an involvement.

Tilden's first meeting with Mary Garden occurred when she came to Philadelphia to sing the opera *Louise.* No doubt through his father's connections, Junior wangled an invitation backstage to meet her and was ushered to her dressing room for a perfunctory hello. He startled her by saying, "I don't think you sing, Miss Garden. I think you, well, you seem to vocalize thought."

"Good God!" Miss Garden cried. "Here's the first person I've found in Philadelphia who seems to understand me. Sit down, boy." And, according to Tilden's account, she held the curtain for several minutes while she talked music with him.

Certainly music was forever a refuge for him. His brother gave Tilden tennis, but music was his mother's signature. So long as he had music, he had something of her. When he was growing up, his gramophone record collection (which eventually numbered three thousand) was his proudest childhood possession. Only a few could intrude upon this corner of his life. Alice Tatnall Franklin, four years younger and musically inclined, was one who qualified. June would invite her to his room, where they could listen to the records, or he would go round to her house to hear her play the piano for him. Many Saturdays he and Alice would take the Chestnut Hill local from the Queen Lane station and go downtown and haunt music stores. In between, they would indulge his sweet tooth too. First they would stop by Whitman's for a chocolate continental with marshmallow topping, and then, after listening to music and buying records, they would be sure to have a sundae for the road before getting on the train and heading back to that unlikely world of his in Germantown.

Sometime in the afternoon, likely as not, he would go upstairs to the music parlor and listen to his mother play the piano for him.

CHAPTER FOURTEEN

"Everything that made life worthwhile lost favor"

THE strange insular childhood of Junior Tilden began to unravel in 1908 when he was fifteen and his mother contracted Bright's disease. Limited to a wheelchair, she was never much of a factor in the house again. The only people still alive to remember her now were young children then, and they recall only the same single sad tableau: Mrs. Tilden sitting grimly in her wheelchair on the terrace in front of Overleigh, attended by a nurse. Linie's husband, with heavy new investments in the Pennsylvania coal fields and the rising likelihood of nomination to the Philadelphia mayoralty, had begun to devote even more of his time to his outside interests. Herbert was finishing up at Penn, about ready to join his father at work and to bring a bride home to Overleigh. So Junior was finally sent to school, Germantown Academy, and for everyone else's convenience he was also farmed out of his own house. He was bivouacked a few blocks away at 519 Hansberry Avenue, just the other side of the Germantown Cricket Club, where he was given the third floor room in the small house owned by his mother's maiden sister, Mary Elizabeth Hey—always Auntie to June. She lived with her niece, his cousin, Selena (that is how her name was spelled) Hey. She had taken the surname of Hey because she had been raised by Auntie, although in fact Selena was the daughter of another sister's failed marriage to a ne'er-do-well Civil War hero.

The reason that Tilden always called Selena Twin was that they shared the same February 10 birthdate, although she was fifteen or so years older. But she adored this small fondness; for one thing, Twin was a considerable improvement upon Slimy, which is what the neighborhood kids had twisted Selena into. Twin was hefty and not attractive, any more so than the older lady she lived with. Nor was Twin especially robust, having lost out on a chance to go to Bryn Mawr because of ill health, so it was a sheer delight for her to suddenly have this lively young man, who took three stairs at a bound, dropping into her life. If it were possible, Twin and Auntie were soon spoiling Junior even more than his mother ever had. In 1930, as a measure of his affection, it was to the two ladies, to their "love and belief in me," that he dedicated his first and only novel.

Their Billy was to keep his bedroom in that house for thirty-three years, more than half his life, until they were gone and he finally sold the property in 1941. There, with the two maiden ladies, is where Big Bill Tilden lived more than any single place in the world. After dining with kings and movie stars, while he ruled the world of tennis, he would come back to 519 Hansberry, place his latest trophies beside the rubber plant with the porcelain birds balanced on the branches and entertain Auntie and Twin with his tales of glory while they served him his every whim and a succession of steak dinners, with ice cream.

Back in 1908, however, when Junior was first sent to live with the Misses Hey, he still spent a great deal of time at Overleigh. Every evening he would cut through the club, whistling loudly, "with great attempts at pianissimos and fortissimos," according to Alice Tatnall Franklin, coming bravely home to be with his sick mother. In the mornings, while the other wealthy boys in the neighborhood trundled off to Germantown Academy (or, for the girls, Germantown Friends across the street), the Tilden chauffeur would crank up the fancy Locomobile and come over to Hansberry from Overleigh to pick up Master Junior and drive him to school. Since the Locomobile was an expensive touring car, with a canvas top and side curtains, the chauffeur would leave it in the garage and, instead, take the Lozier on the days with bad weather. Whatever the car, Junior would sit up front with the chauffeur and they would pick up his younger schoolmates along the way and jam them into the back seat.

June seems to have had no major problems adjusting to a real school. Although for some reason he chose not to participate in dramatics, he was a cheerleader and senior class poet. Buddy Mann played number one on the tennis team when Tilden was a junior, but June was captain and star in the spring of 1910, when he graduated and drew this doggerel from the yearbook:

> I am thin around the waistband,
> And padded in my jacket,
> But proud I stand when my right hand
> Grips firm my tennis racket.

His favorite expression: "curses." His favorite place: with girls who are easily entertained. His ambition: to be a clown. Characteristic: thinness. At seventeen he was, like most thin, long-legged men, a late physical developer; he stood but five feet ten, more than three inches short of his full height, and he weighed only 128 pounds. No one who knew Junior as a boy, however, remembers him as being exceptionally skinny; thin, yes, but he was so graceful that he never appeared gawky.

The one unfortunate physical failing that is recalled was hygiene: bad breath and body odor alike. A woven blue mackinaw with stripes across the waist, a favorite outfit, came literally to stink of perspiration. How his mother, the health addict, ignored or accepted these gaping sanitary wounds is impossible to fathom, although the best of contradictory evidence suggests that he was only periodically neglectful of hygienic care—especially for some time as a teenager and then again in the pathetic last years. While he was never a neat man, when he was at the peak of his fame, on display and proud to be, he was nearly fastidious in tending to his personal appearance.

Yet even to give Junior the best on this count, he was not at all popular among his contemporaries, even considered somewhat peculiar for always seeking out the company of younger boys. Josephine Reeves Walton says that when she played mixed doubles once with Junior in a vacation tournament, she received an anonymous letter advising her not to be upset that everyone would be rooting against their team, for it was only Junior Tilden they all hated. Linie Tilden confided to friends that she worried about her boy.

His loneliness was heightened when he entered the University of Pennsylvania in the fall of 1910. There were no younger boys to pal around with there, and, besides, he had matriculated at the Wharton School of Business only to please his father. He had no interest whatsoever in commerce and was a desultory scholar who seldom studied. Joe Morgan, another younger Germantown neighbor, recalls that whenever he saw Junior at the Queen Lane station, coming or going from the Penn campus, the only books he carried were novels. He made no mark in college. Only a handful from his class ("Give 'em hell, lick 'em clean, Pennsylvania 'fifteen!") even knew that Junior Tilden existed, and some found it quite difficult to believe that such a person had been in their class when suddenly he surfaced as a celebrated world champion a few years later.

And then, in the spring of his freshman year, his life came completely apart at the seams when his mother suffered a stroke and suddenly lay near death. At the end, May 2, 1911, he sat outside her door at Overleigh all through the night, crying uncontrollably—by his own account "utterly in shock." Her dying so shattered his soul that he grew nervous, even physically jittery, shaking. The poor boy was floundering badly. Not only had he lost the anchor of his sacred mother, but he was trapped in a school discipline he could not stand; he was forced to live away from his own house; he understood, surely, by now, that he was a homosexual; he was nearly friendless and literally repelled some people; he was ravaged by nervousness; despondent, confused, lost. The shaking got so bad that St. Vitus's dance was suspected for a time, and at last his father had him withdraw from Penn for a year.

He retreated back to Germantown and his music, and then began to discover himself again at Germantown Academy, where he could coach the little boys he felt comfortable with and fill in as a cheerleader every now and then. On his twenty-first birthday, February 10, 1914, Mr. Tilden gave his son what he wanted most for his present: a dance. Certainly, it was curious for a young man to have, in effect, a debutante coming-out party, but that is what Junior asked his father for, and he invited all his young friends and delighted in the happy evening at the Germantown Cricket Club. He began to make plans to go back to Penn and finish up.

But he was never to graduate. Early in the summer of 1915 William T. Tilden Sr. fell ill with kidney trouble. Sometime after the death of his wife he had assumed residence at the Union League, all but giving over Overleigh to Herbert and his new family. Mr. Tilden was brought back to his house in the midst of a heat wave in July, but debilitated by the climate, his illness compounded by uremic poisoning, he died at eight o'clock in the morning of July 29, with his two sons at his bedside. He was sixty years and one hundred and forty-three days old; his son and namesake was to live sixty years and one hundred and seventeen days. William T. Tilden Sr. was eulogized by the local press as "one of the best-known citizens in Philadelphia," and it was noted that at the Union League "a pall seemed to be cast over the club, members and employees alike speaking in subdued tones." Two days later he was laid to rest next to his wife and mother and his three babies in the plot he had bought thirty years before at Ivy Hill.

Herbert, his father's friend and associate, was as staggered by this death as Junior had been by his mother's. He passed an agonizing summer, drifting in despair, drinking somewhat more. Like his father, Herbert was a hard drinker, but he was by no means the alcoholic that Big Bill melodramatically sometimes later portrayed him; but then, this summer left an impression upon Junior. Herbert's two small children, Miriam and William III, were themselves too young to remember the times, but Miriam has reconstructed what her father was like that summer after his father died. "He was weak, at sea, I'm afraid," she says. "He felt that he couldn't make the contribution that his father did."

Late in the summer the young family at least got away to the seashore, to Cape May, then a very fashionable resort at the southern tip of New Jersey. Herbert caught a little cold swimming one day. It turned into pneumonia. His resistance was low. He just went. From being perfectly fine on a Friday, he was dead the next Wednesday, September 22, 1915. At least they had gotten him back to Overleigh. He was only twenty-nine when Junior watched him die in his bed at seven that morning.

On Friday Junior was there at Ivy Hill when his brother was lowered into his grave at the foot of his father's, where the soil was still turned from that death less than two months previous. "The second bereavement, striking with such suddenness, has aroused profound sympathy for the family," the *Inquirer* wrote. Junior Tilden, twenty-two years old, was the family.

He fell deeper into grief. "Everything that made life worthwhile lost favor," he said later. Alice Tatnall Franklin can recall seeing him some time after his father's death in a black tie; but now, for Herbert, he put on black shirts, which he wore for months, and then white shirts with black-lined mourning sleeves. If he went back to Penn for his senior year (it is not clear), he stayed but a short time, leaving well short of graduation. Aimless, in self-pity, he seems for some time to have done nothing more substantial than to sit about his room at Auntie's and listen to his records.

Apparently Selena Hey dared advise her younger cousin but twice in her life, and this was the first occasion. Twin was a woman cheated. Her health had robbed her of a chance at college, and her aunt had manipulated her away from any possible marriage. What suitors there had been ten-fifteen years ago, Auntie had always found terribly lacking, and Twin, unsure of herself, bent to that advice and let them get away. Now there weren't any callers to choose from. She was left to live out her life as a companion to a fussy old woman in residential Philadelphia. Even when they got away—on a cruise to the Continent, a pilgrimage to Yorkshire, wherever—Twin's presence was defined not by where she was but what Auntie was up to. Whenever Twin gave the slightest hint of striking out on her own, she was reminded how grateful she should be that Auntie had taken her in; besides, even the thought that

Twin might leave her would bring on "the vapors." Twin wasn't going anywhere, and what she told Junior was that he was falling into that same trap. With Overleigh sold now (to a bishop), 519 Hansberry was his only home, and unless he looked beyond it he was going to end up, as she had, living out all his good days as a companion to an old lady. She told him this.

Perhaps he would have overcome the grief and inertia himself in due time. Perhaps he needed Twin to prod him. Whatever, he took her advice, and sometime early in 1916 he set out on his mission. Junior gave his life over to tennis. He was then ranked seventieth in the country, and he lost that summer in straight sets in the first round at Forest Hills. Only four years later Big Bill Tilden was champion of the world, the greatest of all time.

What inspired him to tennis at this point in his life is almost as difficult to understand as how he became so good so fast. The best answer to the latter is that he was a natural athlete composed of valuable raw material that only needed mining. The answer to the former is a good bit more elusive because so many more subtle things were involved. On the most elementary level, he was simply at loose ends. He had no family, and by then he knew he had no prospect of gaining one. "He felt he was short-changed," says his nephew. He did have the reporter's job with the *Evening Ledger*, which he enjoyed well enough without having it intrude too much upon the rest of his life. Besides, he was well fixed with his father's inheritance. When he became champion, the conventional hearsay was that he was a downright *heir*, filthy rich. In fact, and despite Junior's luxurious upbringing, William T. Tilden Sr. suffered some heavy losses in his coal investments—perhaps as much as half a million dollars—in the last few years of his life, and the relatively small size of his will was the subject of some dandy gossip at Germantown Cricket and the Union League. Junior was left about $60,000, certainly a substantial sum, especially if he had tended to it and invested it sagely, but it was a very finite figure, and the usual estimates of his heady resources were considerably exaggerated.

But not to quibble: at the age of twenty-three he not only had a job but something to fall back on, and doting relatives to take care of him. Having learned how to devote herself to one person, Twin found it natural enough to indulge another as well. A friendly black retainer named Dickinson Walker looked after 519 Hansberry, a tidy red-brick end house with green shutters, and Twin taught him to cater to Master Junior's every whim. Almost every night: steak, corn on the cob, some peppers stuffed with rice that Tilden could scoop the rice out of, corn muffins, ice cream of course. Tilden didn't have any everyday details to tend to, like other people. He had nobody to worry about but himself, and he had a great deal of time on his hands. And from somewhere deep in him there surfaced too this incredible drive, this zeal, this obsession.

"He suddenly was compelled to want to be supreme in the game of lawn tennis," says Carl Fischer, who was one of the few people close to Tilden during this crucial stage in his life. "But still I'm sure that Tilden had no concern for anything like the world championship as such. It was the obvious end product, but not the intentional one. Make no mistake, though, that but for this incredible determination, you never would have even heard of Big Bill Tilden. Nobody ever worked so hard at anything as he did at tennis."

And so he turned to tennis, to this game, with a swelling passion, but not only to master it—and herein truly lies his supremacy—but to contribute to it as well. Years later he wrote with disdain about the tennis he knew as a child: "They played with an air of elegance—a peculiar courtly grace that seemed to rob the game of its thrills. . . . There was a sort of inhumanity about it [and] it annoyed me. . . . I believed the game deserved something more vital and fundamental." He sensed a place where he could make a donation in his mother's name.

Chapter Fifteen

"He was starting to walk like a real fruit"

IT was another two decades before Twin again dared to give her cousin advice. By now Auntie had died, and although she had never lived in Yorkshire, Twin moved there, to the land of her forefathers, to finish out her days. Billy made the three-hour trip up from London one time to see her when he was touring as a professional late in the 1930s. It had been some time since last they had been together, and so the changes in Tilden were immediately apparent to her. She fumbled with her tea and sandwiches for a while until finally she got up the nerve to tell him: his homosexuality was becoming more overt, and he must be more guarded.

Furious, Tilden shot to his feet, glared at Twin, and stormed out of the house, never to say another word to her for as long as they lived.

But on his own terms he was at last beginning to peer into a few corners for some understanding of his homosexuality. At the least he was preparing rationalizations, on a tortured journey to rationale. "Women are a lot of bitches," he told Gloria Butler, a young friend he had known for several years, since he played in her father's tournament on the French Riviera. "When someone is a genius, when they have a great task in life, they cannot afford to be depleted by a woman. Women wear down a man. They have no right to make a man of genius share their petty demands."

On another occasion, late in the 1930s, riding on a train from Southampton into London with a young pro, Tilden suddenly felt compelled to bring up the subject of his homosexuality and then, almost stridently, to deliver a message. "Well," Tilden began pleasantly to the younger player, "I suppose you have a date in the city tonight."

"Why, yes, as a matter of fact, I do, Bill."

"Well, I have a date too," Tilden went on, "although, of course, things are a little different with me. Dickie boy has just come over from the States to see me."

"Oh yes," said the younger player, embarrassed.

"Those of us who have my way of thinking, well, we look upon ourselves as the chosen few," Tilden said. "I think it's my responsibility to convert young boys. We are the exceptional. God has smiled upon us."

That was a rare, almost inexplicable revelation. Most often, though, he studiously avoided the subject in tennis company, except perhaps with the French players, who took homosexuality more in stride. Cochet can even remember times when Tilden would poke fun at himself, admitting that he too often concentrated on coaching the cutest players instead of the best ones. "Of course we knew about it all," Cochet says. "He was always having difficulties with the police for soliciting little boys. But Americans are so sensitive about questions of morality. It was his business, and it didn't interfere with his tennis."

Tilden was so uptight about the human body that he never seems to have gone nude in the locker room, choreographing his showers to keep himself turned away from spying eyes. Keeping himself covered seems to have been a lifelong exercise too. Curtis Coggins, one of his earliest friends, was so impressed by this peculiarity, even as a young child, that he mentioned it to his family. Many players cite it first in recalling Tilden. Roy Coffin not only shared many locker rooms with him, but often even the same bed when they made their tennis-and-bridge forays South, and Tilden never revealed himself to him. William T. Tilden III maintains that the issue is overstated, that his uncle's undue modesty was nothing but evidence of his harsh puritanical beliefs, but a Philadelphia psychiatrist familiar with the case says that Tilden's "modesty" was much more than that—a concern not uncommon among certain types of homosexuals who fear they will "tempt" others.

In any event, whatever the reasons for his modesty, it was so pronounced that people began to assume that he must be hiding something. When he was arrested for a sex crime, he was carefully examined in the genital area and found to be quite normal in every respect, although it was noted that his penis was "rather small in comparison with his stature." Perhaps he was himself in agreement with this judgment and embarrassed by it, and therefore all the more anxious to keep himself covered. Unfortunately, for all his efforts at concealing his privates, all he did was heighten speculation. It was widely rumored that he owned but one testicle, a tale that gained such currency that it is still sometimes cited casually as established fact.

In Philadelphia a much more elaborate story began to circulate. This account goes as follows: At age fourteen, playing follow-the-leader at a neighborhood house that was under construction, Junior slipped as he tried to jump over a pile of rocks and lumber, and in the fall ripped off part of his scrotum and half his penis. The boys ran to the Tilden house and notified the coachman, who drove over, picked up the poor boy from a pool of blood and rushed him to Germantown Hospital, where he was operated on by a young resident, William Swartley, who was, of course, the doctor who removed Tilden's finger fifteen years later. Many people in Philadelphia believed Big Bill to be a sexual amputee.

The story was so rich in detail that it encouraged belief. Besides, for a generation that had so little comprehension of homosexuality, it explained away Tilden's aberration in strictly physical terms. But there is no evidence to support any part of the story. He may have taken a fall and hurt himself in some way, he may have gone to the hospital— but he never makes any mention of such an accident, and the hospital records have long since been destroyed. For as much as Tilden was a homosexual, it was because he chose to be one, not because he had to.

Increasingly as he grew older, as his game diminished, as he could no longer, in effect, satisfy himself on the courts, he turned to teenage boys for sex.* By his own admission and from all evidence, however, it is clear that Tilden was never an intensely sexual person. The fact that his mother had instilled such a fear in him about venereal disease no doubt heavily influenced his attitude toward sex with women, but it also appears to have made him back off from intimacies with his own sex. Tilden just never came to grips with *bodies*. Not only did he always try to conceal his own, but he was something of a voyeur with others. Alphonso Smith recalls the time when he was attending the University of Virginia and Tilden came to town touring as Dracula. An exhibition match was arranged, and although it was quite inconvenient for Smith, Tilden virtually demanded that he come to his hotel room to change into his tennis whites. When he undressed, Smith remembers that Tilden kept sneaking foolish peeks at him, rather like a little boy. Finally, there is also the matter of hygiene. In his more depressed periods, especially near the end of his life,

* In modern-day gay parlance such a homosexual is disparaged as a "chicken queen" or a "chicken hawk."

Tilden would neglect his body altogether, as if transferring his shame of self to his physical presence.

By his own account to a court psychiatrist, Tilden had two heterosexual encounters. He said he first had some sex play with a young girl about his age in Germantown when he was sixteen or so. The extent of the intimacies is unclear —perhaps just some petting—but there was no intercourse. Then, several years later, when he was serving in the army at Pittsburgh, around age twenty-five, he lost his virginity —his first and last complete heterosexual experience.

Years later, in the chambers of Judge A. A. Scott, who was presiding at his trial in Los Angeles, Tilden recalled that that one lone full encounter with a woman was "awful." Judge Scott inquired point-blank then if he had actually had intercourse.

"Yes, your honor," Tilden replied, "and it was so repulsive to me that I puked all over."

By contrast, Tilden said that he had his first homosexual encounter around the age of ten, participating in mutual fondling with another boy from the neighborhood. The two met regularly for the next five or six years, eventually having ejaculations in each other's presence. Tilden enjoyed the same kind of relationship with a fellow student at Penn, but that seems to have been the last partner he ever had of the same age. And, just as he always participated in sex with boys, so too was the extent of his sex immature. His usual pattern was to fondle the young partner, and then masturbate himself afterwards, in private.

When Tilden played the French championships in 1927, some European journalists plotted to get the goods on him. At the hotel where they all were staying, there was a bell-hop who was a very small man, nearly a midget, and although he was actually about thirty, he looked hardly fifteen and was blond and chubby, just the type Big Bill liked. Particularly as he got on in life, just being next to "round-bottomed little boys" would get him all fidgety and handsy. Anyway, the newspapermen chipped in a few francs apiece and got the little bellhop to go up to Tilden's room and make a pass at him. To their surprise, he was back with his report in just a few minutes. He told them that despite his best efforts at leading Tilden on, all he would do was fondle the little fellow's genitals. He would not open his own fly, nor did he appear to get an erection.

To the very end, this seems to have been the full extent of his sexual participation. "Anything more would obviously have been too great an invasion of a body—his or whoever he was with," says one psychiatrist. When he was arrested, the court psychiatrist asked Tilden if he had ever engaged in such activities as fellatio or pederasty, eliciting the most livid negative response. In fact, Tilden considered such practices as "perverted," and for that matter he tiptoed all around the very word *homosexual;* nobody can ever recall his using it. His definitive statement on the subject appears in his autobiography, *My Story,* which was written after his first arrest:

> . . . throughout all history there has been a record of occasional relationships somewhat away from the normal.
>
> One knows that this condition exists, that it is more or less prevalent and always will be. History further demonstrates that in frequent instances, creative, useful and even great human beings have known such relationships. . . .
>
> The condition may or may not call for some action in individual cases, but if it does, it calls more for psychiatric than legal or punitive measures. The list of celebrated people in this age and previous ones who have deviated from the norm makes it obvious that this is not a sign of "degeneracy" in the usual sense.

It is, if anything, an illness; in most cases a psychological illness. . . . Greater tolerance and wider education on the part of the general public concerning this form of sex relationship is one of the crying needs of our times, if only for the support which thereby would result for serious studies of the problem.

This was written, of course, after he was arrested and the cat was out of the bag. Beforehand he had made every effort to front as a straight. On those occasions when adult homosexuals tried to approach him, he was brief and rude. Once when a very flagrant queen actually managed to get into the locker room and coyly introduce himself, Big Bill felt so threatened or ashamed that he flew into a regular fit and nearly threw the interloper out bodily. Nothing upset him so as when he caught George Lott mimicking his swish, and when he saw that, he would rage out of control and threaten to call off the tour.

For the public, he invented love affairs that always, by his telling, fell just short of marriage—to actresses like Peggy Wood and Marjorie Daw, for example. Of course, he did like these women, and he got along beautifully with many who shared his artistic interests. Helen Jacobs and Molla Mallory were probably his favorites among the players. Gloria Butler says, "Bill was attracted to . . . well, let's say he *appreciated* two types of women. One was the very sweet girl. There was a German player, Celia Aussem, and he just loved to be around her, play mixed doubles with her. You could almost see, when he was with this type, that he was thinking, If I were different than what I am, this is the kind of woman I would want. But then he liked the complete opposite too, the real tough bitch, because he could demean them and he didn't have to put on airs. He really liked Tallulah, for instance. He'd say *she'd sleep with a swan.*"

Short of that, when she was sleeping with Frank Hunter, Bea Lillie and some other of Tallulah's friends chased Tilden, flirted with him, but nobody ever got to first base. "I thought he was sexless," Hunter says. Technically, Tilden shows a lot of characteristics of the schizoid personality, of which a lack of sex drive is a prime one.

In his fiction, women (if they appear at all) are treated harshly and/or superficially. "Mixed Troubles" is, for example, strictly male chauvinist. Marion takes back the ring and they share "one of those long, lingering embraces that end all movies" after Jack tells her flat-out to stay off to the side of the court and let him hit all the shots—which he does, all for winners. "Love Means Nothing," a serial he wrote for *Racquet Magazine*, featured the beautiful Helen Pendleton, but the thrust of the story was not her but her boy friend's drinking problem. Hooray: love conquers all and he goes on the wagon! Even mothers get short shrift, and the only time one is featured is in a story entitled "The Amateur," where the matter of the mother-son relationship is far subordinate to Tilden's paean for amateurism.

In *Glory's Net*, his novel, he at last faces off a Good Woman vs. a Bad Woman. Mary Jones is as All-American as her name, from the Midwest, where she met the hero, David Cooper, at a church picnic. She dresses rather modestly (not to say drably), cannot abide the foreign taste of caviar, leaves the Folies Bergère in a protest against nudity and, best of all, hates the USLTA and liquor. Whatta gal! Her rival is Arlene Hocker, a beautiful, conniving socialite who is not only the daughter of a USLTA official but also "the recognized leader of the young wealthy country club set of Westchester County." It is Arlene who teaches David to smoke and drink, and when she kisses him in a speedboat, she goes so far (Tilden makes a great to-do about this) as to actually put her arms around his neck. Your complete scarlet woman: "She loved

David. There was no use trying to fool herself. Loved him passionately, overwhelmingly [and she felt that] all Mary did was to attempt to drag David down to her middle-class level."

But if there was one passage Tilden wrote that best sums up his prevailing attitude about women and what they were up to, it is these lines from a story entitled "The Drive from the Sideline." It is about a troubled tennis champion named Blake. Okay, what was the matter with Blake? Tilden explained: "The truth was that Blake had fallen in love and married a bare-back rider in a traveling circus. The girl was young, beautiful, unscrupulous and clever."

So there you are.

Tilden's childhood reads like a textbook of circumstances liable to produce a homosexual male: the neglectful father who was devoted to another brother; the overprotective mother, warning her baby about the dirt and disease of sex. Irving Bieber's classic study of homosexuals found that this type of mother abounded among homosexual-to-be children; the absent or disinterested father appears in 87 per cent of the cases. Mrs. Tilden's overwrought fancies about Junior's supposed illnesses were another common sign, and also it is often the case among incipient homosexuals for them to shy away from children of their own age and form their own coterie of younger children. (That Mrs. Tilden kept Junior from going to school would, naturally, have influenced him even more.)

Bieber wrote, "Boys [who are to become homosexuals] may isolate themselves from their playmates because of felt inadequacy and a sense of deep shame about their over-closeness to the mothers, which includes unconscious guilt about incestuous feelings. The fear of anticipated humiliation drives many such boys from contact with peers." Incipient young homosexuals avoid sports not so much because of a lack of physical prowess but for psychological reasons. Homosexuals appear to be especially anxious about playing baseball; the hard-thrown pitch poses a castration threat, and failure with the bat can mean humiliation, a fear of impotence.

Had Tilden had any aptitude for music, he surely would have drifted into that. As it was, it took a wild series of coincidences to get him started in tennis: the influence of his beloved brother, Herbert; the accessibility of the Germantown Cricket Club courts; the fact of Junior's own natural ability. Beyond that, to keep him going, he required his monumental drive and his intrinsic love of the game, plus a very thick skin indeed. How incredibly difficult it must have been for him: a lifetime in the midst of the most complete, secure heterosexual community. There are virtually no homosexuals in big-time male sports. And, more than in the whole society athletes tend to be antipathetic to homosexuality, seeming both to despise it and fear it alike, and with a vengeance that must have placed Tilden on trial with himself every day of his life.

The fact that homosexuals would be so uncomfortable in athletics is one reason why so few stay in sports. And then, since it appears to be only a small percentage of homosexuals who compete seriously in the first place, we should not be surprised that only a handful ever reach the top. Tennis, alone among the major sports, did suffer the reputation of being a "fairy game." This image originally devolved simply because *lawn* tennis was an upper-class diversion, ladies and gentlemen—Mister Tilden—all dressed in pristine white, playing together and saying such things as "love" and "let." The famous line "Tennis anyone?" which was first uttered on Broadway by, of all people, Humphrey Bogart, was soon seldom ever spoken except in a swish way. The whispers about Big Bill, the sport's greatest player, further damaged the game's repute.

Then Gottfried von Cramm, Tilden's good friend, another champion, was charged by the Nazis with crimes of immorality; politically motivated or not, the charges hung on to tennis more than on to von Cramm. Finally Tilden was arrested, convicted. Tennis was saddled with an image it is only now finally getting over.

In point of fact, however, tennis was never a haven for homosexuals, either in Tilden's time or now (and there even appear to be fewer lesbians in women's tennis than in such sports as golf and track). Since World War II, only one male player, and he an obscure South American journeyman, has ever been suspected among the world-class players of being homosexual. What's more, nobody was really sure about him. Granted, the odd player can get by in any sport living in the closet, but in athletics, in a macho environment, where the players are rooming with one another, running around with one another (often after women), any homosexual would be hard put to conceal his true status for long.

Two major league athletes, Ed Bouchee in baseball and Lance Rentzel in football, have been arrested in recent years for exposing themselves to children; both, significantly, were married, and to all appearances to their teammates they were carrying on normal heterosexual lives. Besides Bouchee, only a couple of other major league baseball players (literally out of thousands) have been considered possible gays. One National Football League first-round draft choice of a few seasons ago was known as a homosexual when he was chosen; he had a hard time being accepted and also playing very well, and was soon out of the game. Hockey, the most macho game of them all, seems devoid of homosexuals. In basketball a sad old drunken college coach was marked with the reputation, but virtually no one else. In boxing a milliner named Emile Griffith, a fidgety bachelor, flew into a rage at a weigh-in in 1962 when his opponent, the welterweight champ Benny Paret, taunted him in colloquial Spanish, raising doubts as to Griffith's masculinity. That night, on the ropes, while the referee watched frozen in horror, Griffith pummeled his tormentor to death.

In those sports where there is some evidence of substantial gay participation, it is invariably a case where it is traditional for the competitors to pick up the sport on their own, after childhood: body-building, for example (although there may be more homosexuals in the audience than in the ranks). When the Roller Derby was thriving a few years ago, many of the men (as well as the women) were homosexual; significantly, Roller Derby is not a sport children play, but one that adults turn to.

Professional football players do sometimes joke uneasily about how things seem to get unnecessarily grabby in the big pileups, and Dave Meggyesy even touched on this in his book attacking pro football. Dave Kopay, who played as an NFL substitute for several years, revealed his homosexuality in 1975, after his football career ended, estimating there were a score or more closet gays in the NFL, including three starting quarterbacks. But so far, nobody has taken such buckshot claims very seriously. John Graves, a professor of philosophy at MIT, who is also an active Gay Liberationist, writes, "Many athletes are highly sexual, but the homosexuality among pro football players that Meggyesy hints at is probably more like prison sex or rough locker-room horseplay than anything involving real tenderness. . . . We must ask whether things would be easier for Tilden today. I fear that an openly gay athlete would still have many difficulties."

The fact is that Big Bill was alone then, as he would be alone now, competitively dominating a cruelly homophobic society that hated all he represented. He was forced to personally pretend to be something he was not, and

publicly he was necessarily a non-person, without substance. At a time when a word such as "pregnant" was not
permitted to appear in most newspapers, when mention of
a subject such as menstruation was utterly taboo, no
journalist would even touch on homosexuality. "You could
not even *talk* to him about himself, much less write about
him," Al Laney says, "because eventually you knew you
would come to that great barrier, and you could never get
beyond it."

Westbrook Pegler, writing in 1930, bemoaned this fact
and tried to let his readers in on the truth at the same time.
"He is as famous as Babe Ruth in his own country and just
as famous in other countries where nobody ever heard of
Babe Ruth [Pegler wrote], but the mysterious Mr. Tilden,
though he glories in his celebrity . . . nevertheless is a
stranger to the public and to the sports writers. . . . His
temperament has withstood description in a thousand
attempts and defied popular understanding, and the people
know him only as a figure, a celebrity, not as a person."
Then Pegler gratuitously added, "Mr. Tilden also fancies
himself as a patron of young boys who wish to play tennis."

Tilden's case was complicated by the fact that different
young boys filled different roles for him. He was hardly
some dirty old man, seducing children indiscriminately. On
the contrary, his greater love was paternal, not physical.
"He was truly fond of these boys," says Carl Fischer, who
had a two-generational experience with Tilden. First he
himself was Tilden's young friend, and then, years later, his
son filled that role (until he began to shave).

His ultimate, most fulfilling relationships were with the
boys who became his surrogate children, his "heirs," his
"successors." To them he was all (but lover): father,
teacher, inspiration, friend. John Graves, professor and Gay
Liberationist, writes, "Many of us (perhaps especially
those in the closet) feel a need to overcompensate for not

having a child. This may lead us, like Tilden, into a need to be unusually creative, or to be perfectionists, or to emphasize drama and showmanship to call attention to ourselves in this life. Certainly these responses may be very good. On the other hand, guilt about repressed homosexuality can lead to Puritanism or extremism in other areas. It is important to note that all of Tilden's protégés speak highly of him as a devoted teacher and coach. From Socrates to Peter Fischer, it has been recognized that gay people have special qualities of concern that can make them excellent teachers, and the Greek notion of pedophilia included a strong educational responsibility."

Indeed, the great conflict in this area of Tilden's life was that he wanted to be father and teacher alike to the same favorite (and cute) boys. Thus, to be his "son," a candidate had to be a potentially good tennis player on the one hand, but on the other he not only had to be physically attractive and bright, but still unformed and malleable. The great irony is that while Tilden spent his life searching for his heir, he found him in Los Angeles in the late 1930s, but he then let the boy get away from him and devoted himself to other less talented young players who would not dispute his philosophy. When he was fifteen years old, Jack Kramer would hook Montebello High School, way out in the suburbs, and take two buses and a streetcar just to come in to the Los Angeles Tennis Club so that he could play with the great Bill Tilden. But Kramer was a strong personality, and he would not permit himself to fall under Tilden's dominion. While the two always remained cordial, they drifted apart, Kramer to become undisputed champion of the world, heir to Tilden's title, Tilden to go off searching for an heir.

Because he selected his tennis successors primarily on the basis of their looks and personality, he was constantly being rejected when the boys grew up and themselves realized how impossible was the goal he had set for them. Perhaps the first was Frederick Staunton, now a retired newspaper publisher from Charleston, West Virginia, who met Tilden in 1918 when he was serving at Pittsburgh in the army. Tilden played tennis with the boy every day— "an exciting teacher and hard taskmaster," Staunton says— and soon began to speak grandiosely of tennis as the boy's life's work. Staunton said he had other things in mind for his life, and Tilden dropped him instantly.

Sandy Wiener, from Germantown, was Tilden's favorite protégé (at least until he took on Arthur Anderson later in his life), and it must have destroyed him when Wiener just gave up on tennis one day, much as he might toss away an old sweater. "I just wanted to play football in the fall," he says now, acknowledging that of course he had no idea at the time how this decision must have wounded Tilden. A few years later, when Junior Coen gave up big-time tennis, Tilden went around with the cockamamie story that Coen didn't want to play anymore because he and Frank Hunter were dropping out of the amateur game, and Coen would miss their friendship. In fact, if anything, it might have been the other way around: Tilden was surely more encouraged at last to turn pro because his little buddy had left him. Coen simply realized that he was too short and physically limited ever to excel at the very top, and he didn't want to spend more years of his youth shuttling around the circuit as a tennis bum. So, he enrolled at the University of Kansas and went about his future. Like the others, like Fischer and Wiener, Walter Thomas, Don Strachan, Frederick Staunton, Coen was immediately removed from Tilden's consciousness.

"He manufactured friendships," Coen says now. "He did that because everyone needs friends, and I guess I would question now whether Bill ever had a real friend. Life would revolve around the people he *made* his friends at that time. The sex thing was there, I know now, although I never once saw it. The key was friendship. He took these little kids and helped them in order to get their comradeship. Then he moved on, he discarded them like products, so to speak, when they could no longer play the role he required them to. They could no longer serve any useful purpose in his life."

Gloria Butler's position as a protégée is especially interesting because she was one of the few girls to win this honor. Tilden was just as demanding with her and the relationship was every bit as intense and loving, if diminished in the one sense that she could not be his heir. But their close association as father-daughter/pro-pupil finally blew apart in a way that Tilden's father-son connections could not: Miss Butler started dating a boy whom Tilden liked. "That made him furious in two ways," she says. "First, he convinced himself that I was leading the boy down the garden path, and in effect, you see, he was somewhat jealous. Plus second, I was flouting his authority by not devoting myself entirely to tennis. One night he waited up and really read us both out when the boy brought me home late. Finally, somewhat later, when Bill had cooled down, I got up the nerve to say, 'I must lead my own life.' And he replied, very formally, 'Okay, from now on it will be strictly a teacher-pupil relationship!' It always remained much more than that, but anyway, that was his reaction."

In his fiction the only genuine relationships among characters are between older men and younger boys. Friendships among contemporaries of the same sex are surface, and boy-girl romances read as if Tilden wrote them strictly off what he saw on the stage or in the movies, all stylistic and banal. Only once, however, in a story entitled "The Ghost of Wimbledon," does he drop any hint of homosexual thought, when he writes about Roy the father figure, and Bob Adams the younger player. He notes that when another older player hangs around Roy, Bob "had an occasional twinge of jealousy where Roy was concerned."

In *Glory's Net*, his most personal and extended document, he deals with a number of themes important to him, but in the end it is the matter of father-son, of succession, that trumps all the others. At the peak of his career, the hero, David Cooper, decides to give up his championship, to let his outlet be his younger brother, Billy. "He and Mary would live their life in Hobsonville, and he would have his tennis career in Billy." And more: *Glory's Net* was written at a time when Tilden was leaving the amateurs, departing the glory, when the need for a son began to swell within him. In the last paragraph of the book David returns to Mary, and she introduces him to the son he did not know existed; he was conceived in happier days but carried and born while David was off philandering.

The final line of the book is Mary saying, "Mr. David Cooper, I want you to know Mr. David Cooper Junior." How, above all, Mr. William Tilden must have wanted so to hear that for himself.

Of course, despite his foremost passion, to have a son, boys were always his sex objects as well. Nonetheless, he does not seem ever to have confused his sons with his lovers, and in the early days of adulthood, when he obtained satisfaction enough from his tennis, he found sex only rarely and discreetly. Mostly then he seems to have slummed: newspaperboys, bellboys, and so forth. Being so close to Tilden at this time, Hunter often dropped by his hotel rooms, even barged in, and never once chanced upon him alone with a young man. George Lott and John Hennessey devilishly spied on Tilden, precisely with the intent to catch him in the act, but without success.

But in the 1930s, as Tilden grew older and was removed from the spotlight, he became less selective and less cautious. He started to advertise more, by action and appearance. "As soon as he got me alone in the car, there was a great deal of knee slapping," says Allen Lewis, a baseball writer for the Philadelphia *Inquirer,* who twice had to resist Tilden's advances "when I was in my cute and chubby stage." And, as Twin had told him, appearances were no longer deceiving. "I mean, he was starting to walk like a real fruit," Lott says. Some instructional movie shorts he made drew snickers from audiences, and Don Budge recalls an afternoon at Wembley in London in 1939 when rain canceled play and Tilden took a cute little unsuspecting ball boy aside in the locker room. "He was looking at that kid the way a man would look at Elizabeth Taylor," Budge says. "It made us all sick."

Effectively, he was even losing control of himself on some occasions. There was, for example, a day in Los Angeles in 1943. Tilden was starring in a play named *The Fighting Littles,* which was opening that night. Featured with him was a pretty young girl he had befriended named Meredith Anderson. This was the second play they had done together, and they had become good friends. Indeed, Miss Anderson's father, who did not know Tilden was homosexual, had initially been concerned at the attentions the older man had paid his daughter. Tilden took Miss Anderson out to dinner, chastised her for smoking, and introduced her to bridge. "You can always tell them that Bill Tilden taught you bridge," he crowed. They had a lot of fun together.

The afternoon before the play's opening, the director called a read-through for the cast. In this exercise, the actors do not go through their paces but merely gather together to sharpen their cues. In the director's living room they all flopped about, Meredith Anderson sitting down on the rug in front of the young actor who played her love interest in the play. Personally there was no romance between the two young people, but they had become good friends, and casually, unconsciously, Meredith slid back closer to him, and soon, to be even more comfortable, she sat back between the boy's legs, so that she was resting up against his chest.

Tilden, in a turtleneck, sitting in a chair across the room, looked up and saw the two kids together. The young man was not, it seems, a homosexual, but Big Bill fancied him. Suddenly, without warning, he shot to his feet, and wide-eyed, screamed, "How could you do this to me?" At first no one in the room even knew whom he was talking to, much less what about. When there was no response, he dashed across the room, reached down and violently yanked Miss Anderson from the boy, literally flinging her away.

"I thought he was going to kill me," she says now. "I did. I was sure he was going to kill me. I swear, I never saw wrath like that in all my life, never before, never after."

The cast froze, fearful and confused. At last the director rushed in and, with some others, tried to calm Tilden down. He stood there in the middle of the room, breathing hard, eyes ablaze, glaring at the poor little girl, who lay there cowering on the floor.

Finally he regained some of his senses and returned to his seat, never apologizing or even acknowledging the tantrum. Uneasily, the cast went back to the read-through. But the incident was so charged, the man so frightening, that all good interplay among the cast had been destroyed, and the play foundered.

The word had long since begun to spread. Even before Tilden left Philadelphia behind and moved to Los Angeles for good in 1939, the doors were closing to him. In Los Angeles the greatest tennis player in the world found that he could not get a job teaching at a club.

CHAPTER SIXTEEN

"You know, Arthur's the only real son I ever had"

S HORTLY after Big Bill arrived in Hollywood, Na-
thanael West wrote of it in *The Day of the Locust:* "As
he walked along, [Tod] examined the evening crowd. A
great many of the people wore sports clothes which were
not really sports clothes. Their sweaters, knickers, slacks,
blue flannel jackets with brass buttons were fancy dress.
. . . Scattered among these masquerades were people of a
different type. Their clothing was sombre and badly cut
. . . their eyes filled with hatred. At this time Tod knew
very little about them except that they had come to California to die."

Tilden, of course, was the second type. Whether he had
lived but five more years, or the fifteen he actually did, or
twenty-five or thirty, he had gone to California to play out
the string. It was, in the first place, a conscious business
decision. There were few indoor courts to speak of in 1939,
and Tilden needed a place where he could be around tennis
all year. He was, in fact, to go on tour (with Budge) one
more time, but even for all his vanity, Tilden understood
that that extended phase of his life was coming to a close.
But quite apart from vocational reasons, California was
even more important as an escape: from the past, from the
East, from Philadelphia, increasingly even from his own

family. Besides, in California he could be among his idols, the actors. Twin went to find her legacy in Yorkshire; Big Bill went to Hollywood for much the same reasons. They both died searching, far from home.

He had made his first visits to the Coast early in the 1920s. Manuel Alonso, the Spanish player and good friend, accompanied him on one California visit in 1923 and was rather embarrassed by how Big Bill carried on with the picture people. "He would have given his life to be an actor," Alonso remembers, "and I guess it was the end of him out there." Tilden often even referred to his favorite stars with an article attached to the name—"the Bankhead," "la Pickford," that sort of thing—and from the first he cavorted with the grandest of stars. On that 1923 trip, for example, he played on Cecil B. De Mille's court, met Howard Hughes, and played tennis with about the two biggest names in town: Charlie Chaplin and Douglas Fairbanks.

Tilden first met the Little Tramp at Fairbanks' private hideaway on a film lot, and the two men struck it off right away. Tilden was to call Chaplin "one of the most amazing people in the world . . . one of the most vital people of my acquaintance . . . I have heard him talk sociology, economics, politics, music, drama and nonsense." And while the two men's egos clashed head-on, they shared enough common interests and respect to suffer one another.

Among other things, Chaplin was nuts about tennis. One time during the 1930s, when Tilden was touring with Vines, they went five sets (one going 23–21) in Los Angeles, in a match that lasted from nine-fifteen P.M. to twelve-forty-five A.M. As Tilden, beaten and exhausted, was picking up his rackets, Chaplin came down out of the stands and, dead serious, complained to him about how there was not going to be the doubles match, as advertised. Chaplin had a bad backhand himself, but he was a dogged little player, and even though he was already in his fifties at this time, he was far superior as a singles player than as a doubles player. No doubt, and not unlike Tilden, Chaplin was too dominating a personality to put up with a partner's restraints.

Blacklisted by tennis and country clubs, Tilden was required to depend upon the kindness of Hollywood stars for work. He did get one job as pro at a fading old luxury hotel, the Château Elysées, which was located up in the Hollywood Hills. The tennis court was laid over a garage and sloped somewhat; Tilden was given a room on the premises, and for breakfast he ate dry cereal that he kept in his bathroom. He also taught at David Selznick's court and at Joseph and Lenore Cotten's; he called them "real folks." One summer Clifton Webb, himself a well-known homosexual, rented Constance Bennett's estate and brought Tilden in to teach some of his favorite girls: the Bankhead, Katharine Hepburn, Garbo, and Valentina the designer.

Big Bill also got onto the San Simeon guest list; and in 1943, at a Bel Air estate, Tilden was the star attraction at a small tennis party that Errol Flynn hosted. It was somewhat later in the proceedings when Flynn was supposed to have assaulted a guest, Beverly Hansen, who was seventeen years old. Big Bill had departed not long after the tennis part of the festivities had concluded, however. Flynn was regular company, though, for he was recognized as the best player in the movie colony. Once, at the Racquet Club in Palm Springs, Tilden separated a hundred dollars from Flynn, beating him by hitting nothing but backhands. Bizarre handicap betting didn't originate with Bobby Riggs.

In fact, there was a lot of tennis action in those days, much of it at the Los Angeles Tennis Club, which was run by Perry Jones, a tennis tyrant who was also something of a fussy old-maid bachelor. Jones was usually antagonistic to

Tilden, possibly because it was rumored that Jones himself was also homosexual. While there is no proof of this, there was talk, and Jones certainly wasn't crazy about having Tilden around bringing the subject to people's minds all the time. But Jones couldn't arbitrarily just ban Tilden from the most important tennis premises in the West.

Big Bill's favorite place to play was not the Tennis Club but Chaplin's estate on Summit Drive, up in the hills overlooking Sunset Boulevard. Sunday afternoons, at the tennis house, Chaplin held what was known as the Big Tea—and tea truly was the beverage served. The most extraordinary mixed bag of players and kibitzers gathered. Tilden protégés, such as Arthur Anderson, Noel Brown and Gussie Moran, would be in attendance, plus some of his better students and other tennis pros, as well as a cadre of stars: Garbo, Tallulah, Flynn, Cotten, Spencer Tracy, Olivia de Havilland, Farley Granger, Shelley Winters. And topping this mélange there would also be various Chaplin children, his wife and, for a time, his teenage paramour, Joan Barry.

Miss Barry had bad teeth and "a weird, faraway birdlike look," according to Gussie Moran, but she also possessed "positively the biggest boobs in Hollywood," which was certainly no mean feat in Tinseltown at that time. For a while Chaplin used his tennis guests as a captive audience in an effort to transform the owner of the largest mammary realty in Hollywood into an actress as well, but to no avail —Miss Barry couldn't even emote successfully into a tape recorder. Most Sundays Chaplin himself would compete with Tilden, telling stories and lodging opinions, entertaining the assembled after tennis. "Charlie would talk about life and war," Arthur Anderson recalls, "but never Communism. Bill, of course, wasn't political, so there was never any conflict in that respect."

Tilden's everyday life in Los Angeles was fluid and scattered, but a routine began to emerge. Most mornings he would rise early and have breakfast at a restaurant named DuPars near Hollywood and Vine. Usually he ate with Ben Alexander, the actor who later became famous as the second banana on *Dragnet*. Then Tilden would tool around the movie stars' estates, cadging courts, coaching or playing for the fun of it for the rest of the day. Most nights were handed over to cards. At the Little Club on Sunset or at another card club over by the Farmers Market, he often played with Betty Grable, who was then at the height of her career. George Raft and Buster Keaton were other regular bridge partners, and Tilden also played some big-money gin rummy, often at Joe E. Brown's house, for two cents a point. But then it was just as likely for him to sit in at the Little Club playing with a bunch of old women who didn't know Big Bill Tilden from Hirohito. He whisked about, first in a big Lincoln Zephyr, then in a 1942 Packard Clipper that soon looked and smelled like a mobile gymnasium, the back seat overflowing with all manner of sweaty paraphernalia. Bobby Riggs remembers: "In all the years I knew Tilden, the only property he ever owned was an automobile, four or five rackets, some kind of blazer, a pair of slacks, and a few sweaters."

As a coach, Tilden was unrelenting and dogmatic, hard on conditioning, and even innovative in some respects; but he never psychologically committed himself to teaching. Noel Brown, one of his best protégés, explains: "Bill's great failing—at least as he grew older—was that he couldn't understand his time and place in life. Noel Brown was a tournament player, but now, in this place and time [rapping his desk] Noel Brown is a business executive. Bill Tilden never let go of the fact that he was no longer a great champion. He carried it all through his life. On the one hand, he was trying to find an extension of himself, to continue as champion through myself and these various other young players. It was his mother-and-father instinct. But on the other hand, he could never follow that instinct completely, do what was best for him and them, and be a real teaching pro. He did the teaching in a half-assed way just to carry himself along. Make no mistake: Bill Tilden was always playing. He was always a player in his own mind. He could never find himself out here as a coach."

Perhaps because of this ambivalence, even a certain frustration, Tilden demanded total obeisance from his students. He treated men, women and children all the same. He could brook no divergence from his views. Noel Brown, for instance, was one of the best young players Tilden ever worked with, good enough to make the top ten, but Brown was a natural serve-and-volley type, and when Tilden couldn't convert him to his one right way, they parted. The so-called big game that Brown played, which Kramer perfected, generally aggravated Tilden. He thought the whole sport was going to hell. In 1920 Tilden had written with confidence: "In 1950, I believe that every leading player in the world will have a drive and chop, forehand and backhand from the baseline." But here it was fast approaching 1950, and far from possessing a variegated all-court attack, most players weren't even bothering to learn to hit balls that bounced.

He liked to play the big hitters. Well, he still liked to play anybody, but he liked to play the big hitters best. Gloria Butler can remember him playing a match once at the Château Elysées against a hard-hitting kid named Donnie Harris. Tilden went out and hit hard with him. The kid won the first set in a best-of-three 6–2 and led 5–0 in the second when Tilden stopped by to chat with Miss Butler as he toweled off. "I think I've taken enough of this now," he said, and when he went back on the court all he fed Harris were chops, slices, backspin. The kid was soon throwing rackets and crying out in confusion; he never won another game: 2–6, 7–5, 6–0. "Well, I know a little more tennis than what they play now," the old man explained with satisfaction when he came off the court.

And yet, as intense a competitor as he remained, he was forever the model of sportsmanship and graciousness. Gloria Butler asked him once how he could endure getting beaten by younger nobodies. "Oh come on," Tilden said, chiding her. "I beat everybody once, and now that I'm over the hill, it's only fair that I give everybody a shot at me." All he required of an opponent was a seriousness of purpose; it was all right for a man to insult Bill Tilden, but he could not insult tennis. Even in his most desperate financial straits, Tilden would run a pupil off before he would take easy money from someone who took tennis lessons lightly.

If anything, he treated women and children harshest, testing them. "You silly bitch!" he would scream if one of the ladies let down in the least. "Get your fanny around! Get it around!" he would holler. (His pet peeve, although not just confined to women, was that Americans ran only from their knees, not from their hips.) His method of instruction also featured tactical impositions. Kathy Checkit, one of his favorite female students (she had been a ballet dancer), remembers that he would not only hit balls to her, but would ask in the process, "Now, if I put the ball there, what are you going to do with it? . . . Why?" Gloria Butler says that when he rallied with her he would yell at her where to return the shot: slice it crosscourt, drive it down the line, lob it, and so on. Miss Butler was not only a student of his for years, but she often lived in the same apartment building. "I know this will sound perfectly foolish to anybody who hears it," she says, beginning somewhat defensively, "but I honestly believe that I may know more about tennis than anyone in the world simply because I listened to Bill Tilden talk tennis for six years."

Like the women, the boys Tilden instructed were given

no quarter. One of his better students was Dick St. Johns, the son of Adela Rogers St. Johns, the Hearst reporter who had known Big Bill for years and had a no-nonsense relationship with him; when she asked Tilden to be her son's coach, she extracted a flat-out promise from him that he would keep his hands off the boy. Under Tilden's tutelage then, Dick St. Johns improved steadily and entered the boys' championships of California at Griffith Park in Los Angeles. Sure enough he won, and thrilled, the new young champion and his mother drove Tilden home after the match.

Eventually, in their excitement, the St. Johnses realized that Tilden was unmoved, even sour. He had not even so much as congratulated the boy. Finally, confused, Dick made some direct reference to his victory to his coach. Tilden only snapped back, "You'd be wise not to discuss that again, ever."

"Why?" asked the bewildered young boy.

"I just saw a Tilden pupil play *not* to lose. Tilden pupils play *to* win," Big Bill replied, and, furious, he folded his arms and went the rest of the drive in angry silence.

Of all his protégés during a period of forty years or more, Arthur Anderson was Tilden's dearest, and the first time he played a tournament he reached the finals. Anderson was a small skinny kid of about eleven, while his opponent was not only older but much larger and more mature. He also happened to have a German name, and since the Hun was on the rampage at this time, Tilden's earlier fond feelings for Germany had been replaced by the most complete, passionate All-American hatred for all things Teutonic.

As soon as the match began, it was obvious that little Anderson had no chance against the stronger boy. Manfully he hung on but lost 6–1, 6–2. As soon as he left the court and walked over to his coach and friend, Tilden raged at him. "You have no guts!" he shrieked at the distraught kid. "You're no Tilden pupil. You play gutless tennis. You let that German beat you." Pausing then only long enough to figure out some punishment, Tilden added, "I won't ride with you. You better find your own way home." With that, he turned heel and stalked away to his big Lincoln Zephyr and drove off by himself. Anderson and his mother had to walk to a bus stop and then get on and transfer to another bus to get back to their house.

It was shortly after this episode that Big Bill got his last windfall—poor old Twin died and left him $25,000. He went East to collect his loot. Bill Tilden III remembers that the lawyer handling the estate inquired how Tilden wanted the bequest; he thought perhaps he might prefer to have some of it invested in securities or other long-term propositions. "Oh, I've got to stay around for a couple more days," Big Bill replied blithely, "but then I'll come over and pick it up in cash." He almost surely picked up the Packard with this haul, but his usual spendthrift ways were overcome by patriotism, and he also bought a lot of war bonds. Of what was left, he skimmed off a great deal to invest in plays that he starred in. One, a comedy entitled *The Nice Harmons*, produced at the Assistant League Playhouse, was also written by William T. Tilden II.

That sank quickly and without a trace, so then Tilden followed up by starring in somewhat more reliable vehicles: *The Children's Hour,* by Lillian Hellman, and *The Fighting Littles,* by Booth Tarkington, both at the Wilshire Ebell Theater. For the money spent, he at least finally found a critic who admired his work. Katherine Von Blon of the Los Angeles *Times* wrote of *The Children's Hour:* "William Tilden played with ease and proved himself a most convincing actor" as Dr. Joseph Cardin. And despite the tempest in the cast that Tilden had created the afternoon *The Fighting Littles* opened, Miss Von Blon decided that he played the role of the father "in high-handed farcical manner, making the most of his every opportunity for comedy."

The war provided Tilden with another chance to show off his comic gifts, for he organized a cheerful little tennis troupe to play service hospitals and camps. He often paid the show's travel expenses out of his own pocket, and it was not unusual for him to rush all over the country to help sell war bonds or to auction off his old tennis equipment. Once, in a hurried trip to Philadelphia, he got $15,000 for an old racket. (Yet consider this: In March of 1940, before his own country had gone to war, Tilden was asked to play a match in New York to benefit the Finnish Relief Fund. For that cause, he not only knocked down a $300 fee, but billed the charity an additional $400 in travel expenses from North Carolina, where he was playing at the time; fare for a lower berth was $45. But then, Tilden didn't give a hoot about Finland, so to him his behavior was quite consistent.)

The tennis vaudeville he worked up starred himself, with a Pasadena pro named Walter Wesbrook, plus Gorgeous Gussie Moran and Gloria Butler. Although Tilden turned fifty in the middle of the war, February 10, 1943, he still appeared remarkably youthful and lean, even if his hairline was beginning to recede and he needed eyeglasses for reading. Sometime in the late 1930s he had begun to wear short pants on the court, and since he possessed such fine long legs and quickly realized how shorts improved his appearance, he soon started wearing daring short shorts. "God, those legs," Gussie Moran coos. "Fantastic. Grable should have had them." Tilden also settled pretty much on robin's-egg-blue shirts, completing his ensemble with the old trademark, the Tilden sweater. He was still, as Miss Moran says, "a very striking man."

However good he looked, Tilden realized that few of the

soldiers appreciated the niceties of tennis, so he and Wesbrook would play each other singles but briefly. Tilden
would then commandeer the microphone and bring on the
sex. He introduced Gussie as "the Hedy Lamarr of tennis,"
while building up her opponent, Miss Butler, as the girl
next door, "my little favorite." While the girls played,
Tilden and Wesbrook would go into the locker room and
dress up in drag.

This was, apparently, the only woman's role he ever
played—although it was really more a period piece. He
and Wesbrook got up in old-fashioned clothes: pantaloons,
long full sleeves, big floppy hats. Tilden had all sorts of
frills and strawberry-size balls hanging from his hat brim.
In falsetto he introduced Wesbrook as Miss Wilhelmina
Shovelshoot and himself as Miss Sophic Smearone, and in
the little piece of business that followed, the two old
spinsters challenged the real girls to a game of doubles.
Choreographed by Big Bill, the match ended with Gloria
hitting him in the chest with a shot, and he stalking off the
court, declaring he would no longer continue because "she
won't play like a lady." That used to bring the house down.

Then, in the finale of the day, Tilden and Miss Butler
would join to play Wesbrook and Miss Moran in a fairly
serious game of mixed doubles. It is difficult to believe, but
the mentality of amateur officials was such at the time that
this match upset them. Because the two young women
were amateurs and the two older men professionals, Perry
Jones of the L.A. Tennis Club, who was also the top
USLTA official in Southern California, actually threatened
the Misses Moran and Butler with suspension from all
amateur play if they continued to compete alongside professionals, entertaining the troops. This sounds too much to
be true, but that is the way tennis people thought in those
days.

Tilden had not had to contend with the USLTA for

many years, but this was more than even he had ever had to suffer. So, according to the best accounts, he called up Perry Jones and told him that if he didn't stop trying to break up his troupe, then he, Tilden, was going to call up his friend Walter Winchell and get WW to blast Jones on the radio as unpatriotic. Jones backed off, but simmering, waiting for a better shot at Tilden.

After the matches, Tilden and the others would visit the wounded soldiers. Miss Butler remembers one afternoon in Van Nuys when they went into a ward in the hospital where "there wasn't a whole man in the room." The place was deadly grim, and the tennis players, stunned to silence, were hard pressed even to look up. In a moment, however, Tilden recovered and took command, jauntily walking right over to the worst case in the ward. The kid had both legs and arms missing. "Well," he said point-blank, "how'd ya lose 'em, son?" By the time he left the ward, that kid and a lot of the others were laughing along at the strange tall athlete telling stories and doing impersonations. Tilden handled these sessions much as if he were telling ghost stories to the smaller children back in Germantown.

He also may have managed to take some personal advantage of these expeditions, reconnoitering for gay young soldiers. Miss Moran remembers no such thing, but Miss Butler claims there were at least two occasions when he ended up with a homosexual GI back in his hotel room. From his Hollywood contacts, Tilden also was able to gain introductions to young homosexuals who had come out to be movie stars but had failed to gain notice. But as ever with his protégés—Arthur Anderson and then Noel Brown—Tilden remained scrupulously proper.

Mrs. Anderson herself was, however, not unmindful of the possibility that her son's handsy adult friend might be homosexual. Early on she grilled young Arthur about the relationship, asking oblique questions that gave her answers without truly revealing to the boy what she was trying to get at. Tilden himself sensed her concern and offered up casual little hints and euphemisms every now and then to assure her. "He was very funny, very particular about Arthur not being permitted to go places alone," Mrs. Anderson says now, pausing to add a bit sardonically, "Of course, perhaps that was because Bill knew the ropes so well himself." Tilden did take young Anderson everywhere he went. "There wasn't a restaurant in Los Angeles we didn't eat at," Arthur says, and in fact he was such a conscientious little boy that he urged Tilden to stop treating him to the best restaurants all the time, wasting his dwindling resources.

The Andersons were the difference in Big Bill's life. His coaching opportunities were circumscribed by his reputation, his touring career ended by the war and his advancing age, but he still had some money, and these first few years in Los Angeles were not necessarily unhappy times for him. He played a lot, coached some, enjoyed his bridge, his acting and his acting friends; and most of all, for the first time since 1908, he was welcomed into something of a real family situation. The Andersons truly loved him. Many times he said to Marrion, "You know, Arthur's the only real son I ever had." And to Arthur, "You and your mother are the only close family I ever had."

The boy, who is now an engineer with an explosives firm in Los Angeles, a tall, gaunt, utterly humorless man, uncompromising on the subject of Tilden, was, of all the protégés, temperamentally most like the mentor. His mother, also still living in Los Angeles, drew as close to Tilden as any contemporary woman in his life. Once as unyielding in his behalf as her son, she is now able to see Big Bill in broader perspective, freckles and all. "There were many things not right about Tilden," she says. "He was a person who had a million faults. God knows I didn't condone Bill, but I had sympathy for him. He was the kind of person who would go to hell for you if you were his friend."

The Andersons first met Big Bill around 1940, when he was coaching at the Château Elysées. Arthur Anderson, ten or eleven at the time, lived close by and would come over to watch the tennis after school. Tilden, always on the lookout for young boys, noticed him, subsequently introduced himself, and was so impressed by the young boy's intense demeanor that he volunteered to give him free lessons. The friendship grew quickly. Marrion Anderson was an outspoken woman, a bookkeeper who knew nothing of tennis, but she saw that Tilden was a kind man and good for her boy, who was an only child. Besides, the Andersons were really a natural for Tilden, since the absent Mr. Anderson was an alcoholic who had abandoned his family and was eventually to drink himself to an early grave. Young Arthur was just as obsessive on the subject of alcohol as Tilden. Although his father did not die until Arthur was in his teens, Anderson always referred to his father's "dying" when he had been age three, the time when liquor overtook the man. When Mr. Anderson finally did die, the boy would not "be a hypocrite" and go to his father's funeral. Although the Anderson situation was obviously sadder, more dramatic and more complete, both young Arthur and Junior Tilden were rejected by their fathers, raised by their mothers. The factors of need and shared identity were present between Tilden and Anderson, where they had not been with Big Bill and other protégés. "I know that I knew Bill Tilden better than any person who ever lived," Anderson declares with conviction.

Mrs. Anderson says that there was never any romance between herself and Tilden, nor was there any real discussion of a marriage of convenience, even though Tilden moved in with the family for two extended periods, once after the death of Mrs. Anderson's mother, and then again years later when Arthur went into the service. Tilden had his own entrance to the premises, and his part of the place soon took on its own distinctive flavor. "You had to wade through that section of the house," Anderson says, smiling, the closest he will come to any criticism of the man. Tilden would just strew his clothes about, sometimes letting them fall one by one as he moved along: a shoe here, then dirty pants, shirt, socks, underwear, all in a line. He also scattered dollar bills about the house, tucking them here and there like Easter eggs—his contributions to the rent for Marrion, for she would not charge him. Whether he lived in with the Andersons or by himself at any of a succession of small apartments, Tilden was invariably around the family, starting at break of day, when he would usually show up to take Arthur out to breakfast, going down to meet Ben Alexander at DuPars. And predictably, as Anderson's tennis game improved, Tilden began to put on him the mantle of greatness that he didn't think would fit Jack Kramer. Anderson was indeed a fine player, and eventually he ranked as high as number seventeen in the country, but at no time did anyone but Tilden even remotely consider him of championship caliber.

It is one baffling inconsistency in his life why Tilden paid so little attention to his namesake, the only son of his beloved brother, Herbert. Here, surely, was the easiest and most logical place for him to play father, but at best he was only perfunctory in the relationship. What makes this even more strange is that Tilden always took some genuine interest in the women in his family: his widowed sister-in-law, who remarried as Hazel MacIntosh (he affectionately called her Haze) and his beautiful niece Miriam. "It was significant of Uncle Bill that he never ceased to think of Mother as the adored bride of his brother," Miriam says. Miriam herself felt so close to her uncle that she turned to him for his advice when she was considering marrying a

British army officer. She had met him when Tilden bought her a first-class trip to London. He always had presents for the women in his family, and once took Twin and a friend of hers on a whirlwind trip to Paris. But for his nephew, Bill III, there was nothing, not even when the young man grew up to be a pretty fair tennis player: captain of the Princeton team and good enough to qualify for Forest Hills.

Instead, Tilden put his nephew's tennis achievements down, and often called him Hopeless. He gave his brother's son not a penny of Twin's bequest, and later, when Bill III, struggling with a young family, couldn't buy his uncle's trophies from him when he went broke, Tilden got furious and shortly thereafter demanded that his nephew ship all his trophies to California. Bill III thinks the problem mainly was that "I was onto my uncle and he knew it"— that is, he was aware of the homosexuality.

Tilden did continue to retain fairly close relations with Hazel, at least calling her every Christmas, but the argument over the trophies was the official break with the family. At that time, symbolically, he gave to Marrion Anderson a famous bracelet that he had been awarded years before. It has seven gold balls, each one representing a national championship. Tilden told Mrs. Anderson specifically that he was presenting it to her because he wanted the bracelet to "stay in the family." But in a sense it seems that this harsh rejection of his natural family was emblematic of his attitude toward his complete past; he had joined it all in his mind—relatives and old friends, Philadelphia, the whole damned East—and tied the lot as a tin can to the USLTA's tail.

Increasingly desperate for money, he pawned a few of his trophies, caring not whose possession they came into; but then when he got sick once in 1950 and made out his first will, naming Marrion Anderson as executrix, he gave both her and her son stern instructions about the disposition of his trophies. "He told me never to give his family any of his trophies," Arthur Anderson says. "In his mind, his own family had ceased to exist by then. And he also told me never to give the trophies to the USLTA either. Ever."

A few of the trophies—including the huge standing cup that Tilden retired in straight years, 1923–24–25, for winning successive national titles—are on display at Mrs. Anderson's apartment. A couple more may be viewed at her son's house nearby, where he lives with his wife and small son. The most valuable of all, the trophy Tilden retired in 1922, the one that Little Bill Johnston wanted so desperately—that one is occasionally brought out for viewing at Arthur Anderson's house. Most times, however, it remains hidden away in a warehouse, along with the bulk of the other trophies, where the Tildens and the USLTA and nobody else, for that matter, can get so much as a peek at them.

In her apartment Marrion Anderson walks over to a closet and opens it up. There is a huge slate-gray steamer trunk there, with the initials WTT 2ND painted on it. It is chock full of his trophies and has been there since he died. Mrs. Anderson says she has never bothered to look inside.

CHAPTER SEVENTEEN

"But, Bill, this time you're indicted"

WHEN the war ended, Tilden led the establishment of the Professional Tennis Players Association, and envisioned that it would be the wedge, at last, to bring about open tennis competition (which was, in fact, more than two decades away). He was no longer a top player and many of the younger pros disliked him intensely— Frankie Kovacs taunted him regularly, in the George Lott tradition, and Frank Shields called him "an old bitch" to his face—but the pros needed him.

Carl Earn, who played briefly on the PTPA circuit then, says, "He held the whole tour together himself. Nobody else could control all those opera stars." More important, Tilden still drew the lion's share of the attention, even when players like Perry, Riggs or Budge were along. Still first class, all the way, he would call up the press as soon as he got ensconced in his suite: "Hello, Big Bill Tilden here"—and they would come down to inspect a phenomenon. Ridiculous as this seems, the professional tennis gate often depended directly on how well a fifty-three-year-old performed.

Tilden was still competitive. In a match at Chaplin's, he beat Frank Parker, the reigning U.S. amateur champion, and in the pro tournaments he regularly reached the

quarterfinals. Because Tilden still attracted so much curiosity and paid the bills for them all, the pros did their best to
stack the draw to keep Tilden alive; but given that, his
wins were all legitimate. In 1946 at Pittsburgh, for example, where sixteen pros were playing for the sum of
$3000, a whopping figure at that time, Tilden, unseeded,
upset the number-eight seed, John Faunce. Later that year,
at Forest Hills in the pro championships, he had Wayne
Sabin, one of the top-ranked pros, down two sets to one
before he gave out. Riggs was then acknowledged pro
champion (Kramer was still in the amateurs), and there
were two or three matches when Tilden took an early lead
over Riggs. Often it was only stamina that defeated Tilden.
The chestnut everybody roasted was that, even at age fifty-
three, Bill Tilden was the best player in the world for one
set.

Yet a more subtle deterioration was taking place. Old
friends who had not seen him in some time were not de-
ceived by the beautiful strokes and the wonderful legs.
Frederick Staunton, the West Virginia newspaper publisher, who had not been with Tilden since World War I,
visited him when he played Charleston. "It was obvious to
me that he was a sick man, and I left with a saddened
heart," Staunton says. An automobile accident left Tilden
relatively unhurt but terribly frightened. Increasingly he
was paying less attention to his hygiene. Carl Earn says
that he stopped showering altogether and became nearly
obsessive that he might be seen in the nude. He wore an
old sweater and dirty, unpressed pants. W. B. Mullan, then
a young room clerk at a small suburban Pittsburgh hotel,
recalls vividly how shocked he was when this famous man
came to check in there. "The other players were well
dressed, quiet and reserved," Mullan says. "Tilden, however, checked in unshaven, in tennis shoes, and in a ragged
old athletic jacket. He had decidedly outspoken comments

on everything. He seemed so out of place, but yet so confident and sure of himself."

Well, there was much reason for hope. The postwar
sports boom was rolling, and pro tennis figured to cash in
too. Even if he could no longer be champion, Big Bill
Tilden was head of the Professional Tennis Players Association, and would be right in the thick of things, the grand
old man of tennis. Obviously, open tennis was just around
the corner, and the USLTA was going to get its just deserts.
Well before the 1946 season ended, the interest in the 1947
tour began to swell, and it was certain that the prize money
would be doubled.

And then, shortly before ten o'clock on Saturday evening, November 23, 1946, two officers in a Beverly Hills
police patrol car saw a 1942 Packard Clipper being driven
somewhat erratically on Sunset Boulevard. The cops
thought the driver looked young. They also noticed that
the man who sat next to him had an arm around him, "holding him very tightly, and, it appeared, with his right hand
in the boy's lap." They flagged the car down at the intersec-
tion of Rexford and Sunset, and when they did, Tilden
quickly changed places with his companion and offered his
driver's license to the officers. Instead, they told the boy to
get out of the car. When he did, the police saw that his fly
was wide open, four buttons undone. Tilden was taken to
headquarters and quickly signed a full statement. He made
no protest, made no requests for counsel, and indeed, since
he did not have his reading glasses, he signed the statement
merely on the basis of what a station-house sergeant assured him it contained. "I have always had a great regard
for the law and respected law enforcement officers," he
declared later in explaining his actions.

When Tilden finally recovered some of his wits, it seems
that he tried to enlist the offices of Jerry Giesler, the
famous Hollywood attorney. Giesler didn't want anything

to do with it, and a bail bondsman, Fred Beacher, suggested to Tilden that he contact a young lawyer named Richard Maddox, who had previously been working the other side, as city attorney and prosecuting attorney in Beverly Hills. Maddox, in his mid-thirties at the time, already "represented a lot of picture people," and no doubt this credential impressed Tilden. Maddox found the message awaiting him Sunday night when he came home from spending the weekend on his boat off Newport Beach.

He met Tilden in a little room in the Beverly Hills jail and was immediately appalled, not only that Tilden had given a statement but that he had such "an indifferent kind of manner." Somewhat with reservations then, Maddox agreed to take the case. "The toughest cases I've ever had," he says ruefully, "are where a dog or a child is the victim." And he soon regretted his decision. Nervous when first arrested, then nonchalant, Tilden grew increasingly uncooperative and even a bit cavalier with his lawyer. He was often disingenuous, and when Maddox at last extracted the truth from him, his client took it all very lightly. For one thing, Tilden told Maddox, these little nuisances had come up before, both in the United States and England, and they'd always been washed out. "But, Bill," Maddox shouted at him, "this time you're indicted." Tilden was no more impressed. "They're going to hang you," Maddox went on. "They're going to chew headlines." Just a couple of weeks before the trial Tilden wrote his sister-in-law, Hazel MacIntosh, assuring her that there was absolutely nothing to worry about.

Mostly Tilden listened to what he wanted to hear. According to Maddox, this was largely Mrs. Anderson. "She was crazy about him," he says, "and he was like an ostrich, depending on her opinions." The Andersons, for their part, were suspicious of Maddox's efforts. To this day Arthur Anderson maintains that the state was out to get Tilden,

and to get him to leave California, and that Maddox convinced Tilden to take the rap—opinions which are simply
contradicted by all the known facts. But then, it is amazing
how many of Tilden's friends, people who knew well that
he was a homosexual who liked little boys, still believe (or
claim) that he was framed.

But if Big Bill was not set up, and surely he wasn't, he
was dumb and he was unlucky. By coincidence, A. A. Scott,
the judge assigned the case in superior court, just happened
to be the son of a famous cause lawyer named Joe Scott,
who had recently represented none other than Joan Barry
in her paternity suit against Charlie Chaplin. And Chaplin,
of course, was Tilden's best-known friend, as well as an
increasingly suspect fellow traveler. It took little of the
public imagination to visualize the spectacular orgies that
must be going on up there on Summit Drive between tennis
matches, with the Commie Symp ravaging all the teenage
girls and the degenerate old champion all the boys. Tilden
himself kept throwing Chaplin's name around so much,
with assurances of his staunch support, that Maddox finally
went out to see him. Chaplin had enough problems of his
own, however, and was hardly interested in getting involved with Tilden. Well, he told Maddox, his idea was
that Big Bill should jump bail and skip the country.

At that point Maddox figured he better stop counting on
Tilden and his so-called friends and go out and win the
case his way. He had a plan and, he was sure, an excellent
shot at acquittal. The state's whole case rested on the boy,
who was a handsome, dissolute fourteen-year-old named
Bobby. Without his testimony, which a minor was not required to offer, Tilden could renege on his statement, made
under stress, and nothing would wash. It was obvious that
the state knew its case was on thin ice. The prosecution
could have thrown the book at Tilden, what was known in
the cops' vernacular as "a two eighty-eight," standing for

"lewd and lascivious behavior with a minor"—a felony. Instead they only charged him with a misdemeanor, "contributing to the delinquency of a minor," or just "contributing" in courthouse jargon.

The whole case, even with the reduced charge, was vulnerable, because Bobby was vulnerable. He came from a divorced family, had been in and out of schools, and was presently furious at his stepmother because she wouldn't allow him to obtain a learner's driver's license. Moreover, he was hardly any babe in the woods. The very day of the Tilden arrest he had also had some kind of sex with a young girl—"Quite an afternoon," he boasted to Big Bill— and Tilden was amazed at his precociousness. At one point in their petting, Big Bill had even paused to ask Bobby where in the world he had learned so much about sex at the age of fourteen. "In the private school I just left," the kid said nonchalantly.

Indeed, there was even some question about who was seducing whom. Bobby was not surprised by the intimacies; he had come back for more of them. The weekend before, after some matches at the L.A. Tennis Club, where Tilden had met Bobby, they had first gone out to dinner together, at Eaton's on La Cienega Boulevard, and then, back in the car, parked, started what Tilden always referred to with court officials as "fooling around"; that is, playing with each other's genitals. It was Big Bill who got bored with that after a while and called it quits. Bobby pushed right ahead and masturbated, ejaculating there in the front seat of the Packard. After a full study of the facts, the probation officer came to the conclusion that Bobby was "not injured as much [by Tilden] as are his parents and the general public."

After their first time together, Bobby directed Tilden to drive past his school in Westwood, so that he would know where to pick him up. This Tilden did that Wednesday

after school, although this time their activities were confined to tennis. It was then Bobby who asked Tilden to take
him to a movie on Saturday. Big Bill picked him up at his
girl's house on Lucerne Avenue about a quarter to six, took
him to dinner at the Castle Steak House on Vermont, and
then to the Pantages Theatre to see *The Jolson Story*. It
was after the show, going home, that Tilden let Bobby
drive, put "my arm behind him to give him a backrest" and
then began to fool around.

Thus Maddox felt quite sure that if he could get Tilden
to plead not guilty and demand a jury trial, Bobby's parents would want no part of interrogation and spotlight, and
would pull the kid out. Moreover, if Maddox sought a jury
trial, the case would be moved up to another court, away
from Judge Scott, and also out of the jurisdiction of William Ritzi, a stern moralist prosecutor. "I've always
thought," Maddox explains, "that if you've got a drunk
driving case, you don't want it tried in a traffic court by
some judge who sees it as a big deal, just as Scott saw the
contributing as a big deal. You want drunk driving and
contributing before some judge who usually handles
murder and rape."

Maddox picked up even more ammunition when both
the social worker and the psychiatrist who investigated the
case urged without qualification that Tilden be treated, not
incarcerated. Bobby's parents also advised the court that
they did not want Tilden to go to jail. Maddox and Tilden
obtained fifteen letters of reference from respected citizens—doctors and corporation presidents, old players like
Frank Hunter, and journalists like Grantland Rice and S.
Wallis Merrihew, the editor of *American Lawn Tennis
Magazine*, who wrote, "I have been like a father to him."
Significantly, not one single letter came either from Philadelphia or from a USLTA representative. The writers
pleaded with Judge Scott for clemency, and some of them

assured him that the incident must certainly be a unique aberration; indeed, a couple of them clearly went overboard and lied in Tilden's behalf.

Yet, with all this going for him, Tilden would not follow Maddox's advice and plead not guilty. "He was hung up on the sportsman thing," Maddox says, and as always under pressure, the best and the worst in Tilden surfaced together. Quite earnestly, even nobly, he worried more for Bobby than for himself. Maddox assured Tilden that if he did plead innocence, Bobby would never suffer, because then his parents would not let him testify—and Tilden would walk. But Tilden was unconcerned, and he acted as if indestructible, certain that no court would dare put the great American world champion behind bars. Somehow he seemed convinced too that his high-placed friends, such as Chaplin, would rescue him, especially if he was contrite. To this end he covered himself with shame. "I sincerely regret my actions and desire that the court have faith enough in me to permit me to prove that this does not reflect my true nature and my better self," he petitioned. And to Graydon Beeks, the probation officer: "I can only reiterate my deep regret, humiliation and shame. I have learned my lesson and will never forget it." For penance he promised to play more matches for charity. And thus, purged and cocky, he waived a preliminary hearing and pleaded guilty.

His assumption was that he would be given something of a tongue-lashing, perhaps a small fine, and then be put on probation, under psychiatric care. Both Beeks, the probation official, and Dr. J. Paul De River, were of a like mind with Tilden. In recommending a suspended four-year sentence, Beeks wrote, "It should be noted that his present attitude is favorable, that because of his notoriety he would be easily supervised and would be watched by the general public as well as police officers throughout the country

. . . and any jail sentence would of necessity be limited and not tend to work as a curative measure, but would probably bring more publicity in the case and hence more harm."

Dr. De River, delving into Tilden's pysche and sex life, found him to be a pitiful creature, unquestionably sick of mind. He assessed him to be "impulsively weak . . . passive autistic with egocentric traits . . . in need of special psychiatric care." He concluded, "In my opinion, whilst the man appears outwardly cool, he is basically a neurotic and in some ways quite juvenile. . . . This man should be regarded as someone who is mentally ill."

Even Ritzi, the district attorney, who is himself now a judge of the superior court in Los Angeles, understood that the person his department was criminally prosecuting was not sane. "The poor man was a sick individual," Ritzi freely admits now. "We realized it then and we realize it now. It's just that society treats it differently today than in those days."

Tilden cooperated with the psychiatrist, Dr. De River, at least insofar as his childhood experiences were concerned. He spoke candidly of his mother's admonitions about venereal disease and of his first boyish homosexual adventures. Tilden claimed, though, that he had not participated homosexually since college, maintaining that he had only fallen into the encounter with Bobby because he had been tired and nervous lately, suffering the aftereffects of his recent automobile accident.

Dr. De River was willing to accept this account, because he suspected that Tilden was troubled with an "endocrine dysfunction so often seen during the evolutionary stage of life when the sex curve is on the decline." He likened the condition to a female's change of life, and added, "During this period there seems to be a weakness in the inhibitionary functions of the will." Dr. De River thought that shock treatment, which was highly favored at the time, would correct the problem. Besides, as Tilden assured him in all honesty, "Sex has never been very important in my life; I have had an outlet through athletics."

Certainly the psychiatrist found no reason for society to fear Tilden and, like the probation officer, was of a mind that jail would serve only as vengeance. Dr. De River thought Tilden to be "mild-mannered and polite and intelligent," and was impressed that he wished to obtain treatment and sincerely regretted his transgression. Indeed, by now Tilden's contrition was reaching new depths. He was flogging himself unmercifully. "I am abject and ashamed of myself beyond all description," he declared at one point, while also hastening to assure the doctor that "Everyone knows I have been of a kindly nature, and I get along well with people; why, I wouldn't harm a hair on anyone's head." All in all, Dr. De River felt that, with psychiatric help, Tilden could be "rehabilitated as a useful member of society."

Against this array of compassionate authority, the court was influenced by the prevailing attitude against homosexuals at that time. Offhand, for example, they were referred to as "degenerates," a term that wounded Tilden deeply. A couple of anonymous letters sent to Judge Scott provide a pungent reading of society's general feeling toward homosexuals in 1946.

> Your Honour:
> Please give him the works! I was the victim of a *social degenerate* myself between the ages of 10 and 14. He was 45 years old then. I do hope he is dead and roasting in Hell! His *degenerate, homosexual* practices on me affected (and ruined) my whole life! Nothing can be done for me now, as I am now an old man and awaiting the undertaker. But please your honour, save

the youth from the "Hell on Earth" thru which I went!
Give this degenerate "The Works"!
   With kindest regards & best wishes of the season

JUDGE A A SCOTT.
   Certain influential Sportsmen of Hollywood are placing big Bets that you will give Tilden probation. They
claim that in a closed room you got him to plead
guilty saying that you would let him go free etc. Please
My Dear Judge for the sake of the other Boys and your
own future Do Not Do This. He ruined my own Boy
who later died and in some ways I will forever think
that this Dirty skunk and degenerate was the prime
cause . . .
                              A Humble Father

   Judge Scott himself was more concerned about potential
victims than about the immediate welfare of the admitted
offender. "I felt very sorry for him," he says now, "but society has to protect the young." The judge was also privy to
a welter of rumors that Tilden had long been a practicing
homosexual and had regularly enjoyed intimacies with
juvenile boys. The court never could uncover any solid
proof of these allegations, but clearly there seemed to be
too much smoke for there not to be some fire. In maintaining that this was his first homosexual experience since his
youth, Tilden was sorely testing the good will and the common sense of the court.
   How strangely he behaved: the formal expressions of
shame on one hand, the private expressions of bravado on
the other, addled bullheadedness throughout. Had he followed Maddox's professional advice and pleaded not
guilty, he surely would have gotten off. Or, had he followed his own stated precepts of a lifetime—"Truth,

Though the Heavens Fall!"—a clean breast may have earned the sympathy of all the court. Instead, and despite his outward show of confidence, he acted in ways that seem to have been almost calculated to bring on his fall. To begin with, to pick Sunset Boulevard on a Saturday night to "fool around" with a brazen young partner illegally driving a car, to blithely sign a full confession, and to dispute counsel.

People who were wrong deserved to be punished. Uncle Bill felt that, down in his heart. Ashamed himself of his own lifetime wrong, it seems to have been time to punish Bill Tilden. If so many people think he was framed, perhaps it was because, unconsciously but purposefully, he framed himself. It would be the honorable thing to do.

The matter of sentencing, with consideration for probation, took place on January 16, 1947, at nine-thirty in the morning: The People of the State of California vs. William Tatem Tilden. The proceedings were brief. Coolly, respectfully, Maddox pointed out to the court that every dispassionate source connected with the case, as well as the more involved, such as Bobby and his parents, wanted Tilden freed, under psychiatric care. Big Bill himself followed with another apology. "I very deeply regret the incident," he told Judge Scott. "I have had a terrible lesson, one which I will never forget."

He then sat back, ready to hear how long his probation would be.

But first Judge Scott went into a little dissertation about Tilden's impact upon youth. "I am just wondering, Mr. Tilden, have you ever given any thought over the number of years that you have been engaged in athletics to the harm that you could do if you were ever caught doing something like this?"

Tilden looked up at the judge, and he lied to him. "Sir, I

don't think I have thought of that, because I have never been involved in anything of the kind."

Judge Scott gave him one more chance. "You mean by that you were never caught," he said.

Tilden lied again. "I mean I was not involved in it, sir, in that kind of thing. Years ago, sir, I was once very stupid, but in recent years I have not been involved."

Judge Scott, simmering at this stupid affront to the court's intelligence, carried on a bit more discussion, and then, without any warning whatsoever, he glared at the defendant and threw down this thunderbolt: "All right, the court at this time is going to sentence you to the county jail for a period of one year. . . ." Tilden gagged, stupefied, his face suddenly "ashen." Punishment—all right, but jail . . . And Judge Scott went on: "I am going to recommend that this time be served at the road camp, and on your release from jail the court is going to order that you place yourself under the care of some competent psychiatrist. . . . In addition to that, you are at all times to be a law-abiding citizen, and you are not to be found in the company of any juveniles, of either sex. . . ."

Big Bill slumped in his chair, aghast and horrified, "near collapse," according to the Associated Press report. Maddox says, "He was absolutely in shock." But Judge Scott kept pouring it on, speaking past the poor crumpled figure into the newspapers: "And I hope, Mr. Tilden, that this will serve as an object lesson to those parents who are not concerned about the types of individuals that their youngsters are going around with. There is just too much of this going on all the time in Los Angeles and elsewhere, and we've got to stop it."

When the judge paused here, Maddox tried to rise and obtain some consideration for his client. "If the court please," he began, "is there an opportunity for a stay of execution to permit this defendant—"

"No," Scott called down. *"Put the sentence into effect immediately."*

Big Bill was still so stunned that Maddox had to help lift him to his feet and support him as he was led away to the custody of the sheriff's deputies and a cell in Los Angeles county jail.

CHAPTER EIGHTEEN

"Judge, I can't help myself"

AFTER a week's confinement in the L.A. jail, which he later confided was the worst part of the entire prison experience, Big Bill, Number 9413, was dispatched to the Castaic Honor Farm, where five hundred inmates were kept. It was a minimum-security facility, located in a state forest forty miles north of Los Angeles, near Lancaster. It was at Castaic that, a few days after his arrival, Tilden celebrated his fifty-fourth birthday. He was still in excellent health:

> He is a white male; well-developed and well-nourished; height 6′ 1½″; weight 175 lbs.; brown hair turning gray; brown eyes; his complexion is medium fair; his face is of the shield-faced type, offsetting a head that is rather small in comparison with the rest of his body; the skin is muscular, glandular, vascular, and the bony systems are negative. The heart and lungs are negative. His extremities are long, particularly the lower limbs. The pulse is of good quality, about 78 to 80 beats per minute.

He said that he belonged to the American Legion and the Episcopal Church, having left the Presbyterians somewhere along the way, but he attended services only slightly more than he did Legion meetings. "While not a deeply religious person," he wrote in this time of travail, "I have very definite beliefs. I believe in a god of love and justice, and trust Him to solve my problems and those of this long-suffering world." With his coaching income, a retainer he had from the Dunlop Tire and Rubber Company that Vinnie Richards had obtained for him, and the few odd dollars he could pick up in pro tournaments, Tilden made about $7500 a year. But from Twin's estate he still had a car and about $8000 invested—every penny of it in U.S. war bonds. He was down but not out. "He always had a great confidence within him," says Carl Fischer. "The fact that he held up so well in jail is a tribute to him."

Certainly Tilden tried to put the best face on things. When he got out, he updated an autobiography he had written twenty years before in England, and he wrote so glowingly of Castaic that it sounded like ad copy for a resort in *Holiday* magazine. He said he would feel "eternally grateful" to Judge Scott for ordering him there, because "a culprit should thank his lucky stars if he manages to get sent" to Castaic. Moreover: "The Honor Farm gave me a wonderful opportunity to undergo rehabilitation, and I took full advantage of it. Among other things, it gave me the rest needed by my nerves, and the time for reflection needed by my soul." He did not note that he had so much time for reflection by himself because the other inmates would have little to do with him. They were jealous of his reputation and in abhorrence of his crime. In the prison caste system, a sex assailant of children ranks at the bottom. Tilden's rejection was as complete in this society as in the one outside.

But, disdained, he served his lonely time without incident. His first job was as a member of the "scouring gang" in the kitchen—polishing aluminum utensils. He did that well for a week and was promoted to table setter and waiter in the main dining room, where he served for another week or so. Having paid his dues in these menial tasks, he was assigned to the commissary store room, where he was put in charge of supplies—"a very responsible post," Tilden noted. So responsibly and manfully did he serve his time that, with Maddox pressuring him, Judge Scott finally relented somewhat and gave Tilden an early release. Of the year, he served seven and a half months; he came out August 30, 1947.

His release was not permitted without stipulations, notably that he undertake psychiatric treatment, and that he never associate with juveniles, as coach or friend. Indeed, when he had the promise of an apartment at 5342 Russell Avenue, it was pointed out to the court that this was a felicitous location since "there are no juveniles in the area." In October, however, hardly a month after he got out, the probation officers came to Tilden with a stern warning; somebody had turned Tilden in for escorting Arthur Anderson, then age seventeen, to a junior tournament in Ojai.

The Andersons were among those who did not desert Tilden. David Selznick and the Joseph Cottens also remained steadfast, and so too did Chaplin welcome him back. But many of Tilden's Hollywood benefactors jumped ship, and also, because the conditions of his parole prohibited him from being with minors, he was denied much of what little coaching work he might still scare up. He moved through a succession of smaller, cheaper apartments in Hollywood and West L.A., began dipping more heavily into his savings, and became even more neglectful about attending to himself. He retreated into writing—always in pencil, in longhand on foolscap, a fine, florid hand. He finished his first play in years, a melodrama entitled *New Shoes*, which was staged at the El Patio Theatre. The L.A. *Times* called it "well-written," but "malodorous" as well, which was fair enough considering that the plot revolved around a mentally ill mother, a kidnaped son and sibling incest. It was much the most depressing work of his—at least the darkest ever to be published or produced.

Yet, about the same time, he was polishing up his autobiography, *My Story*, a cheery opus, chock full of big names and gushy anecdotes, with hardly a discouraging word. Curiously, it was dedicated to Little Bill, long dead. Writing it must have made him look back to the glory days. Tilden often turned to the sky for his images and, true to form, he began *My Story* with this first paragraph:

> Life is like a spring day. Clouds and sunshine alternately fill the restless skies, one succeeding the other with disconcerting abruptness. Sometimes it seems as if there will be no break in either, but the end of both always comes. Just now, I am under a cloud, but I know that somewhere ahead shines the sun. Fighting toward it, already I glimpse a beam tinting the gloom, and I take hope. For all through my career I have loved the brightness, and I long for it again.

The Andersons were his greatest rays of light, rising in his affection all the more as he lost faith in his own family. He was wrong, too, to think the Tildens had denied him. His nephew, despite their disagreements, still remembers almost everything his uncle instructed him in, and he named his first child for him. Bill III and his wife wrestled with changing their young boy's name when his namesake was jailed, but at last they decided that the lasting glory in the name would outlive the brief shame, and they let it stand: William Tatem Tilden IV.

Auntie and Twin were gone, but the women who were left, his sister-in-law, Hazel, and his niece, Miriam, still cared. "We all loved him dearly," Mrs. Ambrose writes of those painful times. "He was kind, amusing and generous, always affectionate toward us, and it would not have occurred to us to exchange him for all the tea in China. The measure of his love for us was his sharing of his happiest times, and his pathetic withdrawal from us when things went badly for him toward the end of his life. His misfortune hurt us deeply because he was and will remain one of us. His sins were our sins. I think of him lovingly now, and I always will."

But the world was closing in on him now, and he decided somehow that these people had rejected him. He even thought the Andersons would abandon him, and he gave them that chance. After the arrest he said to her, "Marrion, I want you to know that you're the one who must decide whether I ever see you and Art again." But of course they would not leave him. In fact, Arthur was with Tilden, alone in his apartment, in complete violation of his probation, when the police showed up on the afternoon of January 28, 1949, with another warrant for Big Bill's arrest.

It was not to catch Tilden with young Anderson that they came there. It was because, through his automobile license number, he had been identified as the tall man who had picked up a sixteen-year-old hitchhiker named Michael that morning at the corner of Westwood and Wilshire Boulevard and had almost immediately begun making advances. Tilden assured the police that there must be some mistake, but there was little chance of that. Michael said that the hand that kept reaching out to touch him was missing the tip of the middle finger. It was Big Bill. By now, pathetically, he was reduced to cruising, trolling the streets around high schools and Y's.

> Michael [at the preliminary hearing]: Well, we ran along, and he had the radio on, and he had his hand on the seat, beating time on the seat with the music, and

then when we got down to Seventeenth Street he moved his hand over on my leg and started to mess around.

William Ritzi [the prosecutor]: Now you say "mess around." . . . What do you mean, son?

Michael: He was playing with my privates.

Ritzi: Were your privates inside of your trousers or outside?

Michael: Inside. . . .

Ritzi: Did he say anything at this time?

Michael: He said his hands were cold.

Ritzi: His hands were cold?

Michael: Yes sir. I pushed his hands off and we kept going.

Tilden made repeated additional efforts to touch the boy, to open his fly, each time explaining that his hands were cold. Michael was calm and unafraid. He had been picked up by a homosexual once before and had been so upset then that he had not remembered enough detail to justify arrest. This time he was an expert witness. He read Tilden's face, noticed the missing finger, his clothes, the jumble of items in the back seat, the missing ornament on the hood, the make and model, the license number. It was an open-and-shut case.

Yet this time Tilden prepared immediately to fight the charge. He concocted an alibi, and he went to Maddox and begged him to handle his defense. Tilden had never before been anything but cool and distant with the lawyer, and Maddox turned him down flat. "I said I didn't want to represent him because he didn't take my advice," Maddox explains. "I said it was my idea to go to court and try to *win* cases and get people *out of* trouble."

Distraught, Tilden promised him that he would heed his counsel this time, and Maddox felt obligated to take him since he was familiar with the case. As an associate, he brought in Charles Callahan, who had only recently left the Beverly Hills prosecutor's office. Tilden was in good hands again. Unfortunately, they had him dead to rights. His alibi featured a program of people he had been with that day—dentist appointment, discussion with a filling station attendant, luncheon with Noel Brown—that were all extraneous to the hour in question; "his escapades," Judge Scott characterized them impatiently. Then, for the crucial time, eight to nine in the morning, Tilden said he had driven Arthur Anderson to Hollywood High and then gone to DuPars for breakfast. For an alibi this was a beauty, similar to an accused murderer claiming that he could not have shot the victim, as he was otherwise occupied in a strangling. If he had taken Arthur Anderson to school, Tilden was guilty of probation violation, and liable to an immediate return to jail.

The alibi was academic quickly enough anyway. The waitresses at DuPars denied that he had come in that morning at the hour he claimed, and poor Anderson told the officers who checked with him that he had not seen Tilden until twelve-thirty in the afternoon. Later Anderson changed his story and said Tilden had driven him to school that morning, the police report noting without any comment that this improved recollection developed after the boy "admitted discussing the matter with his mother and a Mr. Noel Brown, a tennis player and close friend of the defendant's at his home the previous evening." But there was just no getting Big Bill off. Even the sympathetic probation officer recommended incarceration this time.

Chaplin tried to intercede at this point, sending his attorney to see Judge Scott, with an offer to take Tilden out of the country for the remainder of his probation—in Chaplin's custody. Of course, there was no legal way that the judge could even consider such a deal. Privately, about this same time, Tilden was contacted by an intermediary for an old French player named Coco Gentien. He had been a pretty fair player who for a time had partnered Suzanne Lenglen in mixed doubles. Gentien was also a homosexual, and he urged Tilden to leave the United States and come live out his life in France, where there was more understanding of these matters. Tilden was moved by the offer, but, always an American, he never seems to have seriously considered accepting it, if indeed he could have gotten out of the country anyway.

Judge Scott received no anonymous mail this time, nor any letters of reference either. The public had lost interest; Tilden was just another old fag, of which there had always been plenty about in Hollywood. Big Bill went to see Judge Scott to petition for understanding. He pleaded with him not to force him to live in the painful purgatory of probation; give him his sentence and let him square his account in full inside, so that when he came out he would be clean and could teach his young friends again. That was the mercy he really wanted: don't keep him from children. And there, alone in the judge's quarters, Tilden told him the whole truth. "Judge, I can't help myself," he said, haggard, bent, scared, his eyes searching the floor. Judge Scott asked him about the value of psychiatric treatment, and Tilden told him that it was useless. "It doesn't do any good, nor would any more do any good."

This time the court was gentle. The new charge, involving the boy Michael, could easily have been prosecuted as a felony. Instead, Judge Scott merely sent Tilden back up for a year on his probation violation and let the punishment for the new molesting run concurrently. It was on February 10, 1949, his fifty-sixth birthday, when Tilden stood before Judge Scott again and heard himself dismissed as a liar as well as a degenerate.

Judge Scott: "These young fellows who look up to you,

just like thousands of kids still do and like thousands of
adults still do . . . they cannot bring themselves to believe, Mr. Tilden, that a man . . . who gave his word: to
use your own language, you gave your word 'as a sportsman,' that this would never happen again. Certainly the
word of a sportsman ought to be good enough for anybody,
Mr. Tilden, and when you have broken your word, what
can I do for you? . . .

"Maybe the road camp might be a little better for him
this time, maybe some of that snow, opening up some of
these highways, keeping in that cold atmosphere for a
while would help him."

Take him away; Maddox handed him over to the deputies again. He was supposed to get a full year, but they let
him out a couple of months early, for Christmas. There was
no one to meet him when he was taken back down from
Castaic and released in Los Angeles on December 18, 1949.
It was just a few days before the Associated Press poll of
the half-century was announced. It voted Tilden the
greatest athlete in his sport by a margin larger than any
other—Babe Ruth, Jack Dempsey, Bobby Jones, Red
Grange. Of them all, Tilden was voted the most dominant;
he got ten times more votes than his nearest challenger.

To a couple of members of the press that waited there
alone to record his entrance back into society, J. F. Grover,
the jailer, announced, "Well, here's Big Bill Tilden again."

"Yeah, here's Tilden again," he said, and he walked out
of the jail and off into the rain by himself.

CHAPTER NINETEEN

"Jesus, it was awful. The poor old son of a bitch"

H IS opportunities were now even more diminished. People who had been willing to accept the first arrest, or who thought it a mistake, would not forgive him the second. It seemed clear that he had not learned his lesson, despite all his promises and guarantees to the court. More clubs were closed to him, fewer students would dare go to the old queer for lessons. Not even Vinnie Richards, an officer of the company, could get Dunlop to keep up the contract. They had hung in the first time, but after the second arrest Dunlop not only ended the affiliation but sent out an urgent order to all its salesmen to recover all Dunlop equipment marked Tilden from off the shelves; better to destroy a racket than have it soiled with the Tilden name on it.

Many people in tennis were furious at him for how he had hurt the game's reputation; among other things, he was called an ingrate. He came back to Forest Hills one year and realized that as he approached old friends they would literally turn their backs upon him and walk away, or simply act as if he did not exist. "Oh God, it was awful," says Sarah Palfrey Danzig, an old protégée and two-time U.S. champion. "You could see them snub him. He was so kind, so good. He deserved better from us all." In his old home

town, where once he had been saluted officially as the
"Pride of Philadelphia," given the Bock Award, the city's
highest honor to a native son, he became a non-person. At
the University of Pennsylvania his alumni files were
purged, and at the Germantown Cricket Club, where he
was an honorary life member, people would stand in front
of his picture and alternately snicker at him or swear at
him. Finally Frank Deacon could take it no more. He went
to the club manager and requested that the portrait be
taken down for a while. The manager replied that the club
rules required fifty signatures for such an action, which
would mean a big to-do and more shame. So a few nights
later, with a few drinks in him, Deacon—somewhat antici-
pating Mr. Roberts—stayed around the club until everyone
had left, and then just took the portrait down himself and
handed it over to the Tilden family. Play your own sweet
game, Deacon. But in Philadelphia, as in Hollywood, as in
tennis, almost no one rallied to Tilden's side. "They didn't,
they didn't," Carl Fischer says now, shaking his head, and
then lowering it sadly. "They didn't, myself included."

One of the few who did make a special effort was his old
love, Angel Child, Gloria Butler. She went to Los Angeles,
where she found him teaching on a shabby public court
near Grauman's Chinese Theatre that was owned by a
couple of guys named Angelo and Nino Giordano. It was
pay as you play, and Big Bill was a useful curiosity who
might attract some extra customers. "The work does me
good, and I guess it does the Giordanos good too," Tilden
said. "I'll play tennis with anyone who wants to play."

Miss Butler and Tilden saw each other across the way.
She waved. He stopped his instruction, but he did not wave
back. He just stood stock still as she came toward him,
closer, closer. By now he had been rejected so many times
that he no longer had the nerve to approach old friends.
Even when she reached him, Tilden still only stood and

looked down at her, tears forming in his eyes. At last she understood, and she spoke his name tenderly and fell against him. Only then did he put his arms around her, but he was shaking so, that he could hardly hold her. She held on to him. "It's all right, Bill," she said. "It's all right, it's all right."

"Angel Child," he sighed at last between his tears.

Miss Butler helped fix him up in a better apartment in the hills just above Hollywood, and she took another flat for herself in the same building. She stayed for the next six months or so, and early on perceived the depths of his agony. At nights he would become painfully restless, anxious to get out, to drive around, to find a boy. Sometimes she could hear him pacing the floor, and so she would make an excuse and come over—cook for him, play cards with him, read the bad plays he was still writing, take him out for a drive. Anything to contain him.

Tennis still brought him the most of what happiness there was. He was working on a new instructional book, *How to Play Better Tennis;* and as *My Story* had been dedicated to Little Bill, to the past, this one was for Arthur Anderson, for the future. Naturally he could no longer play with his old pals at the Los Angeles Tennis Club. Perry Jones had barred him from the premises as soon as it was revealed that Tilden had met the boy Bobby there. But every September, shortly after Forest Hills, the Pacific Southwest championships, a public tournament, was held there. Gloria Butler asked him one afternoon if he would like to go out to see the matches. The Pacific Southwest was one of the more important tournaments in U.S. amateur tennis and always attracted a top world-class draw, but Tilden shrugged and said that he wasn't the least bit interested. She didn't believe him, of course, and that night she caught him in the lie when she found him huddled at the radio, listening anxiously for the day's results.

So the next day Miss Butler practically forced him to go with her to the matches. He paused a long time before he went through the club gates, and inside he actually began to shake in fear. No one said anything to him. As at Forest Hills, there were some who turned and walked the other way as he approached. He was so frightened and shook so, that at last Miss Butler took up a position on one side of him, and another friend on the other, and they supported Big Bill, as if he were a cripple.

For matches, Frank Feltrop, the well-known teaching pro at the Beverly Wilshire Hotel, was one man who would still let him come by and use his courts. Tilden would drop over to the hotel out of the blue and ask Feltrop if there was anybody around looking for a fourth for doubles. Anyone. No money, no playing lesson, just a game, a chance to play. *Did anybody want to play tennis with Big Bill Tilden?* Sometimes, though, Feltrop wouldn't let him on the courts till he got cleaned up; sometimes his clothes were so rank that he had to give Tilden a clean shirt or pair of shorts. His attention to hygiene was deteriorating all the more. One dirty white sweater reeked with perspiration, and his famous old camel's hair coat (with sash) was crumpled and spotted.

One day he came by Richard Maddox's law office. He had come into a little luck, picked up an extra lesson or two, and with the extra money he had gone out and bought his lawyer an expensive fountain pen set. More than twenty years later Maddox still keeps it on his desk. There was no need for the gift; the account was settled. It was just a gesture typical of Tilden. But when he arrived, unexpected, with the present, Maddox was meeting with another client, and Tilden had to wait in the anteroom. He was so malodorous that after a while the receptionist had to go see Maddox's secretary and urge her to get the lawyer to bring Tilden in, because he was fouling up the whole place.

Alphonso Smith, who hadn't seen Tilden for many years, and always remembered his immaculate white clothes, was appalled when he saw him show up to play an exhibition match wearing a dirty sweatshirt, filthy short shorts, and blue sneakers. Ben Pearson, a Hollywood agent, recalls that Tilden never seemed to switch out of his tennis clothes. He would often drop by the houses of people he knew, just coincidentally around dinnertime, and hang on for a free meal. "There were whole periods when he seemed to subsist mainly that way," Pearson says. Sometimes then Tilden would kick off his sneakers, borrow a blanket and fall asleep on the couch. Feltrop never remembers him showering after matches at the Beverly Wilshire. "Of course, you've got to remember I hardly made an effort to check," he says. "At this point nobody was in any hurry to be around this guy when he undressed."

In 1953 Feltrop, who is now the pro at the Deep Canyon Club in Palm Desert, California, got a sponsor to put up $10,000, which was big money for the pros then, in order to hold what he christened the National Professional Hardcourt Championships at the Beverly Wilshire that spring. Feltrop brought Tilden in as something of a co-promoter. It was a nice gesture, for Big Bill was thrilled again to be doing something for tennis and the pros. He not only induced people like Vinnie Richards to come out and enter the tournament, but he sold boxes to many of his most faithful Hollywood contacts. He was alive again, involved, rabid with enthusiasm, and above all, ready once more to stand in the spotlight. Feltrop invited him to play too. *For all through my career I have loved the brightness, and I long for it again.* Although Tilden had turned sixty that February, Feltrop monkeyed with the draw a little so that the old man had the easiest opponents, and a pretty good chance to actually win one or two matches.

Then, just two days before the tournament was to begin,

Feltrop was summoned to the hotel manager's office and shown a stack of mail from women's groups and other indignant citizens. The manager said he was sorry, but he had a hotel to run; the Beverly Wilshire couldn't afford to be identified with any degenerate ex-con. "My God," says Feltrop, "that was the saddest thing I ever had to do in my life. They didn't even want him ever again to set foot on the place, but I couldn't tell him that, I just couldn't. I just told him that they wouldn't let him play in the tournament. And right there, I think he knew he didn't have a hell of a lot to live for anymore. He said, 'But, Frank, Vinnie's coming out, all the old gang.'

" 'I'm sorry, Bill, I'm sorry.'

" 'I've sold all these tickets to my friends. Joe Cotten, David Selznick. This is their chance to see me play again.'

"I just said, 'I told you, I'm sorry. I can't do anything.'

" 'I'll sue you then, I'll sue the hotel,' he said all of a sudden. Oh, he still had a crust on him, an unbelievable hide.

"I said, 'Come on, Bill, it's your arm that's been hurting, isn't it? You can't play with that arm, can you?' And then he dropped his head and nodded and said, Yes, he would go along and say his arm was hurting, and after that he just turned and walked away. He must have been down to about one-fifty then, and he was all bent over then, so his bald spot in back was showing. Jesus, it was awful. The poor old son of a bitch."

One more place was closed to him. He went back up into the hills to Chaplin's court. Chaplin had left the country and then been forbidden re-entry, but at least Tilden still had use of the court, if he also had fewer students all the time. But he carried on, standing straight, more angular than ever, skinnier than he had been since college. When he stood there on court pointing a racket and screaming at a pupil, the sweat dripping off the tip of his nose, he reminded Kathy Checkit of a game old hawk. "I felt he was on stage most of the time," she remembers. "But he never looked humble. He was proud to the end." If a student asked him to lunch, he would go, but he would not accept that generosity again until he had saved a few bucks and repaid with his own luncheon treat. Bill Tilden was not just a hired hand. "He never showed a thing," Marrion Anderson says. "He was a great person for bravado." Arthur Anderson, who feels he knew him better than any man, swears that he never saw Tilden down, not for a day, not for a moment.

But a thoughtful man will insulate his heir from seeing some of life's little bothers. When there was no money at all, and Big Bill had to pawn his trophies to pay the rent, he could not take them himself. "He had someone else bring them in," the pawnshop proprietor reported. He got forty-five dollars for three silver cups. Then one day in May Tilden wrote Vinnie Richards at Dunlop: "Vinnie, could you please send me a couple of dozen balls and a racket or two? If I had them I think I could get some lessons to give. I need the money badly." Richards immediately prepared a packet to send.

A few days later, on Tuesday, June 2, Tilden called on a regular student, Herbert Brenner, at his office. He had a deal for Brenner, and when it turned out that Brenner would be away for a few more hours, Tilden was so anxious that he borrowed some stationery from the secretary and left Brenner a long note offering him forty hours of instruction for $200. This was a cut-rate five bucks an hour, but only if Brenner would pay in advance, now. Tilden wrote, "I am in real need of money, therefore this offer."

What Tilden needed money so urgently for was a trip he had planned, first to Texas for some exhibitions, and then up to Cleveland for the U.S. professional championships at

Lakewood Park. It was a lark, really, only a chase after the brightness, but Big Bill was still a player, and Cleveland was where they were playing. Bob Rogers, one of three other pros who were going to accompany Tilden, says, "We were going along just for Bill. We didn't expect to make any more than expenses, but it would help Bill."

Tilden was not in the best of health either. The enforced idleness of the two jail stretches had surely not been good for a man whose whole life had been spent daily in hours of strenuous physical exercise. Even though he was sixty years old, Big Bill would still often spend most of every day on the court, playing or teaching. At this point he also had a nagging cold he couldn't shake. Sometimes he would cough so hard—and coughs deep and rasping, not just from the throat but from way down in his lungs, rattling his whole body—that he would have to put his racket down and go back and lean up against the canvas for support. But then it was always right back to the game. Big Bill Tilden was getting ready for the U.S. pro championships again, and there was neither the time nor money for a doctor. "I'm a little better," he noted to Herbert Brenner.

A few days before he was going, Tilden drove out Wilshire to Westwood and picked up Anderson at UCLA, where he was attending college now. There he met two of Anderson's teammates, a couple of top Canadian players named Don Fontana and Bob Bedard, who had been recruited to play tennis for UCLA. Tilden invited them to come along with Anderson and work out with them at Chaplin's, and when they all got up there he suddenly announced that they were going to have a Davis Cup match—Canada vs. the United States.

Fontana and Bedard looked tentatively at each other and then over at the gaunt old man with the beautiful long legs and the dirty white sweater. He was exhilarated. He conducted a draw, and as they played he said things like "Advantage, United States" and "Canada leads, four games to three, first set." It was a beautiful, eerie absurdity, the four of them, alone on the abandoned estate, playing out this fantasy all afternoon. "Bob and I won both singles," Fontana says, "and then the doubles too. Tilden was beside himself when he and Anderson lost that, because it gave Canada the match. We were just playing to get some good practice, but he was like a real tiger, and he agonized when they lost, when the United States lost. It was all very real to him." Big Bill had to get ready for the U.S. pro championships. When Herbert Brenner came through with the $200, the trip East was on for Saturday morning.

The night before, Friday, June 5, the Andersons invited Tilden to come over for a going-away dinner. He and Arthur played several sets earlier that day, and Tilden also picked up a couple of lessons as well before he went back to his little apartment at 2025 North Argyle Avenue, just up from Hollywood and Vine. On his way home he stopped at a drugstore to get something for his cold. Then he went to his room to change for dinner. "Bill had a habit," Anderson says, "of getting all dressed to go out, coat and tie, everything, everything but his shoes, and then he would lie down on the bed until it was exactly the time to leave. He was always very punctual. Then he would sit up, pat his hair down in back from where the pillow mussed it up, put on his shoes, and get up and go out."

When Tilden did not arrive exactly on time for dinner, the Andersons waited only a few minutes before calling. It was just not his nature to be late, especially for dinner. When there was no answer, they assumed he was on the way over; but his apartment was hardly a mile away, and after more time passed without his showing, Arthur drove over to Tilden's apartment. He got the landlady, Mrs. John Bray, to let him in. Big Bill was dead across the bed. He already had his shoes on. He had almost gotten up. Beside the bed his bags were already packed, for playing in the U.S. pro championships in Cleveland.

Officially, cause of death was coronary thrombosis. The coroner said, "Just a case of a chap sixty years old who outlived his heart." Most people agreed with Frank Hunter, who calls it "a blessing." Besides the trophies that had not been pawned, Tilden left practically nothing: $142.11 in cash, $140 worth of American Express traveler's checks—and $200 had to be returned to Herbert Brenner. He was due a six-dollar refund from the Automobile Club of America. That and what else there was went to Arthur Anderson: "because of his loyal friendship, and the loyal friendship of his mother, and because I consider him to be my logical successor in tennis."

A memorial service at the Pierce Mortuary the following Wednesday drew a spotty crowd. "A scattering of personal friends" was how the AP characterized it, kindly. There were a few tennis people there—Ellsworth Vines, Pancho Segura, John Doeg, Gussie Moran, Noel Brown, Frank Feltrop—but, of course, there was no one representing the USLTA, no one representing tennis. From tennis, there was not even a wreath.

Tilden was in a nice brown suede jacket and in a new clean white sweater with red deer figures running across the chest, which Joseph Cotten had bought for him to lie in. Then Big Bill was cremated, because it was cheaper to get him across state lines that way, and shipped back to Philadelphia. For $115, a small stone was bought, and it reads WILLIAM T. TILDEN 2ND 1893–1953. That is the only monument of any kind, anywhere in the world—at Forest Hills, at Wimbledon, in Germantown, anywhere—that pays tribute to the greatest tennis player who ever lived. And the trophies are in a warehouse. There is nothing else at all.

On a warm June afternoon, while the U.S. professional championships were taking place at Lakewood Park in Cleveland, a handful of relatives and friends in Philadelphia came out to Ivy Hill and watched as Bill Tilden was lowered into the ground, seventy years after his older brother and sisters were put there, forty years after the rest of his family. He was placed by the side of his brother, Herbert, and at the feet of his mother, so that at last he could be her child again, for good, at peace.

Index